Gradual Economic Reform in Latin America

Gradual Economic Reform in Latin America

The Costa Rican Experience

Mary A. Clark

STATE UNIVERSITY OF NEW YORK PRESS

Published by
State University of New York Press, Albany

© 2001 State University of New York

All rights reserved

Printed in the United States of America

No part of this book may be used or reproduced in any manner whatsoever without written permission. No part of this book may be stored in a retrieval system or transmitted in any form or by any means including electronic, electrostatic, magnetic tape, mechanical, photocopying, recording, or otherwise without the prior permission in writing of the publisher.

For information, address State University of New York Press, 90 State Street, Suite 700, Albany, NY 12207

Production by Diane Ganeles
Marketing by Fran Keneston

Library of Congress Cataloging-in-Publication Data

Clark, Mary A., 1962–
   Gradual economic reform in Latin America : the Costa Rican experience / Mary A. Clark.
     p. cm.
   Includes bibliographical references and index.
   ISBN 0-7914-5031-7 (alk. paper) — ISBN 0-7914-5032-5 (pbk. : alk. paper)
    1. Costa Rica—Economic policy. 2. Structural adjustment—Costa Rica. I. Title.

HC143 .C54 2001
338.98—dc21

00-045052

10 9 8 7 6 5 4 3 2 1

To my parents, John and Shirley Clark

Contents

List of Illustrations — ix

Preface — xi

1. The Gradual Road to Reform — 1

2. The Legacies of 1948: Democratic Institutions, Social Welfare, and Economic Development — 17

3. "Easy" Structural Adjustment: The 1980s — 43

4. Reforming the Welfare State: The 1990s — 69

5. Costa Rican Outcomes — 105

6. Conclusion — 135

Notes — 147

Bibliography — 177

Index — 193

Illustrations

Tables

2.1	Costa Rican Presidents and Party Representation in the Legislative Assembly	25
3.1	U.S. Bilateral and Multilateral Assistance to Costa Rica, 1982–1995	48
3.2	U.S. Economic Assistance as a Percentage of Costa Rican Imports and GDP, 1982–1989	49
4.1	Basic Development Indicators for Costa Rica	83
4.2	Distribution of K–12 Students in Costa Rica, 1996	96
4.3	K–12 Educational Institutions, 1996	96
5.1	Income Distribution among Urban Households in Costa Rica	115
5.2	Costa Rican Nontraditional Export and Tourism Regimes	126

Figures

5.1	Top Four Nontraditional Exports and Tourism	107
5.2	Households in Poverty in Costa Rica, 1980–1994	114

5.3 Costa Rica: GDP and Real Minimum Wages, 1978–1996   116

5.4 Costa Rica: Inflation and Unemployment, 1978–1996   117

5.5 Costa Rica: Real Effective Exchange Rate, 1979–1996   125

6.1 The Quality of Democracy and the Speed of Reform in Latin America   141

Preface

By the late 1990s, market-oriented economic reform had become the guiding policy orientation of virtually every Latin American country. But a clear unevenness characterized the execution of market reforms. Some countries had nearly completed them, some moved very slowly toward measures like trade liberalization, deregulation, privatization, introducing market mechanisms into public administration, and reducing state spending, while others saw reforms reversed. Despite the apparent ideological dominance of the "Washington Consensus,"[1] it is far from fully implemented in Latin America. Why?

This question is particularly interesting in the case of Costa Rica. I arrived in Costa Rica in late 1989 to find a country that had lived for the better part of a decade under intense pressure from the United States, the World Bank, the IMF, and certain domestic technocrats to abandon its previous development model and adopt neoliberal economic policies. It seemed that economic policy had already changed a great deal and that this small, vulnerable nation would quickly succumb to the international trend toward sweeping market reform. But by the time I completed a dissertation on export promotion, in the early 1990s, it was clear that expectations of a rapid conversion were mistaken. Successive Costa Rican governments did not question the general goal of market reform, but they did encounter significant political and technical obstacles to certain measures. The reforms of the 1990s, in particular, involved key elements of Costa Rica's welfare state and they ran into vested interests, institutional obstacles, ideological barriers, and administrative complexities.

The main goal of this book is to explain why economic reform has taken a gradual pace in Costa Rica, especially in the last decade. I focus on politics, specifically, the qualities of Costa Rica's democracy, as well as the complex requirements of the reforms themselves, as the main explanations for the slow adoption of market-oriented adjustment. The book presents ten case studies of key structural adjustment measures, five from the "easy" decade of reform, the 1980s, and five from the more difficult 1990s. Before concluding, I also evaluate the outcomes of Costa Rica's gradualism, that is, the economic, social, and political effects of the reforms completed thus far. My hope is that this case study will shed light on some of the general reasons for slow and uneven reform throughout Latin America and contribute to the broader debate over the benefits of gradualism versus shock therapy. Toward this end, the last chapter concludes with a brief comparison between Costa Rica and several peer Latin American welfare states: Uruguay, Brazil, and Argentina.

I would like to thank Tulane University for its extensive support of this project. The Center for Latin American Studies Faculty Mellon Grant program provided funding for research in Costa Rica during the summers of 1994 and 1997, the Graduate School supplied a research grant for the summer of 1995, and a Bernstein Newcomb College Fellowship allowed me to take a semester leave in 1996. In Costa Rica, FLACSO provided an institutional home during the summer of 1994, and Research Director Carlos Sojo gave his time generously during subsequent visits to discuss the development of the book. Researchers at the University of Costa Rica's Instituto de Investigaciones en Ciencias Económicas also helped me to obtain data during several visits. Discussions with Patricia Alvarenga, Eugenia Rodríguez, and Iván Molina helped to sharpen the main themes of the book. Countless government officials and private businesspeople patiently explained the intricacies of Costa Rican structural adjustment and gave me feedback about the book's arguments as they were developed. And the comments of three anonymous reviewers for the State University of New York Press corrected mistakes and strengthened the overall quality of the book.

Parts of articles previously published elsewhere appear in original or modified form in two chapters. Sections of chapter 3, including tables 3.1 and 3.2, as well as a previous version of table 5.2 (chapter 5), first appeared in: Mary A. Clark, "Transnational Alliances and Development Policy in Latin America: Nontraditional Export Promotion in Costa Rica," *Latin American Research Review*

32, no. 2: 71–97. Portions of capter 5, including previous versions of figure 5.1 and figure 5.5, first appeared in: Mary A. Clark, "Nontraditional Export Promotion in Costa Rica: Sustaining Export-Led Growth," *Journal of Interamerican Studies and World Affairs* 37, no. 2: 181–219. I am grateful to these journals for allowing reprinting of this material.

As for personal support, I owe a great debt to don Bhotto, doña Cecilia, Federico, and Mario for sharing the warmth of their family life and helping me to feel at home in their country over these last twenty years. I also want to express my gratitude to my husband, Mark Gasiorowski, who never doubted that I would complete and publish this project. My parents always gave unquestioning support for my fascination with Costa Rica and I deeply regret that my father did not live to see the publication of this book.

1

The Gradual Road to Reform

Costa Rica consistently lands at the top of lists ranking Latin American democracies.[1] To political scientists, it represents a sort of Third World paradise, a regime that is superlatively democratic, stable, and respectful of human rights. But for economists, the last fifteen years of structural adjustment in the country have been a very frustrating experience. Some Costa Rican technocrats complain that "too much" democracy makes market-oriented policy reform nearly impossible. Officials at the World Bank and Inter-American Development Bank privately admit that they find Costa Rica to be one of the most difficult Latin American countries in which to work. Whatsmore, they indicate that the obstacles to policy reform may jeopardize Costa Rica's long-term economic prospects and thus indirectly its social and political stability.

The importance of reconciling these viewpoints extends beyond one small country. For Costa Rica is one among many slow-moving economic reformers in democratic Latin America. After the early 1980s, virtually all Latin American countries attempted to impose one or more components of structural adjustment.[2] The resulting track record is mixed. There exist a few standout performers, such as Chile, the vanguard model, which have completed far-reaching reforms. But the majority of Latin American countries occupy a large category of cases ranging from gradual adjustment projects, distinguished by their continuous forward motion, to completely stalled programs.[3] All of the countries in this latter group are at least nominally democratic. Most of them quickly implemented stabilization programs and the easiest structural adjustment measures only to become mired in the more complex reforms. So what we need to know is: Why are most Latin American countries taking so long to implement market-oriented economic reforms? Might gradualism be more recommendable than many economists believe?

This book does not pretend to offer definitive answers to these broad questions. Rather, it will present findings from a theoretically informed study of an important case in the hope that they will be used in cross-national comparisons. The case study approach allows thick description of economic reform. Close examination of each major reform measure and within-country comparison are indispensable for understanding the unevenness of implementation and its consequences. A case study approach also allows us to examine a country's entire history of structural adjustment, now fifteen years and counting in Costa Rica, thus providing the opportunity for longitudinal analysis.

In comparative context, the best reason for choosing a Costa Rican case study is that it appears to be the quintessential example of the strained relationship between democratic process and rapid economic liberalization. Although much has been made of the problems "new" democracies face in implementing economic reform,[4] it is just as advantageous to study policymaking in older ones. Of course, "new" democracies can only be new for so long and this category is already fading with age. More importantly, an established democracy offers a stable set of political institutions and values that can be held constant while we examine the problem of changing economic signals and responses. It is much more difficult to determine causality when economic and political structures are moving at the same time. Costa Rica has enjoyed uninterrupted democracy since 1948, the longest such record in Latin America. Costa Rica also makes a convenient case study because the sequencing of its economic reform programs has proceeded in textbook-style, moving from stabilization to easy adjustment in the 1980s, and then to more difficult retrenchments of the welfare state in the 1990s. Finally, it is significant that Costa Rica has a well-functioning welfare state, inviting comparisons not only to similarly-situated Latin American countries, but to welfare states in western Europe and elsewhere.

The most unique aspect of the Costa Rican experience with structural adjustment is its reliance on large sums of foreign aid, particularly the politically tied concessionary assistance given by the United States Agency for International Development (USAID) in the 1980s. In some ways, this aid helped to make structural adjustment easier in the 1980s. But because this was geopolitically motivated assistance, sent by the United States for the express purpose of obtaining Costa Rica's help in overthrowing the Sandinista regime, accepting it dragged the country deeper into the regional political crisis. Thus, in other ways, the management of the country became more difficult because of the presence of external donors during the 1980s. In the 1990s, U.S. aid dropped out of the picture as Costa Rica relied largely on the World Bank and Inter-American Development Bank for a smaller amount of donor assistance. Almost all Latin American countries have borrowed from the international financial institutions (IFIs) to support portions of their structural adjustment programs, but Costa Rica's extensive interactions with them makes it a good case in which to study variations in these relationships.

This book is also aimed at addressing some of the shortfalls in contemporary scholarship on Costa Rica. Changes in economic policy and the role of U.S. influence in them during the 1980s have received a great deal of attention, both from Costa Rican scholars[5] and from outside observers.[6] These studies have produced invaluable detail, but they are limited by their fixation with the 1980s and tendency to boil down to debates over the extent to which the United States infringed on Costa Rica's sovereignty.[7] This book moves beyond the politics of the Cold War-driven 1980s by examining the economic policy record as it has developed well into the next decade and by undertaking an assessment of the outcomes of all the changes.

The State of the Literature

The field of comparative politics has long been concerned with the question of whether democratic regimes perform as well as authoritarian ones in responding to changing economic conditions with policy adjustments. This concern has been heightened during the last two decades because the nature of the required adjustments has meant the retraction of state subsidies, protectionism, monopolies, employment, and other benefits. On the negative side, it seems logical to argue that market-oriented economic reforms will be extremely difficult under democratic regimes because the potential losers of adjustment measures, who may be small in number but highly concentrated in interest groups, will use their civil liberties and systems of checks and balances to block the new policies. And there will be losers under stabilization and structural adjustment, even if only temporarily.[8] In addition, the greater the scope of the welfare state and thus the ranks of public employees and beneficiaries of social programs, the larger and more organized the opponents of retrenchment.[9] Nor will politicians want to alienate these large constituencies.

On the other hand, public opinion research on Latin America shows that under some circumstances, the rich and the poor will support painful economic reforms.[10] Third World democracies also seem to share a few general features which can be beneficial for structural adjustment. One is known as the honeymoon period, that interval between the installation of a new democratic regime or new government (if the past administration had a disastrous economic policy record) and the return of "politics as normal." The honeymoon period is understood to be a special time in which distributionist claims should be suspended and the government allowed to take extraordinary steps to deal with an economic crisis. Another benefit that democracy offers is its attractiveness to foreign aid donors, particularly bilateral agencies who want to support showcase democracies in troubled regions in which they have geopolitical interests.[11] Costa Rica, Jamaica, Botswana, and Israel have become particularly good at convincing foreign donors to lend massive levels of assistance during rough economic episodes. Finally, democracies may also enjoy a basic legitimacy in the eyes of citizens which, combined with the expectation of regular elections, reduces the probability of social and political destabilization when painful economic reforms alienate constituencies.

Until recently, researchers have been mainly concerned with testing these conflicting logics, trying to find out whether democratic or authoritarian regimes are more likely to impose economic reform and gain successful outcomes. Comparative studies and statistical analyses[12] have not found systematic differences between democratic and authoritarian regimes in their responses (in terms of policy choice and economic performance) to economic crises. In fact, recent Latin American experience makes it clear that democratic countries can make substantial changes in economic policy.

What the regime-level analyses do not address are the variations among democratic regimes and within individual countries as they implement economic reforms. For instance, some countries move quickly and others more slowly. And few countries experience uniformity in the speed, degree of difficulty, or sustainability of the entire spectrum of reform measures. Thus, the current research agenda is here, on the sub-regime level. In particular, the new wave of literature on the management of economic reform attempts to identify the political, organizational, and technical obstacles to implementation as well as the best strategies for overcoming them. Scholars and practitioners working in this vein also demonstrate concern for the social and political, as well as economic, outcomes of the new policies. As it has become clear that structural adjustment in Latin America will not be an overnight affair, but rather a long and complicated process, there is greater recognition that the feedback from one round of implementation will affect subsequent steps.

One important area of agreement within this literature is that, although regime type cannot be reliably correlated with economic policy change, certain democratic institutional configurations are much more propitious for structural adjustment than others. Another key observation concerns the nature of the reforms themselves: some may be categorized as "first-stage" or easy and others as "second-stage" or more difficult. Accordingly, the latter take more time and face greater obstacles than the former.

In the following pages, I argue that these two insights go a long way toward explaining the apparent slowness of structural adjustment in Latin American democracies and particularly in Costa Rica. They serve as the cornerstones of two complementary perspectives oriented toward understanding the unevenness of economic reform. The logical next step is then to consider whether gradualism is a good or bad thing. Accordingly, the last segment of the theoretical section considers arguments about the optimal speed of economic reform. The literature reflects little agreement over this issue but I shall delineate the case for and against.

The Quality of Democracy

The response to the failure to detect general laws about the interaction between democratic regimes and economic crises has been a movement toward looking for relationships between individual configurations of formal institutions and policy outcomes. Institutionalists consider the presidentialist regimes of Latin America to be far more likely than parliamentary governments to suffer from the "dual legitimacy" that leads to policy gridlock.[13] Nevertheless, a great deal of variation in institutional design exists among presidential systems, and scholars stress that such differences affect the possibilities of implementing economic reform.

Chief among these differences is the degree of independent

power endowed in the president's office. An open and transparent decisionmaking system may impede rapid response to deteriorating economic conditions, especially when interest groups oppose the proposed changes. Therefore, experts in the management of economic reform tell us that a centralized institutional structure which insulates a powerful executive branch would produce the fastest results with the least need to compromise.[14] We can predict the ability of a president to pursue his or her own agenda, in this case economic reform, by using three measures of executive strength.

Constitutional powers refer to the president's prerogatives vis-à-vis the legislature. These consist primarily of veto and decree powers as well as the exclusive right to introduce legislation in particular policy areas.[15] Scott Mainwaring and Matthew S. Shugart explain that decree power is the strongest of these, as it allows the president to bypass congress and pursue his/her agenda by declaring new laws.[16] For example, Argentine President Carlos Menem has pushed forward a radical reform program through the extensive use of decrees. In contrast, Costa Rican presidents have no power to decree legislation. Veto powers and exclusive introduction also enhance the strength of the executive but are considered more reactive tools. Presidents may veto unwanted legislation or defend the status quo by refusing to submit new proposals to congress. Costa Rican presidents have very limited veto powers; they may not veto the national budget as determined by the legislature nor use a pocket or line-item veto. They have the power of exclusive introduction only during special legislative sessions. Mainwaring and Shugart describe the Costa Rican president's constitutional powers as potentially marginal, the weakest category in their ranking.[17]

A country's party system also affects the executive officer's power. A president's partisan powers are greatly enhanced when his or her party holds a majority in congress and enjoys substantial internal discipline. Because fewer parties best produce legislative majorities, Costa Rica's two-party system would seem to lend some balance to the fragmentation of political authority created by the president's weak constitutional powers and multiple veto players (see below), especially as it is supported by concurrent elections for all offices. But dual four-year term limits (presidents may never be reelected and Legislative Assembly incumbents must sit out one term before standing for reelection), weak presidential authority, and ambiguous standards of discipline within the two main parties offer the executive few formal instruments for securing copartisan support in the legislature. The president is treated more and more as a lame duck as his or her term progresses and Assembly members spend their latter years in office seeking a position in the next administration.[18] Thus, the window of opportunity for passing reform legislation is very short in Costa Rica. And as we might expect, the behavior of the Legislative Assembly given this set of incentives makes passing economic policy changes agonizingly slow, likely to be held hostage to unrelated political disputes, and vulnerable to compromises that distort the original intent of the legislation.

Other branches of government, state agencies, and constitutional provisions may also check the power of the president (and the legislature). These can be called "veto players" or "veto points."[19] Besides the Legislative Assembly, in Costa Rica, three other bodies function as important veto points in the policymaking process: the Supreme Court, the Comptroller, and the semiautonomous institutions. Costa Rica's constitutional chamber has powerful rights of judicial review and they are often applied to economic policy. In similar fashion, the Comptroller (Contraloría General de la República) has the authority to annul contracts when the rules of public financing are not followed. Lastly, Costa Rica's more than one hundred thirty semiautonomous state agencies can and do slow the implementation of new policies with which they disagree. Subsequently, we will see that all three of these types of veto players delayed reforms during the 1990s.

Informal qualities stemming from a country's political culture may also influence the rate of policy change in Latin American democracies. For example, traditions of consensus-building and compromise have been noted in Costa Rica, Uruguay, and Venezuela (at least until 1989). A government's attempts to build consensus around a new development strategy and a willingness to compromise about the speed and scope of particular polices may convince potential opponents to allow the changes and perhaps even to embrace them, thus enhancing sustainability. On the other hand, use of such methods definitely slows down the implementation of market-oriented reforms and may result in suboptimal economic outcomes.

The last major quality to be considered when Latin American democracies attempt economic liberalization is the significance of their welfare states. The size of a welfare state can be roughly judged by the scope of social protection programs such as pensions and health insurance, and by the size of public-sector employment. Then we must consider a more intangible quality: the extent to which citizens equate their democracy with the rights of social citizenship or access to social services. A social safety net, in as much as it represents governmental responsiveness to citizens' basic needs, may reduce the social and political costs involved in the transitions effected by structural adjustment. But in large welfare states, we can expect little support for retrenchment from either the system's vested interests—the workers who deliver social services and those who receive them—or from the broader public.[20]

The qualities of an individual democracy are most useful for explaining the general pace of its structural adjustment process and for providing insight into the unevenness of reform across countries. But these factors do not fully explain microlevel results, such as the variation of implementation outcomes within a country. For this we must disaggregate the concept of structural adjustment to examine it as a problem of development management.

Managerial Aspects of Reform

When we disaggregate structural adjustment into a set of related but distinct policy changes we immediately see that some are much more technically and politically challenging than others. In concurrence with or after stabilization, Latin American countries have initiated structural adjustment policies in either "bundled" (all at once) or "unbundled" (separately) form. No matter what the case, the general trend is that some policy changes have been accomplished more easily and quickly than others. Those accomplished first—usually trade and financial liberalization, the removal of other subsidies, and "easy" privatizations—tend to present low technical and administrative complexity and are sometimes attainable by executive decree. Thus, they are relatively quick, and do not rely on the bureaucratic structures of semi-autonomous institutions or on extensive societal consensus-building.

Most Latin American countries are now attempting some of what Moisés Naím calls "second-stage" reforms, but only very slowly. Second-stage adjustments comprise complicated privatizations and what is known as "state reform": measures such as overhauling the civil service and restructuring government ministries and institutions, especially social service agencies.[21] Second-stage reforms usually require extensive legislative consideration and run headlong into the vested interests of statist legacies. This is why, paradoxically, that the states with the most extensive public social service capacities often experience more difficulties in improving delivery systems than their poorer neighbors. In the former set of countries, primarily welfare states such as Costa Rica, Brazil, and Uruguay, a loose path dependence operates in which institutions, interests, and even coherent belief systems about the provision of health and education already exist.[22] In these cases, reform efforts often turn into battles between complex alliances of state and societal interests over plans to dislocate employees, demand new competencies, disrupt organizational charts, change work rules, and modify standard operating procedures.[23]

Relatedly, the incentive structure facing would-be reformers for carrying out first and second-stage policy changes is less favorable for the latter. First-stage reforms often create losers, typically those hurt by the removal of subsidies and trade liberalization. But when successful, they also create winners, especially those who benefit from the new business opportunities fostered by international integration and financial deregulation. These interests are likely to organize quickly into powerful business lobbies and pressure governments to sustain the policies they depend upon. Thus, the winners tend to out-muscle the losers.

With second-stage reforms, the political fallout often outweighs potential gains. The losers are represented by large public-sector unions and professional associations while the potential beneficiaries of state reform, that is, taxpayers and clients dependent on public services, are typically poor, unorganized, and disperse. In this case, politicians and their reform teams may feel that there is little to gain by attempting second-stage reforms at all. The incentive structure facing domestic interests also helps to shape the possibilities of international cooperation. If politicians and private interests believe that they stand to gain something from a set of economic reforms, they are probably more willing to form transnational coalitions with external donors in order to pursue them.

Besides the different degrees of difficulty found in certain types of reforms, another set of technical and managerial considerations arises when we acknowledge that those who would implement the changes must back their plans with resources. Visionary leadership constitutes one such resource. Assuming that the idea of structural adjustment in the form of a "coherent framework of policy-relevant knowledge"[24] is available to the country, the reform team must adopt it and translate the concept into specific policy changes on the macro- and microlevels. This process is best organized by an overarching vision of the development model toward which the country is moving. Leadership for such strategies usually comes from public "policy elites,"[25] exemplified by the state technocrats who led the shift to export-led growth in East Asia[26] and neoliberal reform in New Zealand.[27] But in some Central American, Andean, and African countries, transnational alliances, or coalitions of domestic and external actors, have filled a leadership gap by designing and implementing all or part of a structural adjustment program.[28]

The backing of the president or substitute authority facilitates resource flows, positive public opinion, and interagency cooperation. This observation would seem especially important for second-stage reforms, which involve more complex public administration problems. In fact, the relevant literature stresses strong leadership, both inside and outside of a reforming institution, as a key component of managing successful reform.[29] Overhaul of an entire public institution requires that the minister in charge be committed to and focused on the reform goals, as well as possessed of the managerial capacity to bring subordinates, their unions, and the client base on board.

Reform teams also need adequate technical and financial resources to carry out their plans. Structural adjustment programs lead countries into areas in which they have little experience and require fresh capital. Hence, the oft felt need to hire consultants, open new regulatory agencies, train state managers in international best practices, and attract foreign investors. These tasks are expensive, as is the need to design welfare programs targeted at the poor and compensate other "losers" of reform such as laidoff government employees. Again, in Latin America, international donors such as the World Bank, Inter-American Development Bank (IDB), International Monetary Fund (IMF), and USAID have become important suppliers of technical advice and the financing of compensation packages, consultants' fees, new equipment, and physical infrastructure.

As we shall see in chapters 3 and 4, these two perspectives, the quality of democracy and the managerial aspects of reform, complement each other and explain Costa Rica's slow reform quite well. We now turn to what the literature tells us about the expected results of such a choice. Does gradualism yield positive or negative results?

The Debate over Gradualism

At least until recently, scholars and practitioners interested in the political management of economic reform tended to prefer rapid policy change to a slower route. Those in favor of shock therapy argue that it is the superior choice,[30] judging by economic, social, and political criteria. On the economic level, these proponents hold that as long as reforms remain incomplete, a country accrues "procrastination costs,"[31] for it sacrifices the potential benefits thought to accompany the optimal policy mix, one supporting a free-market system. In addition, Ańders Aslund contends that eastern European countries which carried out radical reform accomplished better results than their neighbors in GDP growth and inflation control as well as on social indicators such as consumption, unemployment, and income distribution.[32]

Political strategy also motivates this approach: radical reformers believe that it is important to move quickly, before opponents (whether they be labor unions, business elites, or an old communist nomenklatura) can organize to halt or reverse the reform program.[33] Even if opposition is not that fierce, shock therapists fear that politicians and the populous alike may succumb to reform fatigue. They think that leaders should take advantage of moments of "extraordinary politics," occurring after previous structures or assumptions have broken down. The disintegration of communist regimes and the onset of hyperinflation often usher in such intervals. During such periods, people will be unusually forgiving about suffering transitional costs, whereas if adjustment continues on into "normal" times, they will lose patience.[34] In addition, if the government's commitment to market economics or painful changes is at issue, the best way to achieve optimal economic policy may not be to creep toward the new position. Rather, a more effective strategy would be to overshoot the actual goal, thus establishing credibility.[35]

Arguments for radical reform probably apply best to cases of runaway inflation because the costs of this problem are immediate, affect the entire economy, and fall disproportionately on the poor. In addition, stopping inflation requires the control of expectations, making it important for a government to show a "firm hand." But dealing with hyperinflation is only one sort of economic reform, and, besides, it tends to occur in countries where democratic institutions are not well established, as does the sudden disintegration of political regimes. What then for countries in which checks and balances are a reality?

Gradualists approve of a step-by-step program whereby each stage produces groups of winners who can be expected to coalesce and form the basis of political support for further undertakings. These winners should push the reform program along in two ways: by lobbying for subsequent policy changes needed to lock in their new-found benefits and by serving as a counterbalance against losers.[36] Presumably, negotiated reforms are also more sustainable because all parties have found ways to agree to the new policies. Gradualists might also justify their position by observing that radical reformers are rare among stable, long-lived democracies. With the exception of New Zealand, gradual economic policy change is the norm in advanced industrialized countries. This fact implies that the most constructive strategy for policymakers would be to forgo shock therapy and identify strategies which help politicians make incremental progress on economic reforms within a democratic milieu.[37]

At this time, the proponents of gradualism are not arguing that slow reform produces superior economic outcomes or social solutions across the board. And we have no cross-national studies which test the two models to see which is better. Such a study would require historical perspective and multivariate analysis to control for the many other factors which would affect these outcomes in any given country. But there is some evidence that gradualists could challenge radical reformers on the question of outcomes. For instance, in his study of Latin American adjustment to the economic crisis of the 1980s, Samuel Morley finds fast and slow reformers to fit both the successful and unsuccessful categories; speed is not the main issue.[38]

Other scholars have begun to look at the requirements of certain types of state reform and found that technical considerations might call for slow instead of rapid change. Mathias Dewatripont and Gerard Roland point out that in certain situations, massive public-sector layoffs will cost a government more in compensation if they are done all at once than if the changes can be phased in over time.[39] And Ravi Ramamurti finds that gradual pacing may result in better conceived plans for the privatization of state-owned enterprises.[40] Still others worry that serious political instability (definitely not part of a good business climate) could result from social dislocation provoked by radical reform.[41] This book will present Costa Rica as a case whose gradual reform has produced mostly positive economic, social, and political outcomes. But we will still need a great deal more research before determining what speed is recommendable for economic reforms.

Organization of the Book

The literature on the political management of economic reform shows great interest in those countries which move quickly toward free-market policies and almost as much in nations which try and fail. But we do not know much about a growing middle group of nations which is muddling through. By design or default, most Latin American countries are pursuing the same ends at a slower pace. To explain this phenomenon in Costa Rica, this book contrasts the easier, first-stage reforms of the 1980s with the more difficult second-stage reforms of the 1990s. It then presents data on the economic, social, and political outcomes of the Costa Rican experience. The bulk of the book is based on field research, including over one hundred fifty interviews with Costa Rican policymakers and external donors. Information on the minicase studies as well as the outcomes data were collected during stays in Costa Rica lasting between three weeks and eighteen months in 1990–91, 1994, 1996, and 1997 and supplemented by several brief research trips to Washington D.C.

Chapter 2 describes the origins of the institutions central to this story and outlines the social welfare and economic development models which are the main objects of policy reforms. The aftermath of the 1948 civil war set the stage for the constitutional division of power, political parties, and welfare state that exist today. Costa Rica has a two-party system, something usually considered a positive point for development in as much as it pushes politicians toward consensus. Nevertheless, gridlock is a recurring feature of Costa Rican politics as the constitution of 1949 gave the president very weak powers vis-à-vis the legislature. There are several other notable veto points in Costa Rica's institutional structure including an independent Supreme Court, the Comptroller's office, and the semiautonomous institutions.

Since 1948, the Costa Rican state has supplied excellent public health, education, and pension systems to its citizens. The state also absorbed a growing portion of the labor force in the subsequent four decades as it increased the size of public bureaucracies. In fact, retrenching the welfare state has been much more unpopular than was the original expansion. Finally, chapter 2 describes the evolution of the postwar state in economic development and the addition of import-substitution industrialization to the traditional agricultural export model. To date, the clearest accomplishment of the economic reforms has been to greatly reduce protectionism and return

Costa Rica to a classic export-led growth model.

Chapters 3 and 4 cover four complete administrations evenly divided between the last two decades. This way we can easily compare and contrast the easier reforms of the 1980s with the more difficult second-stage adjustments attempted in the 1990s. While this study's purpose is not to perpetuate the debate about why countries attempt structural adjustment in the first place,[42] both chapters begin with an explanation of the domestic and international stimuli pushing Costa Rica toward the policy adjustments of that decade. Then each chapter presents a series of minicase studies, five from each decade, which illustrate the factors which facilitated or inhibited implementation.

Chapter 3 focuses on a major privatization, nontraditional export promotion, demonopolization of the banking industry, removal of agricultural subsidies, and reductions in import tariffs. In the first three cases, transnational reform coalitions composed of USAID officials and members of the Costa Rican private sector were able to take advantage of a severe economic crisis to pass simple enabling legislation quickly. After that point, the reform coalitions pursued their goals with virtual independence via private-sector institutions. Policy reforms gained strength as the new measures quickly produced beneficiaries. The two deprotectionist measures did produce substantial numbers of losers. But the changes were made by executive decree and the opposition was forced to concentrate on negotiating the terms of surrender.

Chapter 4 deals with the main second-generation reforms attempted in the 1990s. Unlike the first round, these have met with much less success. They turned out to be as difficult as we might have predicted in a democratic welfare state. The five reforms—public-sector layoffs, controversial privatizations, changes in pension regulations, and improvements in health and in education services—are administratively complex and politically contentious. Myriad institutional obstacles, such as short electoral cycles and multiple veto points within the Costa Rican government, halted progress on almost all of the measures. Certain reforms, particularly those involving the opening of state monopolies, provoked resistance from organized labor, professional associations, and community groups. The lackluster performance of the health sector modernization project demonstrates the power of passive resistance and problems presented by weak domestic "ownership" of an externally funded reform program.

The bulk of this book aims to explain why economic reforms

have been implemented or not, without explicit consideration of their desirability. But in the final substantive section, chapter 5 evaluates the economic, social, and political outcomes of this gradualist experience. The economic outcomes of the 1980s private-sector development policies have been tremendously positive. New export, banking, and tourism industries surfaced almost immediately and have served as engines of economic growth as well as mopping up unemployment, especially among those pushed out of the agricultural non-tradables sector. In regard to the social impact, poverty peaked during the economic crisis of the early 1980s but has dropped down to pre-crisis levels due to macroeconomic recovery, government wage policy, and targeted welfare programs. The political effects have also been stabilizing as the "winners" have formed strong lobbies to protect the new incentive system, while, for various reasons, the "losers" have forced concessions but not organized to roll back the policy changes. The greatest question mark is whether Costa Rica will succumb to reform fatigue and not complete the process of state reform.

The conclusions in chapter 6 first recap my explanation for the contrast between the relative ease of structural adjustment in the 1980s and the difficulties of the 1990s. Then I compare Costa Rica's experience with second-stage reforms with those of three other Latin American welfare states: Uruguay, Brazil, and Argentina. The Uruguayan case looks remarkably similar to Costa Rica's and the Brazilian only somewhat less so. But Argentina has pursued a deeper and more rapid set of second-stage reforms. What do Costa Rica, Uruguay, and Brazil have in common that Argentina does not? Three things: political institutions which deprive the executive of centralized decision-making authority, interests capable of forming autonomous pockets of resistance to structural adjustment, and elite preference for a continued welfare state.

What we should draw from these comparisons is that rapid and deep second-stage reforms are possible in Latin American welfare states, but under conditions that do not obtain in most of them. Theoretically, this comparative exploration reinforces the idea that institutions are crucial in determining whether gradual or rapid structural adjustment is more likely in a given country. Yet other variables are probably important as well. Future research should test more broadly to see if leaders' preferences for refined statist models and autonomous actors capable of resisting second-stage reforms independently predispose countries toward slow or no reform. The policy implications are clear: gradualism is logical and predictable in a significant number of Latin American countries. It would be most helpful for them if international experts concentrated on developing best practices for cases in which slow, piecemeal implementation will be the norm.

2

The Legacies of 1948: Democratic Institutions, Social Welfare, and Economic Development

Debate continues to rage over the true origins of Costa Rica's modern democracy. Did the personalities and events of 1948 bring abrupt change to Costa Rica's political development or should we see the current institutional configuration as the outcome of long-standing socioeconomic structures? The latter argument went long unchallenged. In its original version, the argument held that the privations of the colonial period produced an unusually egalitarian society from which democracy naturally evolved.[1] Because the colony lacked Indians or gold to exploit, the conquistadors made due with subsistence farming. The leveling poverty of farming supposedly made the European colonizers into settlers who respected one another as equals. But it turns out that the distribution of wealth in colonial Costa Rica was not so egalitarian after all,[2] and that rural inequality increased rapidly after the introduction of coffee as a cash crop.[3]

Today, a modified version of the evolutionary argument focuses less on rural equality and more on linking Costa Rica's culture of political tolerance to the social relations that developed around the cultivation of coffee. In the nineteenth century, the coffee-growing region and political center of Costa Rica was dominated by small and medium-sized farms on which family members provided the core labor force.[4] These farms depended on the processor-exporters (*beneficiadores*) to finance their cultivation needs and to buy the crop at harvest time. Without any indigenous population or large pool of dispossessed laborers to draw upon,[5] the large estate owners, very often *beneficiadores* themselves, had to pay high wages to coffee pickers and maintain relationships with the family farmers to secure help in the harvesting of their own crops.

The upshot of this situation of class interdependence was that the wealthier property owners and businessmen could ill afford to abuse those laboring under them. According to one influential author, what developed was a "coffee pact" in which smaller farmers and seasonal workers would continue to supply the wealthy with their product and labor in exchange for decent treatment. Such treatment came to include the right to opine about matters of state and even to vote. Because coffee growing was Costa Rica's principal economic activity for over one hundred years, this social pact led gradually to greater political participation among the masses and a national ideology valuing equality and consensus.[6]

Those who attribute Costa Rica's modern democratic institutions to pre-1948 conditions emphasize the gradual broadening of the franchise. Hallmarks include the first free and competitive election (1899) and the introduction of direct voting (1914). Ronald H. McDonald and J. Mark Ruhl tell us that between 1899 and 1948, ". . . democratic elections, honest civilian public administration, and peaceful transfers of power gradually become standard practices. . . ."[7] Remarkably, however, those who understand the civil war of 1948 to have been a major realignment of power and a break in political institutions see the previous era as a much more violent and unstable one. Fabrice Edouard Lehoucq says that: "Until well into the twentieth century, most presidents in Costa Rica came to power though the force of arms or in elections marred by fraud and violence."[8] And Cynthia Chalker reminds us that between 1899–1949, there were four coup attempts, eleven revolts, and a three-year dictatorship.[9] These political institutionalists argue that only in the aftermath of the 1948 civil war did Costa Ricans remove violence from politics and create stable democratic institutions.

The institutionalists do not deny the broad outline of the coffee pact idea, for rural relations in Costa Rica were uncommonly good and tended to promote national unification rather than ethnic and class-based violence as in the rest of Central America. Nevertheless, their account of electoral conflict indicates that even with high levels of societal consensus, elites found plenty to fight about in the realm of formal politics and this disaccord was destabilizing. Just as important, the institutionalists cannot accept the notion that positive socioeconomic factors inevitably or automatically beget liberal democratic regimes.[10] They demand a more explicitly political explanation of why and how a stable democratic regime developed in Costa Rica.

The present chapter does not attempt to resolve this debate but is sympathetic to the view of the political institutionalists. Here we see that a new political regime was constructed in the aftermath of the 1948 civil war. The decisions and ideological orientations of those who won the 1948 conflict are critical to understanding the institutional order set down by the 1949 Constitution, the party structure, and the development strategy upon which Costa Rica then embarked.

The Events of 1948

A tangle of complicated events and unusual alliances led to the civil war of 1948. While it is not necessary to retrace all of these here,[11] a brief description of those events sets the stage for the postwar reforms. We know that competitive elections began in 1899, but electoral fraud was common and still prevalent in the 1940s. In 1948, a particularly grievous case of vote fraud in the presidential election precipitated a civil war as political tensions spiraled out of control.

The 1940s: Elite Dissention

Most accounts covering the political history of the 1940s agree that division among elites set the stage for civil war.[12] The decade opened with the election of Dr. Rafael Angel Calderón Guardia of the Partido Republicano Nacional (National Republican Party or PRN) to the presidency. The PRN's leader and previous president, León Cortes Castro, pulled Calderón into politics, presumably thinking that he was a conservative. The son of a wealthy coffee family, Rafael Calderón was a member of the agro-export elite which had governed Costa Rica since the nineteenth century. Yet President Calderón soon found more than one way to offend members of the oligarchy.

First, in December 1941, Calderón declared war on Germany and expropriated the property of Costa Ricans of German descent. This turned many members of the oligarchy against the president as men of German descent dominated the activities of processing and financing coffee harvests, the main avenues for generating wealth in Costa Rica at that time. Second, Calderón's PRN and the Partido Comunista (Communist Party or PC) drew together in an alliance, bringing urban lower class and organized labor support to the president but further alienating the elite. Calderón did have some personal interest in social welfare issues, but tactical, as opposed to ideological, considerations seem to provide the best explanation for this arrangement.[13] To make the alliance even more strange, the Catholic Church soon joined.

Thus, the Calderón administration took on a populist flavor which encouraged labor organizers, especially those affiliated with the PC and working in the banana plantations among Costa Rica's relatively large rural proletariat. Under pressure from the union movement, the alliance also produced several pieces of progressive legislation establishing a social security institute (1941) and a labor code (1943). In addition, the PC and the PRN worked together in the 1944 presidential elections to bring Calderón's friend Teodoro Picado to office (the Constitution barred President Calderón from running for immediate reelection).

By the mid-1940s, then, the Costa Rican elite had split over Rafael Angel Calderón's relationship with the Communist Party and his social reforms. The opposition groups among the oligarchy coalesced around León Cortes, Calderón's former patron and the leader of a new party, the Partido Unión Nacional (National Union Party or PUN). The anti-Calderón elite engaged in their own odd alliance. They were joined by the progressive Partido Social Demócrata (Social Democratic Party or PSD), formed in 1945. The PSD represented the marriage of middle- and upper-middle-class intellectuals from the Centro para el Estudio de los Problemas Nacionales (Center for the Study of National Problems) and a less programmatic group called Acción Demócrata (Democratic Action or AD), the latter run by men who would become principals of the 1948 civil war.

The leader of the AD was José (Pepe) Figueres Ferrer, a charismatic young man who had been working his own farm when he was thrown out of Costa Rica for an anti-Calderón radio broadcast in 1942. While living in exile in Mexico during 1942–44, Figueres helped to found the Caribbean Legion, a group of Latin American and Caribbean reformers who planned to overthrow a number of regional dictators. José Figueres convinced the group that Calderón was as serious a threat to democracy as Somoza in Nicaragua and Trujillo in the Dominican Republic.[14] For after his return to Costa Rica, the Caribbean Legion helped Figueres stockpile arms while he prepared to launch a military offensive from a farm in San Isidro del General, south of the capital.

The Centro para el Estudio de los Problemas Nacionales provided the political platform for the PSD. It included: (1) opposition to Costa Rica's personalistic party system, corruption, and electoral fraud, all of which were strongly associated with Rafael Calderón; (2) anticommunism; (3) the need for state intervention to curb the excesses of the capitalist economy; and (4) economic modernization in the form of agricultural diversification and better access to bank credit for the non-elite.[15] Organized labor was notably absent from the PSD and its program. In addition, although it is often asserted that the PSD represented the interests of small farmers, there is little evidence that they formed a significant component of the PSD even though the party platform clearly included policy prescriptions on their behalf. Victorious in the 1948 civil war, the PSD became the PLN in 1951.

Political Friction Spills over into Violence

Tensions grew as the 1948 elections approached. In 1947, legislation establishing income and property taxes and Calderón's announcement that he would again run for president fanned the flames of opposition. The PSD and PUN joined to support the latter's candidate, Otilio Ulate, a moderate conservative. Ulate seemed to win the 1948 presidential election, but the *calderonistas* cried fraud and used their majority in Congress to have the results overturned. At that point, the opposition declared that the election had been stolen and Figueres initiated his armed attack on the government. After a six-week civil war pitting Figueres' rebel troops against a small national army and communist party members who had come from the banana plantations to fight, the opposition won.

The Eighteen-Month Junta

The 1948 war did not constitute a true revolution. Representatives of the coffee elite had fought on both sides and the victorious forces did not aim to annihilate the previous social, economic, and political systems. Yet the constitution and policies produced by the new regime would change Costa Rican development permanently. The victorious opposition represented an amalgam of ideological forces led by Pepe Figueres of the PSD and Otilio Ulate of the PUN. The two signed a pact which allowed Figures to head a revolutionary junta for eighteen months in exchange for his commitment to call a Constituent Assembly and turn the presidency over to Ulate in 1949.

It is perhaps ironic that the groundwork for Costa Rica's modern democracy was laid during a year-and-a-half of extra-constitutional rule. The Constituent Assembly, in which the PSD held a small minority of seats, hammered out compromises which produced a document supporting both a welfare state and classic liberalism.[16] Meanwhile, the junta took decisive action on several issues. The junta quickly abolished the army, nationalized the banks, and passed a one-time wealth tax.[17] These moves essentially eliminated the possibility of a countercoup[18] and shifted economic power from the oligarchy toward the new government. The only armed bodies created by the state would be urban police forces, which employ a minimum of military hierarchy and change personnel every four years with the incoming president, and a rural guard. Although Costa Rica upgraded these forces somewhat during the 1980s by accepting military aid from the United States, they are still notoriously ill-equipped and incompetent. On the economic front, subsequent administrations would use the national banking system to modernize the coffee sector, fund small and medium farmers, and finance urban businesses. Thus, the new economic institutions helped to develop a middle class.

Pepe Figueres and his junta also acted in another area that was to have far-reaching consequences for the Costa Rican polity. The junta outlawed the Communist Party (PC), jailed its leaders, and dismantled the radical Confederación de Trabajadores de Costa Rica (Confederation of Costa Rican Workers or CTCR) as well as its member unions. Labor organizations were dealt a heavy blow as any union linked with the PC, CTCR, or suspected of harboring communist influence was banned. Deborah J. Yashar reports that between 1948–1953, the number of registered unions declined from 204 to 74.[19] During the following decades, both major party groupings encouraged the development of milder, liberal and Christian Democratic-oriented unions as well as a movement called "*solidarismo*." *Solidarismo* is a company union system which strives to maintain harmonious relations between management and workers. On-site *solidarista* associations encourage the two sides to cosponsor savings and loan organizations and recreational opportunities for employees instead of organizing workers for collective bargaining and confrontation. This system now dominates the private sector.

Political Institutions

The Executive, the Legislature, and the Electoral System

The 1949 Constitution lays down Costa Rica's modern political institutions. The first elections under its rules took place in 1953. One of the chief concerns of the Constituent Assembly was to reduce the power of the presidency vis-à-vis other branches of government, thus avoiding repetition of past abuses. As a result, the Costa Rican system probably has the weakest executive in Latin America. Costa Rican presidents cannot: (1) veto the national budget as determined by the legislature; (2) use a pocket or line-item veto; (3) assume emergency powers without a supporting vote by a two-thirds majority of the legislature; (4) legislate by decree; or (5) stand for reelection.[20] The president independently appoints and dismisses cabinet members, however. And, in as much as executive branch bureaucracies are responsible for implementing legislation and setting rules, the president can pursue policy changes independently. The president can also call a special session of the Legislative Assembly to consider only legislation proposed by him or her. But this power is constrained by the inability of the president to control the procedures used or the amendments attached to legislation during a special session.

The Legislative Assembly is a unicameral body with fifty-seven seats representing Costa Rica's seven provinces. Presidential, Assembly, and municipal elections are held concurrently every four years. Assembly incumbents must sit out one term before standing for reelection. The president is selected by direct, popular vote and must receive a plurality of at least 40 percent of the vote to avoid a runoff between the top two candidates. Costa Rica has not needed to hold a second round election since the Constitution was written in 1949. Legislators are elected via a closed-list proportional representation system.[21] Costa Rica's seven provinces serve as multimember electoral districts in which the number of seats range from four to twenty-one; the average effective magnitude is 8.1.[22] The Tribunal Supremo Electoral (Supreme Electoral Tribunal or TSE) oversees all elections. Its magistrates are appointed to six-year terms by the Supreme Court. In Costa Rica, electoral laws and regulations, voter registration, and public campaign funding are exclusively reviewed and administered by the TSE. The TSE is designed to make elections as fair and honest as possible. In fact, in an important public ceremony held shortly before each election, the TSE takes legal control over the country's police and rural guard.

Although the 40 percent threshold required to elect a president and concurrent elections limit party fragmentation and tend to increase partisan support for the president in the legislature, the net effect of Costa Rica's institutional design is to undermine executive authority and party cohesion. Weak presidential power, dual term limits, and ambiguous standards of discipline within the two main parties offer the executive few formal instruments for securing copartisan support in the legislature. Instead, John M. Carey informs us, Costa Rican "presidents frequently must stitch together policy-specific cross-partisan coalitions, inevitably requiring concessions to coalition partners in the Assembly."[23] Executive-legislative gridlock is common. The president is treated more and more as a lame duck as his or her term progresses and Assembly members tend to spend much of their second two years in office seeking a position in the next administration.[24] As we might expect, the behavior of the Legislative Assembly given this set of incentives makes passing economic policy changes agonizingly slow, likely to be held hostage to unrelated political disputes, and vulnerable to compromises that distort the original intent of the legislation.

Costa Rica's seven provinces are divided into eighty-one *cantones* (roughly counties), each of which has a municipal government elected from a closed list. At present, each municipal council appoints a city manager but voters will directly elect mayors beginning in 2002. In any case, the municipal governments have little real power as the national government controls most of their financial decisions and provides almost all services.[25] People with political ambition have typically bypassed local government and attempted to gain national office directly.

Political Parties

As we can see in table 2.1, after 1948, Costa Rica evolved toward a two-party system with the axis of political competition dividing the Partido Liberación Nacional (National Liberation Party or PLN) and coalitions of conservative anti-PLN forces. In 1951, José Figueres and other principals of the PSD founded the PLN. Party leaders worked to establish the PLN in every electoral district in the country. In the 1953 elections, the PLN harvested the fruits of the party's organization and Pepe Figueres' charisma as the hero of the 1948 war. That year the PLN won the presidency, a

Table 2.1
Costa Rican Presidents and Party Representation in the Legislative Assembly

Year	President (Party)	PLN	Conservative Alliances	Left	Minor Parties[a]	Total Seats[b]
1953	Figueres (PLN)	30	15	-	-	45
1958	Echandi (PUN)	20	21	-	4	45
1962	Orlich (PLN)	29	27	1	-	57
1966	Trejos (PUNIF)	29	26	-	2	57
1970	Figueres (PLN)	32	22	2	1	57
1974	Oduber (PLN)	27	16	2	12	57
1978	Carazo (UNIDAD)	25	27	4	1	57
1982	Monge (PLN)	33	18	4	2	57
1986	Arias (PLN)	29	25	2	1	57
1990	Calderón (PUSC)	25	29	1	2	57
1994	Figueres (PLN)	28	25	-	4	57
1998	Rodríguez (PUSC)	23	28	-	6	57

SOURCES: Yashar, "Civil War and Social Welfare." Table 3.3; Carey, "Strong Candidates for a Limited Office." Table 5.1; and William Méndez, "PUSC con un diputado más," *La Nación*, 19 (February 1998).

a. Minor parties are very small, usually regional parties not clearly identified with the conservative coalitions or the Left.
b. The number of Assembly seats was increased from 45 to 57 after 1958.

majority in the Legislative Assembly, and secured its position as the dominant political party, a situation that would last until the 1990s. In the 1950s and 1960s, rural zones (peasants and owners of medium-sized farms), as well as the middle strata in urban areas composed the strongholds of PLN support. Indeed, the discourse of the party has always emphasized the defense of small farmers and the construction of a middle-class society.[26] Thus, the party has always counted on multiclass support. But in later decades, the PLN's electoral base, like that of the opposition, became more fluid and diverse by incorporating larger numbers of both wealthy businesspeople and labor organizations.

Although the PLN identifies itself as a social democratic party and is a long-time member of the Socialist International, the working class neither played a significant role in its formation nor can be counted on for solid electoral support. Speaking practically, this situation dates back to the political alliances of the 1940s when the many labor unions affiliated with the Communist Party wound up on the losing side of the civil war and were dismantled by Pepe

Figueres and his junta. But it also says something about the PLN's definition of socialism. In a 1966 interview, José Figueres explained that:

> In Costa Rica, the word socialism simply conveys images of the good life, of honest elections, of economic well-being. By no means does it bring to mind ideas of class struggle as it does in the United States or parts of Europe.[27]

As we will see in the following sections, the PLN has focused on improving conditions in rural areas, universalizing social security, economic diversification, and the defense of small property. PLN administrations increased state intervention and expanded the welfare state while remaining committed to a capitalist framework. These policies resulted in the rapid growth of white-collar state-sector employment, some income redistribution toward the middle quintiles[28] and considerable alleviation of rural poverty.[29]

Personalist followings have always controlled the inner workings of the PLN. Until the mid-1980s, the 1948 generation dominated. José Figueres, Daniel Oduber, and Francisco Orlich were particularly important and all three of them served as president. Decision making within the party still reflects struggles among personalist factions which may or may not represent coherent ideological viewpoints, but there has been a generational turnover. When he was elected in 1986, Oscar Arias become the first PLN president who was too young to have been involved in the 1948 war. And beginning in the 1980s, the party developed splits over whether or not to break away from the state interventionist model toward something more neoliberal. José María Figueres Olsen, the son of don Pepe, is the party's first "New Democrat" and served as president from 1994–98.

After 1948, the groups which opposed the PSD/PLN regrouped into a set of conservative parties which changed names several times until 1983 when they crystallized as the Partido Unidad Social Cristiana (United Social Christian Party or PUSC). Like the PLN, these parties have also been organized around the prominent persons and factions of the 1940s. When electoral politics resumed in the 1950s, Calderón's PRD and Otilio Ulate's PUN (this conservative leader permanently split with the PSD/PLN) challenged the PLN for the presidency. The two parties joined forces and put forth a candidate, Mario Echandi, who beat the divided PLN in 1958. Rafael Angel Calderón Guardia was allowed to return from exile in that year and run for president in 1962, an election he lost. The senior Calderón died in 1970, leaving leadership of the PRN to his son, Rafael Angel "Junior" Calderón Fournier. When Otilio Ulate died in 1973, though, the PUN disintegrated.

Beginning in the 1950s, the conservative parties usually formed fragile coalitions to run a single candidate in the presidential elections. Opposition candidates were elected in 1958, 1966, 1978, 1990, and 1998. Much like the PLN, these opposition parties had multiclass support. Their strongest support came from the owners of large coffee estates and urban industries. But, because of the alliances forged during the 1940s and the persecution suffered by many labor unions in 1948–49, these parties also counted on a sizable allegiance from the urban working class. Also, much as in the case of the PLN, the conservative parties have attracted a more diverse and fluid electoral base from the late 1970s on.

When in office, the opposition coalitions express a combination of principles born from the hardline liberal economic ideology of the Asociación Nacional de Fomento Económico (National Association of Economic Development or ANFE), to which prominent members have belonged,[30] from Christian Democratic ideas about public responsibility for alleviating poverty, and anti-PLN rhetoric. As a result, opposition governments have usually featured the promise of reducing state intervention in the economy, combined with a commitment to welfare programs. But surprisingly, conservative governments made almost no progress in shrinking the size and scope of the state until after the PLN did so itself in the 1980s. What explains this apparent contradiction? As Yashar notes, we lack good research on the inner workings of the opposition coalitions.[31] Nevertheless, any explanation would include two factors. One is that the working-class support and concern about poverty within the opposition parties themselves impedes attacks on the welfare state. Another is that until the mid-1980s, the conservative parties had not established their presence in all electoral districts of Costa Rica as had the PLN. The result was that conservative alliances only first won a majority of Assembly seats in 1990. Even though an opposition candidate was elected president in 1958, 1966, and 1978, it was extremely difficult for each of them to pass legislation while his already fractious coalition held a minority of seats in the Assembly.

The conservative parties have always been the vehicles of personalities linked to the events of 1948 as well as landowners and businesspeople who for some reason were out of favor with the

PLN. On occasion, PLN defectors have helped the opposition to defeat their former party. For example, Rodrigo Carazo, a former Legislative Assembly deputy who had lost the 1970 PLN presidential nomination to José Figueres, left to found his own party. In 1978, his party joined others from the opposition to form the Unidad (Unity) coalition. As the presidential candidate for Unidad, Carazo won the presidency in 1978. Unidad was a bundle of contradictions between the liberal economic leanings of the conservatives and Carazo's own dedication to the welfare state and increased public support for some business sectors such as rice farmers. What the alliance partners did have in common was a concern about corruption apparent in the administration of Daniel Oduber (1974–78) and in the PLN in general.

In a twist of fate, however, the Unity administration would coincide with an economic crisis and Carazo's mismanagement of it would help keep the opposition out of power until 1990. While out of office, the conservative factions finally merged into a single party, the PUSC, formed in late 1983. The party is led by Rafael Angel "Junior" Calderón who has helped shape it into a professional, nationwide organization with permanent representation in all electoral districts. This shift was represented in the PUSC's success in the February 1998 elections in which its candidate, businessman Miguel Angel Rodríguez, won the presidency and more Assembly seats (28) than the PLN (23). In as much as the PUSC has established itself as a real party and ended organizational factionalism among the conservatives, we can say that a true two-party system now governs Costa Rica instead of a dominant PLN constantly under challenge from anti-PLN forces.

In Costa Rica, the left has always pursued party politics and union organizing instead of insurrection. But even in the electoral arena, leftist parties have exercised minimal influence since 1948 when the Communist Party was constitutionally banned. Between 1962 and 1975, when the constitutional prohibition on Marxist parties was lifted, the PC ran candidates under alternative party names.[32] Most support for the left parties came from San José and the banana-producing areas of Puntarenas and Limón provinces.[33] The electoral draw of the left parties peaked in 1982 after a coalition called Pueblo Unido (United People or PU) garnered 3.3 percent of the vote in the presidential race and four seats in the Assembly.[34] But after 1982, internal divisions within PU and later the demise of the left in Central America spelled doom for the Costa Rican parties. Since 1994, left parties have not won any seats in the

Legislative Assembly. There are no parties representing the Far Right although an organization called "Movimiento Costa Rica Libre" (the Free Costa Rica Movement) was a visible and rabid anticommunist presence in the 1980s and early 1990s.

Additional Veto Points in the Costa Rican System

We saw above how the Costa Rican executive's powers vis-à-vis the legislature are quite circumscribed, a situation which makes passing bold reform measures difficult unless the president's party holds a majority in congress and can agree on the proposal at hand. In this way, the legislature forms the most obvious veto point through which another level of government can derail a president's policy package. In Costa Rica, however, the legislature is only the first obstacle a policy reform might face. Three other official bodies—the Supreme Court, the Comptroller, and the semiautonomous institutions—deserve mention as additional veto points in the Costa Rican system.[35]

In 1989, the power of judicial review was substantially strengthened when the Legislative Assembly passed a bill mandating the Supreme Court to establish a new chamber (Sala IV) charged with determining the constitutionality of any legislation or government action brought before it. The legislators were apparently responding to faltering public confidence in a slow-moving judicial system faced with a large case backlog and the need to move more quickly in hearing a recent series of corruption cases. It is thought that the legislators did not forsee the level of activism the new court would adopt.[36] The Sala IV has struck down numerous laws and rules, many relevant to economic reform. For example, in 1995, when the state energy and telephone company ICE decided to lease the rights to sell cellular phone packages to a private firm (Millicom), the Sala IV struck down the deal by declaring it unconstitutional.[37] In early 1998, the Sala IV found unconstitutional several articles of a new law (#7494) that would have eased the ability of public institutions to contract private administrative services. Opponents of economic reform laws and rule changes routinely lobby the Sala IV to review the specific item with which they are concerned. This strategy is particularly effective because such cases go directly to the Supreme Court without being heard by lower courts first.

In similar fashion, the Comptroller (Contraloría General de la República) can review the administration of laws involving public finances and has the independent authority to annul contracts when the rules are not followed or corruption is discovered. For example, in June 1997 the Comptroller annulled the first contract made under a new public works law allowing the state to award concessions to private companies for the construction and operation of infrastructural projects. Thus, the first project in decades which would have allowed a private consortium to finance and build a badly needed highway fell apart because proper procedures were not followed during the bidding process by which the Ministry of Public Works awarded the contract.[38] The law (#7404) was eventually sent back to the Assembly for rewriting.

As a group, Costa Rica's more than one hundred thirty semi-autonomous institutions form a last veto point. These state agencies include the administrator of the health system and pensions (CCSS), the monopolies on telecommunications and energy (ICE), insurance (INS), and oil refining (RECOPE), the body that oversees development projects and runs the ports in the Atlantic Zone (JAPDEVA), the regulator of the free zones (Corporación Zona Franca), and the organization that distributes public funds to welfare programs (FODESAF). They are typically run by boards composed of seven directors, three each from the public and private sectors and one labor representative. The boards of directors set policy for the agencies in accordance with their mandates and executive directives as well as overseeing internal administration. Because directors cannot be removed by any official for political reasons, boards can and do slow down or impede the implementation of new policies they do not like. For example, under President Monge (1982–86), USAID officials set up an alternative structure for liquidating the assets of the state development enterprise CODESA, because it was clear that its board would refuse to carry out the sales. More recently, JAPDEVA did not cooperate at all with President Figueres' efforts to open stevedoring contracts to outside bidders in the country's main port. Of course, as is the case with state ministries, all sorts of bureaucratic politics take place within the semiautonomous institutions that may further hamstring change.

The Question of Governability

The discussion thus far shows that although Costa Rica's state is unitary, its institutional structure offers multiple avenues for obstructing policy changes proposed by the president and cabinet officials. Interest group fragmentation reinforces the decentralized nature of decisionmaking. Neither business nor labor is represented by well-functioning peak associations. There is a peak organization for private sector capital, the Unión Costarricense de Cámaras y Asociaciones de la Empresa Privada (UCCAEP or Costa Rican Union of Private Sector Chambers and Associations), but it has no authority over the smaller and more active business chambers such as those representing industry, commerce, agriculture and producers of particular items like milk, coffee, bananas, and textiles. Labor unions divide their loyalties among three main confederations: the Confederación de Trabajadores Costarricenses (CTC, whose orientation is Christian Democratic), the Confederación Costarricense de Trabajadores Democráticos (CCTD, affiliated with the AFL-CIO), and the Confederación Unitaria de Trabajadores (CUT, which represents communist unions).

Several things temper this fragmentation and help bring a certain level of governability to the country. One is the way that Costa Rica's two-party system and tradition of bipartisanship foster compromise. In 1995, for example, President Figueres and former President Calderón (acting as leader of the opposition) agreed to a pact whereby PUSC deputies would allow the PLN's tax package to pass in the Assembly in exchange for the President's commitment to privatization and deficit-reducing measures. In addition, the country benefits from periodic tripartite negotiation. For example, a tripartite board representing government, business, and labor determines minimum wages biannually. Sitting governments also normally hold a few weekend workshops or *encerronas* with business and labor leaders to seek agreement on matters of national policy.

There are two other factors which balance against the ungovernability that could arise from Costa Rica's fragmented institutions. Interestingly, they are also identified by Peter Katzenstein as features that helped the small European countries make constant adjustments to economic change while minimizing social conflict.[39] First, the frequency with which business elites serve as government ministers, sometimes more than once in their lifetimes, reduces the ideological distance between the public and private sectors. On matters of economic development, government officials consult extensively, formally and informally, with businesspeople. Second, in Costa Rica, a sense of social solidarity is constantly reinforced by the state's welfare programs, particularly the public health and pension schemes to which there are few alternatives.[40] We now turn to the role of the state in social welfare and economic development.

Origins of the Universal Social Welfare Programs

During electoral campaigns, PUSC candidates make a point of reminding the populace that Costa Rica's social security programs did not originate with Pepe Figueres and the PLN. They are quite right. President Calderón Guardia's administration actually established the public pension and health insurance programs that would later be universalized. President Calderón was a medical doctor who had become familiar with state-sponsored social security programs while studying in Europe. When he allied with the Communist Party, organized labor had little trouble in convincing President Calderón to establish these benefits in Costa Rica. The Costa Rican Social Security Fund (CCSS), founded in 1941, launched sickness and maternity health insurance and a pension program in 1943. Before that time, only certain public-sector employees enjoyed pension plans: teachers (established in 1886), the military (1888), and workers in telecommunications (1918), the postal system (1923), railroads (1935), the judiciary (1939), and customs (1940).[41] Likewise, people acquired health services by paying private doctors, finding help from limited government programs or charities, or by working for one of the multinational banana companies that did have a clinic.

During the 1950s, little effort was made to expand social security coverage beyond the lowest paid urban wageworkers. The Ulate, Figueres, and Echandi administrations preferred to commit scarce state resources to building the new autonomous institutions instead of promoting a vestige of Dr. Calderón Guardia's prewar government. The well-organized doctors' union also opposed the expansion of coverage. Physicians feared the loss of their private practices and the invasion of their profession by government bureaucrats.[42] But CCSS administrators continued to press for expansion and in 1961, PLN legislators recognized the political benefits of doing so. They convinced the Assembly to pass a law mandating the universalization of social security. Coverage consequently rose from approximately 15 percent to 50 percent of the population during the decade.[43] But only when President Figueres' second administration took interest in social security in 1970 did the CCSS receive the authority and resources to truly universalize coverage.

The CCSS offers the only pension and health insurance programs in Costa Rica[44] as well as most of the curative services available in the country. Membership in the national health insurance and pension programs is compulsory for those employed in the formal sector, including domestic service. Workers pay combined monthly premiums equal to 8 percent of their wages (employers contribute 14 percent of each employee's wages and the state 0.50 percent).[45] Health insurance extends to all of each worker's dependents. There are also strong incentives for the self-employed and seasonal workers to join the CCSS insurance plans. By the 1980s, all citizens enjoyed the security of old-age pensions.[46] Public health insurance coverage through the sickness and maternity program reached 89 percent of the population in 1991.[47] The state extends virtually free membership to the uninsured poor (via a means test) and so it is thought that most of the truly uninsured retain this condition voluntarily and buy medical services from private providers.[48]

While the CCSS expanded coverage during the 1960s and 1970s, the activities of other state agencies complemented its goals. For example, the Ministry of Health launched massive and successful disease eradication and inoculation campaigns bringing Costa Rica's rates of infant diarrhea, infectious diseases, and malaria down to far below those of its neighbors. The work of the state enterprise in charge of sewerage and water (Instituto Costarricense de Acueductos y Alcantarillados) to bring safe drinking water and waste disposal to all corners of the country, especially rural areas, complemented the Ministry's campaigns. Finally, the Instituto Nacional de Seguros (INS) started providing worker's compensation insurance. Sixty-five percent of the population now receives this benefit and the CCSS provides the necessary services and pensions to the uninsured if they are injured in a job-related accident.

The Costa Rican state committed itself to raising popular education standards even before establishing a concern for public health. In 1886, Mauro Fernández, then secretary of the finance and public instruction ministries, led educational reforms aimed at spreading basic education to a larger segment of the population. These reforms proved tremendously profitable, as Costa Rica's literacy rate rose quickly. Before the reforms, Costa Rica's literacy rate lingered below 20 percent of the population along with all the other Central American nations. But by 1950, the Costa Rican rate had reached 80 percent, far surpassing progress in neighboring countries where literacy spread much more slowly.[49] Again, since 1948, much of the expansion of public educational services has focused on improving schooling in rural areas. The 1949 constitution explicitly directed the state to provide free and compulsory education to all citizens. During his first elected administration, President Figueres pushed through the Fundamental Law of Education to ensure the Ministry of Education adequate funds to carry out this mandate. The Constitution also guaranteed funding to the University of Costa Rica and was subsequently amended to extend the same guarantee to three newer public universities.

As is the case in many other welfare states, an expansion of public employment accompanied the growth of state institutions and services. Between 1948 and 1977, 119 new state institutions were created.[50] And the size of the public work force increased more than sevenfold in thirty years, or from 23,023 employees in 1954 to 162,600 in 1985. In 1985, public-sector workers accounted for 18 percent of the total work force.[51] Because there are no unemployment insurance or cash assistance programs in Costa Rica (although in-kind transfers do exist and are discussed in chapter 5), the state relies on full-employment policies and a strong formal sector to maintain its own taxation needs and individual livelihoods. The growth of public-sector jobs has helped buoy full-employment, especially among females who began to enter the formal-sector economy in large numbers only during the last few decades. Women have come to dominate many of the lowest paid state occupations such as teaching and entry level office work.

The State in Economic Development

The social democrats who won the civil war of 1948 did not seek to abolish private enterprise or even to discourage foreign investment. But they did set out to make export industries pay higher taxes, ensure a stable existence for small and medium-sized farms, and diversify the economy.[52] While tax increases were legislated or decreed, the newly nationalized banking system and the Central Bank of Costa Rica, established in 1950, gave postwar governments the financial power to pursue the latter two goals. Until the mid-1980s, the Central Bank channeled credit via the four state banks by setting *topes*, or lending targets, for the economic activities and types of producers it wished to promote. At first, economic development efforts focused exclusively on agriculture, but in the 1960s, the state established policies to promote industrial enterprises.

Agriculture

In 1948, the junta made good on its commitment to small, domestic agricultural enterprises by creating the Consejo Nacional de Producción (National Production Council or CNP). The CNP was a state marketing board which monopolized the import and export as well as the domestic purchasing and wholesaling of basic grains. Specifically, the CNP purchased beans, corn, sorghum, and later rice from domestic farmers at subsidized prices. The CNP then sold all of these grains, at controlled prices, onto the domestic market. In addition, the CNP monopolized the importation of wheat. Very small farms grow most corn and beans in Costa Rica, so the prices paid by the CNP supported a decent standard of living for many rural people. State institutions also backed a few private initiatives to diversify agricultural exports, most notably those of the cattlemen of the Pacific region. Unlike the case with basic grains, very large farms dominate beef production.[53] The cattle industry took 10 percent of state banking system credit to the private sector in 1956 but peaked at 29 percent of the same in 1975.[54] Despite these efforts, coffee and banana exports remained, as had been the case since the turn of the century, Costa Rica's top two agricultural exports. Hence, successive governments have aimed policy at tying them into national development goals.

The social democrats wanted two things from the coffee industry: more tax revenue and a reduction in the economic power of the largest enterprises, especially vis-à-vis smaller growers. The first government elected after the war increased coffee taxes significantly.[55] In 1952, after overcoming substantial opposition from coffee exporters, the legislature passed an ad valorem tax on coffee that reduced the profit rate *beneficiadores* were allowed from 16 to 9 percent of total sales and required them to pay 5 percent of earnings to the state as a tax. This move would seem to indicate growing power on the part of the state over the top export sector, although one observer notes that international coffee prices were high in the 1950s and that the Ulate government probably would not have been able to impose the tax in less favorable economic conditions.[56] In any case, these laws remain in effect to this day, although exporters have won the right to tax breaks if international prices dip below a certain level. In the 1950s and 1960s, the state used the new tax proceeds to make badly needed improvements in rural infrastructure. Today they are mixed into the general revenue pool.

The state further reduced the power of the *beneficiadores* by siding with small and medium growers attempting to form cooperatives to process and export their crops. Declining international prices beginning in the late 1950s stirred conflict between producers and processors. Farmers demanded that the state help them establish coffee processing and export cooperatives as well as lines of credit independent of the *beneficiadores*. The state agreed and in 1962 the Central Bank established the Federation of Cooperatives of Coffee Growers (FEDECOOP) to assist in the processing and international marketing and of coffee grown by its members. By 1975, the cooperatives processed about one-third of the country's coffee crop; thirty-one cooperative plants had been built by 1979.[57] Outside of these actions, the state generally limited itself to improving the conditions for private coffee production, chiefly through credit and subsidy programs designed to help growers boost productivity by replanting with new varieties and increasing the use of chemical fertilizers.

It would prove far more difficult to manipulate the foreign companies dominating Costa Rica's banana industry. After 1956, the United Fruit Company (now United Brands), a U.S.-based transnational, would share the export business with Standard Fruit (Castle and Cook), and Del Monte's subsidiary BANDECO (now under Mexican ownership). In a manner similar to the coffee industry, the two main goals of successive post-1948 governments in dealing with the banana companies were to secure the position of smaller domestic producers and extract more taxes from exporters.

In the mid-1960s, state development banks began channeling credit to domestic banana growers. By 1973, these independents controlled 46.5 percent of the land under banana cultivation in the country,[58] although the transnationals still monopolized exporting. All other banana cultivation in Costa Rica takes place on the plantations of the foreign companies. The state banks further assisted the local growers by helping them to form the National Banana Association (ASBANA) in 1971, an organization which provided agronomic and management services to growers. Nevertheless, in the early 1970s, tensions ran high as production contracts forced the growers to absorb rising input costs and the Costa Rican government still extracted less than satisfactory revenue from banana exports.

In 1974, President Figures initiated an offensive on the banana transnationals, a strategy continued by the Oduber and

Carazo administrations. As a result, the banana export tax reached an all-time high of $0.95 per box in 1981 as did the minimum price that transnationals had to pay growers ($3.40 per box).[59] The proceeds from the tax were divided between state coffers and a fund to assist the independent growers. But these victories proved all too fleeting. A series of events led the Monge and Arias governments to reduce the tax burden on the banana industry to $0.15 per box by 1989.[60] Thus, while state intervention in the sector improved the situation of independent growers substantially, government revenues collected from the banana industry have come full circle by returning to pre-1974 levels.

Industry

At the beginning of the 1950s, industrial development in Costa Rica was in a nascent stage, dominated by Costa Rican artisans who mainly produced processed food and tobacco items. The average industrial establishment employed 5.7 workers in 1951.[61] Although throughout the 1950s the Chamber of Industries lobbied energetically for legislation aimed at promoting manufacturing, several such bills failed in the Assembly. Import merchants opposed any potential competition to their business and there was a general lack of interest in industrial promotion at a time of very high coffee prices.

Near the end of the decade, however, international coffee prices and banana sales dropped sharply. Consequently, the idea of protecting the balance of payments by encouraging domestic substitutes for imported items became more appealing. The PLN, and especially deputy Daniel Oduber, had been won over to the Chamber of Industry's viewpoint, and agreed to vote for the Industrial Promotion Law even though it had been submitted by the opposition Echandi administration.[62] The 1959 law increased tariffs on many imported items and offered industrialists exemptions of virtually 100 percent on local, import, and export taxes. There were no local content or nationality restrictions on benefits.

Negotiations to enter the Central American Common Market (CACM) came on the heels of the Industrial Promotion Law. For that reason, Costa Rican industrialization was virtually simultaneous with regional integration. Throughout the 1950s, Central American countries had been slowly taking steps, such as signing bilateral free trade agreements, toward a regional integration scheme. Technocrats from the United Nation's Economic Commission on Latin

America (ECLA) nudged the negotiations along. The four northern countries brought the CACM into effect in 1960 but Costa Rica did not join until 1963. For despite passage of the Industrial Promotion Law, President Echandi's administration feared that Costa Rica had little to gain and much to lose by tying its economy to those of neighboring countries. It took the support of the Orlich administration and pressure from the United States to convince the Legislative Assembly to pass the integration treaty in 1963.[63]

The CACM was set up as a customs union whose central features were a Common External Tariff (CET) and abolition of import duties among the members. Nominal protection rates provided by the CET plus the San José Protocol of 1969, under which countries added a 30 percent surcharge to import duties, drove some external tariffs into the many hundreds of percent. Traditional commodity exports and basic grains were exempted from CACM rules, however, so that countries could maintain national agricultural policies. The Central American Convention on Fiscal Incentives for Industrial Protection standardized the tax benefits and subsidies each country offered to firms exporting within the CACM. Costa Rican macroeconomic policy, principally a fixed exchange rate, which became overvalued in the 1970s,[64] complemented the sectoral incentives offered to industrialists producing for the domestic and regional markets.

Disagreement exists over the performance of Costa Rica's industrial sector and the CACM. In regard to their accomplishments, we can note that real average annual growth rates in Costa Rican manufacturing sector outstripped that of the GDP between 1963–78.[65] In addition, the CACM appears to have aided the diversification of Costa Rican manufacturing. Between 1957 and 1980, the percentage of industrial valued added accounted for by processed foods and tobacco declined to 45.6 percent, and the categories representing heavy industry increased from 7 to 28 percent of the total.[66] For the first time, direct foreign investment flowed into manufacturing concerns in Costa Rica during the 1960s and 1970s and this capital was significant for industries involved in the CACM. One source estimates that foreign capital accounted for 58 percent of investment in medium- and large-scale factories between 1960 and 1970 and that, by 1978, over three-quarters of Costa Rica's industrial exports (the majority of which went to CACM partners) originated in foreign or joint-venture firms.[67] In 1980, at the peak of Costa Rica's involvement in the CACM, 28 percent of all exports went to regional partners.[68]

But other economists emphasize the distortions the CACM

brought to Central American economies. According to Victor Bulmer-Thomas, high tariffs on finished products and very low ones on raw materials and intermediate goods encouraged capital-intensive, import-dependent industrialization which produced mainly consumer goods and developed few backward linkages.[69] Claudio González-Vega adds that the dependence on imported inputs too easily translated into negative economic growth when external shocks necessitated corrections in the balance of payments.[70]

There are three important points of agreement, however. First, even optimists admit that Costa Rica's easy phase of ISI (import-substitution industrialization) growth had exhausted itself by the end of the 1970s. Second, the incentives aimed at domestic and regional industry discouraged the few efforts at promoting new nontraditional (extraregional) exports that did occur in the 1960s and 1970s. Third, by the mid-1980s, political instability in the other Central American countries had virtually halted trade between them and Costa Rica. In particular, sales to Nicaragua collapsed because the latter was unable to pay its debt to Costa Rica.

The final phase of state-sponsored industrial development occurred in the 1970s when it purchased the country's only oil refinery, RECOPE (Refinadora Costarricense de Petróleo or Costa Rican Petroleum Refinery), and established a holding company called CODESA (Corporación Costarricense de Desarrollo or Costa Rican Development Corporation). Rather than finding their roots in the ideology of the late 1940s, these developments coincided with an upswing in nationalism and interventionism within the PLN.[71] The Costa Rican state had owned 15 percent of RECOPE from its inception in 1963. The state gradually bought the rest of RECOPE's shares from the consortium which held them, gaining full ownership in 1974. Given that full nationalization took place on the heels of the oil crisis, that the private sector did not feel threatened by state ownership in this strategic sector, and that RECOPE was a profitable company, its purchase was never very controversial.

CODESA, on the other hand, would turn out to be a political disaster for the PLN. The Legislature finally passed a bill creating CODESA in 1972, after years of initiatives by PLN activists who believed that the state should take responsibility for developing projects which required more capital than the national business sector could marshal. The original idea was that CODESA would develop mixed-capital (public-private) ventures which would be sold to the private sector. But public-sector funds provided all of CODESA's investment capital and no companies were sold off until

CODESA was shut down in the 1980s.[72] This financial reality made CODESA, in effect, a state company.

The PLN governed during CODESA's most active period (1972–78), and public controversy surrounded accusations of corruption and cronyism involving Presidents Figueres' and Oduber's use of the company.[73] CODESA's economic performance was equally unsuccessful. By the early 1980s, CODESA had used an extraordinary proportion of available public-sector credit to make mostly unprofitable investments. Industrialists became increasingly annoyed as CODESA's draw on bank lending crowded out the private sector's access to credit.[74] The business community's backlash against CODESA and public perceptions of PLN corruption would help the opposition candidate, Rodrigo Carazo, win the presidential election in 1978.

Three Decades of Growth and Stability

The Costa Rican economy performed exceptionally well during the 1950s and 1970s. Between 1951–1979, the GDP grew at an average annual rate of 6.1 percent, or 2.3 percent per year in per capita terms.[75] There were positive social effects as well. The proportion of the population living in poverty dropped from about 50 percent in 1961 to 20–25 percent in the mid-1970s. During the same period, the Gini coefficient dropped from 0.52 to 0.44.[76] While the industrialization and economic growth brought about by grafting the CACM onto the traditional export model made the 1960s a golden era for all of Central America, Costa Rica stood out among its neighbors because these positive effects lasted through the 1970s[77] and were accompanied by improving conditions for the poor. In sum, the post-1948 development model discussed here, in as much as it emphasized human capital development, closing the urban-rural gap, and concern for the lower and middle classes, paid off handsomely in economic, social, and political terms. Many scholars credit these policies and Costa Rica's aversion to repression for maintaining its political stability instead of experiencing the violence found in the rest of the region during the 1980s.[78]

Conclusion

This chapter describes the political, social, and economic aspects of Costa Rica's development model as it stood on the eve of economic crisis. Although it is true that Costa Rica had a competitive electoral system and an incipient social security program before 1948, the aftermath of the brief civil war clearly delineates the beginning of a new political regime and greater state involvement in human welfare and economic development. To a greater or lesser degree, we can see the ideological imprint of the social democrats in all three areas.

The 1949 Constitution helped to eliminate electoral fraud and the abuse of presidential authority by spreading power more evenly throughout the political system. The Supreme Electoral Tribunal independently controls elections. Relative to other Latin American countries, a Costa Rican president's powers are weak vis-à-vis the legislature. There is also no regular army at the president's disposal. The Sala IV, the Comptroller, and the semiautonomous institutions act as additional checks in the Costa Rican system, making the passage and implementation of legislation an often slow and frustrating experience. To some extent, cooperation between the two major parties, tripartite negotiations, a custom of extensive public-private consultation, and a sense of social solidarity temper the gridlock encouraged by Costa Rica's institutional structure.

Despite the fact that Costa Rica has become world famous for its health and education programs, there was considerable delay in developing a full-fledged welfare state. Postwar governments moved fairly quickly to expand educational services to the farthest reaches of the countryside and to build the state university system. But public health and pension programs were not universalized until the 1970s. Founded in 1943, the social security funds were the offspring of President Rafael Calderón Guardia, and thus tainted in the eyes of postwar governments. More importantly, the expansion of the state health and old-age coverage meant confronting the physicians' union and pouring an enormous amount of public finance into building the necessary infrastructure and paying out benefits. As a result of these realities, social security coverage expanded in stages, but virtually all Costa Ricans now benefit from this system.

The nationalization of the banks in 1948 gave the state an immensely powerful vehicle for guiding economic development. Postwar governments used the banks to act on one of the PSD's and PLN's chief concerns: that small and medium-sized domestic growers be helped to participate in the production of domestic food stuffs and export products. In the spirit of further diversification, state policy assisted industrialists producing for the domestic and regional markets via subsidies, tax breaks, and import tariffs beginning in the 1960s. The state itself then became an industrialist through ownership of RECOPE and CODESA.

As we shall see in the following chapter, key aspects of the economic model have been radically altered by the reforms of the 1980s. Private banks may now offer all of the services once reserved for state banks. CODESA's assets were divested and the company has met its legal death. Finally, agricultural and industrial protectionism is, with a few exceptions, a relic of the past. Export promotion and international competitiveness have become the core themes of economic policy. Attempts to reduce public-sector employment, privatize core state enterprises, and tinker with social programs, in contrast, have been less successful. Chapter 4 explains that those who would reshape these components of the welfare state in the 1990s must confront their general popularity, vested interests, and the hurdles presented by Costa Rica's decentralized political system.

3

"Easy" Structural Adjustment: The 1980s

Costa Rica was one of the first Latin American countries to default on international debt payments and enter the "lost decade." Over a quarter century of growth and progress in human development ground to a halt in the early 1980s as Costa Rica faced the worst economic crisis of its modern history. Virtually all observers concur that President Rodrigo Carazo Odio (1978–82) handled the situation poorly. By the end of his term, key groups were looking for international aid and advice to help restart the economy. Politicians moved to repair relations with external donors and industrialists lobbied the United States for a private-sector bailout. Like many of their foreign counterparts, prominent economists saw the crisis as proof that the regional import substitution industrialization scheme had exhausted itself.

At the same time, major external donors found their own reasons to help Costa Rica with its economic difficulties. The United States attempted to trade economic aid for Central American allegiance to its undeclared war against the Nicaraguan government. The World Bank became convinced that Latin American states should reduce their involvement in economic development and began offering structural adjustment loans to countries which promised to do so. This chapter will first elaborate further on the coincidence of interests between international donors and the Costa Rican public and private sectors in the 1980s. The bulk of the chapter then explains how the resulting transnational alliances and the nature of the economic reforms themselves contributed to the successful implementation of five-key adjustment measures.

An Economy in Desperate Straits

The irony of Rodrigo Carazo's presidency was that although his coalition swept into office on promises of reducing the size and scope of the state, he could not impose these liberal reforms even during a crisis that seemed to confirm campaign allegations about an out-of-control public sector. Carazo, an economist who began his political career as a member of the PLN, left the party in 1969 to form Renovación Democrática. In 1978, Renovación Democrática allied with three other small parties to form a coalition called Unidad to oppose the ruling PLN. Unidad represented a diverse group—neoliberal intellectuals, industrialists, and populist Christian Democrats—united only by their opposition to the PLN in that year's national elections.

Two successive PLN administrations, led by José Figueres (1970–74) and Daniel Oduber (1974–78), had preceded Carazo's election and were best remembered for public-sector expansion and corruption. In particular, President Oduber increased the public sector's role in economic investment and production through the state holding company CODESA. As CODESA grew so did its image as an ineffective white elephant, an entity most useful for siphoning off public funds to the president's cronies. President Oduber also allowed Robert Vesco, the fugitive U.S. financier and friend of José Figueres, to remain in the country and avoid extradition to the United States.

Thus, in 1978, the Unidad coalition campaigned against corruption and shady characters, concepts it was able to associate with public-sector involvement in the economy. Beyond the CODESA issue, Rodrigo Carazo himself did not object to statist development strategies, but others within the Unidad alliance hoped to use his administration to reduce state intervention across the board. The anti-PLN campaign garnered popular support from several sources: an electorate worried that a third consecutive PLN administration would result in too much corruption; economists, agroexporters, and bankers who saw an opportunity to carry out a liberalization program; and industrialists who felt threatened by CODESA's competition for domestic credit. Although Carazo won the presidency, he would never enjoy control over the Legislative Assembly where his coalition came up two seats short of a majority and suffered continuous disunity over economic policy issues.

After Rodrigo Carazo took office in May 1978, severe economic difficulties cut short the new president's honeymoon period and came to engulf the rest of his term. Almost immediately, coffee prices fell and those of bananas stagnated. The cost of imported oil skyrocketed in 1979 as did payments owed on the external debt in 1981. In the latter half of Carazo's term, Costa Rican industrialists panicked as they lost markets in the Central American Common Market (CACM) which was decimated by regional warfare and longer-term trends toward slowing growth.[1] These problems amounted to a balance of payments crisis, rising inflation, and pressure on the *colón*.

During 1978 and 1979, the president had pursued an expansionary fiscal policy funded by domestic and external borrowing (the legislature refused to increase taxes). But as the balance of payments worsened, the public-sector deficit grew to 12 percent of GDP, inflation accelerated, and borrowing became difficult.[2] The government soon faced the necessity of designing an austerity package and securing assistance from the IMF, tasks which the Carazo administration bungled.[3] The president's vulnerability to interest group mobilization and poor executive-legislative coordination led Costa Rica to miss budget reduction targets in each of three austerity plans negotiated with the IMF in 1980 and 1981, resulting in a total breakdown in relations.[4] Without IMF credits, Costa Rica's hard currency reserves continued to shrink and on September 18, 1981, the Central Bank stopped all payments on the foreign debt held by commercial banks. By the time Costa Ricans voted Carazo's party out of office in February 1982, the economy was in a nose-dive, hitting rock bottom in the same year.[5] Added to growing panic about the economic situation, terrorist incidents in San José, involving supposed Sandinistas, and two years of massive strikes by the country's most radical labor unions, only inflamed fears that real social unrest was imminent.[6]

One lesson that President-elect Luis Alberto Monge (1982–86) had learned from watching the Carazo debacle was that Costa Rica could not pull out of the crisis by quarreling with providers of external capital. Consequently, Monge began to repair the country's standing with international donors and creditors before he took office. In fact, the future PLN president had sought support from the United States even during his campaign. In June 1981, Monge met U.S. State Department, congressional, and private-sector representatives to ask for financial support in order to help keep Costa Rica from falling prey to "the marxism-leninism which comes from Havana" and to assure business that foreign investment would be encouraged as part of his economic recovery program.[7] He astutely played Costa Rica's trump card, threatening the possibility that his country might "go communist," or become another Nicaragua, without economic assistance. A few years later, then presidential candidate Oscar Arias would be quoted as saying: "As long as there are nine comandantes in Nicaragua, we'll be able to get $200 million [a year from Washington], more or less, in aid."[8]

Within the private sector, the industrialists in particular suffered from the conditions of the early 1980s. These included the collapse of the CACM, the increasing size of and interest rate on liabilities held in dollars, and a lack of available credit from the public banks. Small groups of them actually made the initial requests to the United States for private-sector aid; Costa Rica's BANEX bank finally got $10 million loan from the United States Agency for International Development (USAID) at the end of 1981. When the new USAID chief arrived a few months later, he began to meet informally with BANEX representatives and other businessmen, and these contacts served to germinate the transnational alliances that would prove so important during the first phase of adjustment.

A final domestic consideration is the impact of the economic crisis on the two major parties. While Rodrigo Carazo's failure tarnished the opposition's prospects in the 1982 and 1986 presidential elections, his party (renamed the PUSC or Partido Unidad Social Cristiana in 1983) continued to attack what it saw as a bloated and inefficient state apparatus. Prominent members of the PUSC are associated with the conservative think tank ANFE (Asociación Nacional de Fomento Económico), whose publications and seminars have served to create domestic intellectual support for economic liberalization. During the 1980s, few *liberacionistas* championed such a sweeping retreat of the state from economic development, let alone social welfare functions. Nevertheless, much as was the case in other social democratic parties around the world, a core group within the PLN did start to lobby for partial liberalization to remove the most costly drains on state coffers and to reorient the economy away from the regional market and toward fuller international integration.

The Changing International Environment

U.S. Aid

At about the time that Luis Alberto Monge was elected, the United States involved itself more deeply in Central American affairs and this directly affected Costa Rica in three ways. First, Nicaraguan *contras* began organizing in Costa Rican territory and thus became a serious security concern for the country. Eden Pastora, the future leader of *contras*' "Southern Front," as the *contras* in northern Costa Rica were called by Reagan Administration officials, was already working with U.S. operatives.[9] Relations between the Costa Rican and Nicaraguan governments grew tense and provoked squabbles between Monge's own foreign and security ministers, the former taking a much harder line than the latter. The United States would become more deeply involved in covert activities in Costa Rica, causing great tension between these two nations as well.

The second turn of events came when President Reagan announced the Caribbean Basin Initiative or CBI in February 1982 (eventually passed by Congress as the Caribbean Basin Economic Recovery Act in 1983). This unilateral assistance program was to stabilize Central America and the Caribbean politically by promoting economic development in the region, thereby reducing the appeal of revolutionary movements. The centerpiece of the legislation provided for duty free entry of certain exports into the United States from member countries between January 1984 and December 1995. CBI provisions also charged other U.S. agencies such as the Overseas Private Investment Corporation (OPIC) and USAID with developing programs to support the legislation, especially in terms of encouraging American investment in the region. Twenty-two Caribbean and Central American countries became beneficiaries of the CBI (the Administration excluded Suriname, Guyana, and Nicaragua for political reasons).[10] Costa Rica soon became a star CBI beneficiary. It dramatically increased CBI-eligible (or nontraditional) exports to the United States and obtained additional economic assistance through a $70 million congressional CBI supplemental allocation to USAID in 1983.

A third aspect of the United States' increased focus on Central America in general and Costa Rica specifically involved extraordinary concessionary aid to the country. Table 3.1 shows that the United States provided Costa Rica with more aid, a total of about $1.2 billion, than the three main multilateral institutions combined during the 1980s. According to Table 3.2, U.S. economic aid between 1982–89 provided the annual average equivalent of 3.6 percent of Costa Rica's GDP and 11.4 percent of imports for these years. The United States allotted most of this money in grant form through the Economic Support Fund (ESF), a mechanism used to

Table 3.1
U.S. Bilateral and Multilateral Assistance to Costa Rica, 1982–1995
(in millions of U.S. dollars)

	1982	1983	1984	1985	1986	1987	1988	1989	1990	1991	1992	1993	1994	1995
U.S. BILATERAL														
ESF	20.0	155.7	130.0	160.0	123.6	142.5	90.0	90.0	63.6	25.0	10.0	0.5	-	-
Other Economic[a]	30.8	57.5	40.1	49.9	36.4	42.7	15.3	28.3	14.1	28.5	9.6	21.8	6.4	5.6
Military[b]	3.5	2.6	9.2	9.2	2.5	1.8	0.5	0.5	0.5	0.7	0.5	0.5	1.0	0.5
MULTILATERAL														
World Bank	-	-	-	80.0	-	-	-	200.0	-	-	-	23.0	22.0	-
IMF	98.6	-	-	54.8	-	51.7	-	53.8	78.2	45.0	-	29.9	-	78.0
IDB[c]	68.6	42.6	96.7	6.1	180.0	111.3	63.5	191.7	49.5	87.5	53.9	379.6	11.9	180.0
TOTAL	221.5	258.4	276.0	360.0	342.5	350.0	169.3	564.3	205.9	186.7	74.0	455.3	41.3	264.1

SOURCES: Raw data provided by the U.S. Embassy, San José, Costa Rica; USAID, "U.S. Historic Assistance Levels"; USAID, *Latin America and the Caribbean: Selected Economic and Social Data*; Development Group for Alternative Policies, *Structural Adjustment in Central America: The Case of Costa Rica*; Economic Intelligence Unit, *Country Report: Costa Rica, 3rd Quarter 1995*; Inter-American Development Bank, *IDB Annual Report*.

a. Includes Development Assistance, Central American Peace Scholarships, Peace Corps, and food aid (PL-480 Titles I and II and Agricultural Act of 1949, Section 416 assistance).
b. Includes military aid, training, and counter-narcotics assistance.
c. Inter-American Development Bank. Despite the large sums, IDB lending did not include balance of payments support or entail macroeconomic or sectoral policy conditionality until the 1990s. In previous decades, IDB lending was limited to infrastructural and agricultural projects.

Table 3.2
U.S. Economic Assistance as a Percentage of Costa Rican Imports and GDP, 1982–1989

	Economic Aid (millions of $)	Percent of Imports	Percent of GDP
1982	50.8	5.7	1.4
1983	213.2	20.3	5.6
1984	170.1	14.6	4.1
1985	209.9	16.9	5.1
1986	160.0	11.0	3.7
1987	184.2	10.8	4.0
1988	105.3	6.2	2.2
1989	118.3	5.9	2.4

SOURCES: Economic assistance data from Table 3.1; import and GDP data from Inter-American Development Bank, *Economic and Social Progress in Latin America*.

assist countries of geopolitical importance. Other recipients in the 1980s included El Salvador, Honduras, Guatemala, Israel, and Egypt.

Conditionality

Of course, these levels of assistance came with strings attached. Beginning with the Monge administration, Costa Rica was drawn into an extraordinarily complex web of cross conditionality among USAID, the IMF, creditor banks and governments, and the World Bank. As one of the earliest reformers in Latin America, Costa Rica served as a testing ground for U.S. private-sector promotion programs and World Bank structural adjustment loans. USAID took the role of lead donor because it supplied more aid to Costa Rica in the 1980s than the World Bank and the IMF combined, held stronger motivation for involvement in the country's economic recovery, maintained the largest staff,[11] and had day-to-day contact with local actors. A division of labor developed whereby the IMF took the lead in hammering out specific macroeconomic targets with the Costa Rican government and the World Bank worked on reducing protectionism by demanding the elimination of agricultural subsidies and the liberalization of import tariffs.

USAID itself concentrated on private-sector development, privatization, and on reinforcing the macroeconomic conditions set in IMF agreements (upon which World Bank disbursements and negotiations with external creditors depended).[12] The United States either tied specific tranches to, or reserved the right to suspend disbursements for, (non)compliance with certain conditions contained in each year's assistance agreement signed with the Costa Rican government. In addition, USAID secured Costa Rican promises to carry out an array of covenants (255 between 1982–1990) sometime during the aid period. Various agreements contained threats to withhold disbursements should previous covenants not be completed.

But the most controversial type of conditionality was the unwritten quid pro quo arrangement the United States attempted to extract from Costa Rica whereby the former would provide economic aid in exchange for the latter's assistance in overthrowing the Nicaraguan government.[13] The United States wanted Costa Rica to allow the *contras* to build bases in the northern part of the country from which they could launch attacks on Sandinista forces. Fragmentary evidence indicates that the United States actually used economic aid directly to attempt to gain Costa Rica's cooperation in its Central American policy.

For example, USAID suspended a disbursement in November 1983, officially because Costa Rica revalued the *colón*.[14] Yet the suspension came on the heels of President Monge's formal declaration of neutrality, U.S. Ambassador Curtin Winsor's public denouncement of the declaration as "bullshit,"[15] and Costa Rica's vote in the United Nations against the U.S. invasion of Grenada. In addition, a document submitted as evidence in Oliver North's 1989 trial demonstrates that the United States intended for its aid to Central American allies to produce support for the *contras*. The document reports a June 25, 1984 meeting in which CIA Director William Casey asked Ronald Reagan, George Bush, and other officials to "provide Honduras and Costa Rica with increased economic assistance as an incentive for them to assist the Resistance [*contras*]."[16] Costa Rica did get an extra $73 million in aid in 1984.[17] Finally, USAID also temporarily withheld funds in 1986 and 1987, ostensibly for failure to meet economic covenants but coinciding with periods of intense U.S. unhappiness with President Oscar Arias' opposition to CIA-*contra* operations in Costa Rica and his Central American Peace Plan.[18]

The other reason the United States granted Costa Rica so much aid in the 1980s was to forestall potential political instability and leftist revolutionary activity that State Department officials believed might develop under conditions of economic crisis and thus threaten the country's showcase democracy status within Central America.[19] To this end, the Reagan administration sent a new USAID director to Costa Rica in January 1982 with a mandate to keep Costa Rica afloat as a "beacon of democracy" in the region.[20] Because the State Department did not provide the director with a blueprint of how to fix Costa Rica's economy, he had substantial autonomy in designing USAID's approach. As we shall see subsequently, this flexibility allowed USAID to sponsor a reform program agreeable to its domestic allies.

**Transnational Coalitions and
Private Sector Development: Cases 1–3**

When President Monge took office in June 1992, he moved quickly to reschedule the public external debt and stabilize the economy. A standby letter signed with the IMF in December 1982 led to a new Paris Club agreement in January 1983 and to a pact with commercial creditors in September. Despite substantial resistance to utility rate hikes, the government cut costs, raised revenue and slashed the fiscal deficit from 14.3 percent in 1981 to 3.4 percent in 1983.[21] When officials decided to unify exchange rates in 1983, they estimated that the (most used) free-market *colón* rate had overshot and so partially revalued the currency. This move actually dampened inflation and countered capital flight.[22] The IMF loan and increased U.S. aid helped reduce pressure on the balance of payments. Within two years, the economy rebounded with reduced inflation, a positive growth rate, and improving real wages.

Monge's efforts to cooperate with the IFI's paid off and the cabinet should have been able to turn its full attention to structural reforms. But the government was still absorbed in the security crisis on the northern border produced by the Nicaraguan conflict. In addition, the cabinet and the PLN itself had fallen into a paralyzing split over the desirability of changing the country's development model. So the impetus for structural reforms came from outside the government where USAID was building coalitions with domestic allies to carry out the first three measures discussed below: the privatization of CODESA, nontraditional export promotion, and opening the public banking monopoly.

One reason the transnational alliances met with so much success is that they pooled complementary resources. USAID brought leadership, money, and technical know-how to the mix. Daniel Chaij,

USAID's director of Costa Rican operations during 1982–87, provided vociferous and unswerving ideological leadership for market-oriented economic reform. Raised in Uruguay and Costa Rica, Chaij was a native Spanish speaker and a self-proclaimed free marketer who was emotionally committed to the success of his programs. He also had enormous resources at his command during the 1980s and used them to gain the maximum leverage, autonomy, and flexibility possible to carry out projects, as well as to contract technical advice from a variety of international sources. The Costa Ricans, working in partnership with USAID, were prominent within the business community and well-connected in the PLN. They provided direct access to business chambers, the cabinet, and the president.

These USAID-backed transnational coalitions also worked so well in the 1980s, because everyone involved shared the goals of private-sector development and eliminating certain public-sector enterprises and monopolies. In addition, the Costa Rican partners sometimes stood to gain financially from their involvement in the alliances, most clearly so in the case of banking. Moreover, the three major reforms carried out by these coalitions would have large and immediate payoffs, effectively expanding supportive constituencies rapidly. The sale of CODESA shored up state coffers while businesspeople profited handsomely from measures promoting new exports and private banking.

In the first three cases considered in this chapter, the Legislative Assembly did have to pass enabling legislation, but only the banking laws drew controversy. In none of the cases was it necessary to overhaul a major government institution to carry out the reforms. The new laws did not affect public banks directly, rather, private banks were gradually allowed to offer competing services. In order to privatize CODESA and promote nontraditional exports, USAID created and funded new institutions which were run by domestic and expatriate managers and remained financially dependent on foreign aid. Under Costa Rican law, these institutions qualified as private entities and thus were unaccountable to domestic public authorities (although entirely beholden to USAID). This status allowed them almost complete autonomy from domestic political interference and provided USAID and its allies with a mechanism to circumvent existing institutions. In addition, these institutions hired from outside of the civil service using higher wages to attract better-qualified workers of various nationalities. The institutions were also flexible, that is, able to rapidly change organizational goals and strategy.

Finally, reforms in the three policy areas examined below provoked relatively little societal resistance. The most significant opposition came from public agencies and legislators who rightly felt that their control over the economy was being reduced and that the power of their private-sector counterparts would be enhanced. Thus, CODESA managers appointed by President Monge were unmotivated by the goal of privatization, the state export promotion agency engaged in turf battles with the organization USAID founded for the same purpose, and a group of PLN legislators mounted intense protest to breaking the public monopoly on banking. This resistance proved no match for USAID, its resources, and domestic allies.

The Privatization of CODESA

The Figueres administration founded the Corporación Costarricense de Desarrollo, S.A. (Costa Rican Development Corporation) or CODESA in 1972 as a vehicle through which the state would make investments that the private sector alone could not afford. Ten years later, CODESA had become a giant state holding company with whole ownership in thirty companies and part in ten others. During these years, CODESA also gained a reputation as an inefficient and corrupt enterprise subject to croynism on behalf of PLN presidents. So much so that by the late 1970s many in the private sector wanted to dismantle it. President Carazo had promised to do precisely this but did not follow through during his chaotic administration. So CODESA continued to inflict enormous losses on the Central Bank and drain off a large portion of state bank system credit[23] while giving back very little to the economy: only 2,122 direct jobs and 1.1 percent of GDP in 1983.[24] CODESA's main subsidiaries operated at a loss throughout most years of their existence.[25]

It is not entirely clear who originated the idea that USAID help privatize CODESA. One author credits a group of Costa Ricans with asking the U.S. Ambassador to demand it.[26] No matter who came up with the scheme, it is obvious that a transnational alliance between USAID, the Costa Rican private sector, and, later on, domestic technocrats, cooperated to accomplish the goal. This coalition helped write enabling legislation, establish a private institution to fund the divestiture process, secure the necessary technical assistance, and actually carry out the privatization.

The CODESA divestiture began in 1984 with a series of

preparatory actions. First, USAID and its allies contributed heavily to language included in the Public Sector Financial Equilibrium Law or Emergency Law passed by the legislature in February 1984. Besides several measures important to exporters, the bill included Article 55 which established that shares in CODESA's subsidiaries could be sold to anyone, regardless of nationality, with the following exceptions: (1) the three public utilities owned by CODESA would be transferred to other Government of Costa Rica entities; (2) a sugar mill (CATSA) would be sold to private Costa Rican cooperatives; and (3) only 40 percent of the shares of the fertilizer company (FERTICA) and a cement firm (CEMPASA) would be sold to the private sector. Later the same year, USAID secured an agreement with the Central Bank that it would make no new loans to CODESA. In February 1985, the Costa Rican government published regulations and a Cabinet resolution supporting the immediate commencement of the privatization of CODESA.

But is was easier to resolve to sell CODESA than to actually do it. While there was never significant union or public opposition to its divestiture, other obstacles arose. One major impediment to the privatization of CODESA's companies was that the market value of most of them was not anything near the investment they had gotten over the years from the Central Bank. In fact, many of CODESA's firms sat idle or existed only on paper; seven companies accounted for 90 percent of CODESA's investment.[27] Under these conditions, privatization was unattractive to PLN administrations because it would publicize the failure of a long-standing PLN development strategy, give the appearance that the government was giving away public resources, and do little to reduce CODESA's debt with the Central Bank. Another stumbling block, at least at the beginning, was that CODESA's management showed a lack of enthusiasm for selling off its assets.

USAID devised a clever strategy to overcome these problems. In September 1985, USAID established a trust called Fiduciaria de Inversiones Transitorias, S.A. or FINTRA with a board composed of five top Costa Rican businessmen, each paid between $1,709 and $3,077 per month.[28] USAID made up to $140 million available to FINTRA which it was to use for purchasing CODESA's companies, running them temporarily, making preparations for privatization, and then selling the firms.[29] In addition, USAID contracted technical assistance for FINTRA from Price Waterhouse, First Boston, and International Resources Group.[30] FINTRA would buy the companies from CODESA at a value set by the Comptroller General of

Costa Rica. The Comptroller set the prices much higher than most of the companies were really worth (i.e. at replacement cost),[31] but FINTRA was able to use its endowment to pay full price, sums which the Comptroller transferred to the Central Bank, thus helping to retire CODESA's debt. In this way, USAID actually paid for the privatization of CODESA.

Thus, the FINTRA mechanism had several advantages. First, it offered an institution through which to circumvent CODESA's management, hostile to privatization during the Monge administration, although much more favorably disposed under President Arias (1986–1990). Second, USAID officials were keen to avoid the public controversy that may have ensued had the United States appeared to directly manage CODESA's divestment.[32] Third, FINTRA supplied critical technical and financial assistance to the Costa Rican government. Finally, similar to the situation in export promotion studied below, FINTRA held an advantage by simple virtue of its technical status as a private entity. Once CODESA's companies had been legally transferred to FINTRA, public-sector regulations did not apply to their resale or liquidation, making the whole process less bureaucratic.[33]

Although USAID originally allotted about two years for the privatization process, the divestiture of CODESA has taken much longer than expected because of legal and technical complications.[34] CODESA did not actually close its doors until July 29, 1997. During the process of divestiture and closure, twelve companies were sold, twenty-three were liquidated, and five transferred to other state agencies. Because most of these involved idle companies or the sale of shares in partially owned affiliates, the sale of the largest four companies took most of CODESA's and FINTRA's time and money. Of these, FINTRA directly managed the sale of ALUNASA, an aluminum concern, in 1987, and CATSA, a sugar mill, in 1989. In a departure from the original plan, CODESA itself would manage the sale of its two most profitable firms, CEMPASA (the country's largest producer of cement), and FERTICA (a fertilizer company). These dragged on for years with the former finally being sold off in 1995 and the latter in 1997.

Interestingly, after 1986, the official discourse surrounding the CODESA matter switched from concerns about state finances and the misuse of public funds to the positive social goals that could be achieved through its privatization. The Arias administration sought to reap political advantages from the sale of CODESA companies by advertising the process as one of "economic democratization." This label best applied to the sale of all of CATSA's shares to several agricultural cooperatives during 1988–89. The trend continued during the Calderón administration when the Legislative Assembly amended Article 55 of the original privatization law to require the sale of all of FERTICA and CEMPASA's shares to unions, cooperatives, and other Costa Rican groups.[35] CODESA sold the two companies according to this formula and FINTRA contributed to the law's social goals, for example, by making loans to Costa Rican groups for the purchase of 63 percent of CEMPASA.[36] But as soon as the sales took place, local and international companies moved in to buy up shares from these groups, thus defeating the spirit of the law. An American firm (Austin Powders) now owns 54 percent of FERTICA's stock with a Chilean company controlling another 25 percent.[37] Outside of the sale of CATSA, then, the attempt to put ownership of these companies in the hands of smallholders failed.

The privatization of CODESA was a slow process, but not a politically disruptive or financially destructive one. By the early 1980s, CODESA was thoroughly discredited and what problems did arise where deftly handled by USAID's endowment of FINTRA and Costa Rican governments' ability to link privatization to the promise, however imperfect, of economic democracy. In the case below, we will see that USAID and its Costa Rican allies promoted nontraditional exports by creating a nongovernmental institution very similar to FINTRA. Like FINTRA, this organization, CINDE, constituted a way around an existing government entity and had the same advantages of large endowment, flexibility, and freedom from public-sector regulations.

Nontraditional Export Promotion

The government of Costa Rica began to promote the sale of nontraditional products (defined as anything but the traditional exports of coffee, bananas, sugar, beef, and cotton) to extraregional markets in 1968 when it created CENPRO (Centro de Promoción de Exportaciones e Inversión or Center for the Promotion of Exports and Investment). The officials who founded CENPRO sought to diversify exports in order to augment Costa Rica's foreign exchange earnings. CENPRO's mandate was to provide market information and technical assistance to (potential) exporters already in Costa Rica, bring new foreign export-oriented investment into the country, and advise other government agencies on policy measures needed by the exporters. Besides the headquarters in San José, CENPRO opened offices in Panama, Venezuela, Puerto Rico, and the United States during the 1970s.

CENPRO failed to produce much increase in nontraditional exports in the 1970s and its foreign offices were closed in 1981. An extensive consultants' report blames CENPRO's disappointing performance on internal problems such as poor training and high turnover of personnel, politically based hiring practices, inattention to the investment promotion task, and the failure to identify and lobby for the removal of regulations which impeded new exports.[38] But in interviews, former CENPRO officials and businessmen stressed that the private sector responded weakly to CENPRO's efforts because government incentives favored investment in import-substitution industrialization. Without an economic crisis, policymakers had no motivation to change key economic signals (e.g. the exchange rate) in favor of export promotion.[39]

Of the three issue areas studied here, USAID most clearly demonstrated its leadership within the transnational alliance specifically concerned with nontraditional export promotion. USAID began to pursue export diversification in Costa Rica in late 1981, in fact, this was the Mission's rationale for loaning $10 million to BANEX bank. The BANEX representatives wanted the loan to fund traditional industries but the two sides compromised and formed what one consultant's report called a "symbiotic relationship."[40] When the new USAID director arrived in January 1982 and began a series of informal biweekly breakfast meetings with a subgroup of the BANEX businessmen, he continued to press the idea of export diversification.[41] The new director quickly offered to fund a private nonprofit export promotion center called "CINDE" (Coalición Costarricense de Iniciativas para el Desarrollo or Costa Rican Coalition of Development Initiatives).

Thus, CINDE became the organizational nexus of the nontraditional export promotion alliance. USAID provided the organization's monetary resources and technical assistance. Between 1983–1990, the United States contributed $47 million as CINDE's sole source of support.[42] USAID also brought in technical consultants from Puerto Rico, the United States, and Ireland to design CINDE's strategy at crucial points. For their part, the Costa Rican members of the Board of Directors (a bipartisan group including prominent businessmen and a few well-respected members of the PLN) led CINDE's lobbying effort during its critical first three years. The standing of these men in social and political circles gave them access to top policymakers, and time after time they would obtain audiences with President Monge or his ministers to push CINDE's case.

CINDE's activities provoked no societal resistance. But in as much as CINDE had exactly the same mandate as CENPRO, the latter felt threatened. USAID decided to bypass CENPRO in favor of a new organization because of the aforementioned negative consultant's report on CENPRO's performance, the disdain with which CINDE's board members viewed public-sector institutions,[43] and the fact that creating a private organization provided a way to avoid civil service regulations and government oversight. The decade saw turf battles between the two organizations until a truce was arranged in 1989. CINDE agreed to maintain foreign offices and carry out investment promotion and technical assistance functions while CENPRO retained a program focusing on running product fairs and helping small national firms learn how to export.

CINDE accomplished a great deal in the areas of policy change (1983–85) and the promotion of foreign export-oriented investment (1986–1990). As for policies affecting nontraditional exports, only modifications in the exchange rate were not the direct result of CINDE lobbying. An agreement between Costa Rican authorities, the IMF, and USAID led to exchange rate unification in late 1983 and to putting the *colón* on a crawling peg in early 1985. Cross conditionality between the IMF, USAID, and former CINDE board member Eduardo Lizano, Central Bank president between 1984–1990, limited political interference with the exchange rate. All other important changes related to nontraditional exports owed their origins to CINDE. For example, because of CINDE's behind the scenes actions, Law 6955 (also known as the Emergency Law) promulgated in February 1984 contained policy modifications crucial to nontraditional exporters. Key among them was legislation providing for the export contract, through which the government provided nontraditional exporters a lucrative fiscal incentive known as the CAT,[44] and 100 percent tax relief on profits and imported inputs.[45] Law 6955 also improved drawback regulations making that option more attractive to assembly industries. Finally, the legislation provided for the creation of a "one-stop investment center," opened in 1988, which simplified and centralized the paperwork required of firms to export from the country. Consultants contracted by CINDE drew up these sections of the legislation and CINDE board members took a lead role in lobbying them through the Legislative Assembly by meeting with government functionar-

"Easy" Structural Adjustment: The 1980s 59

ies, congressmen, ministers, and President Monge himself, usually on an informal and individual basis.

CINDE also joined forces with a private firm, Zeta Investments, to pressure the government into allowing the private sector to participate in running the state-administered free zones. A public corporation created two free zones in 1981, but they failed to attract investors. CINDE and the Zeta group teamed up to push legal modifications in 1984 and 1985 that allowed free zones to operate in the Central Valley (a much more attractive location) and permitted the private sector to administer them. There are now nine free zones in Costa Rica.

During 1986–1990, USAID drew heavily on foreign expertise to help rebuild CINDE into an investment promotion organization. Basing itself on a model borrowed from the Irish Development Authority, CINDE used its foreign offices to target light assembly firms (especially U.S. garment makers) and bring them to Costa Rica where they could take advantage of the export incentives CINDE had lobbied for in previous years. The strategy worked spectacularly well.

Costa Rica's nontraditional export drive has been dramatically successful. Between 1983 and 1990 alone, the value of nontraditional exports soared from 90 million dollars to 635 million, while the proportion of export earnings they represented quadrupled from 10 to 43 percent over the same period.[46] In 1990, the leading Costa Rican nontraditional export products were textiles ($359 million)[47]; flowers, ornamental plants, and foliage ($58 million); fresh, frozen, and dried fish and shrimp ($45 million); and fresh pineapple ($38 million).[48] CINDE itself claimed responsibility for attracting 146 foreign investment projects and 18,000 jobs (55 percent in apparel and textiles) to Costa Rica between 1986–1990 and for at least 17 percent of nontraditional exports.[49] Chapter 5 indicates that improvement in Costa Rica's macroeconomic indicators accompanied export success. By 1990, USAID was touting CINDE as a model for private-sector export promotion. And in a 1991 statement before Congress, USAID used Costa Rica as its chief exhibit when arguing that aid-backed economic reforms (primarily nontraditional export promotion) had brought benefits to Latin American countries.[50]

Chapter 5 also notes that Costa Rica's nontraditional export sector continued to expand and evolve after the 1980s and after USAID had ended its involvement in CINDE. By 1998, nontraditional exports were valued at 3.8 billion dollars or 68 percent of

Costa Rica's total exports.[51] An important shift in Costa Rica's export profile occurred that year when the Intel Corporation opened two microprocessor (computer chip) plants and instantly became the country's largest exporter. Manufactured nontraditional exports now far outweigh agricultural products. In 1998, Costa Rica's leading nontraditional exports were: microprocessors and electronic circuits ($959 million), textiles ($775 million), fish and seafood ($169 million), and flowers, ornamental plants, and foliage ($130 million).[52]

Creating a Private Banking Sector

Pepe Figueres, the leader of the victorious forces of the 1948 civil war, nationalized Costa Rica's banks in the same year. The primary reason for doing so was to give the government full access to national savings which it would use to promote the development goals described in chapter 2.[53] Indeed, during the following three decades, agriculture and industry grew, state-owned enterprises and semiautonomous institutions mushroomed, and urban and rural standards of living improved immensely. Proponents of the state bank monopoly have argued that a direct link exists between public control over bank credit and the peace and prosperity experienced by the Costa Rican population.[54] To let private banking come to dominate the country again would somehow endanger these traditions.[55]

At the opening of the 1980s a few private banks existed, but they could not accept checking or savings accounts, make loans in foreign currency, or receive international funds. Instead, the four state banks dominated and followed policies dictated by the Central Bank of Costa Rica (BCCR). Lending policies in the state banks featured preferential interest rates and *topes*, a system of allocative minimums and ceilings determined by the Central Bank. Through this guidance system, the state directed credit toward development priorities in over fifty categories.

Some in the business community held long-standing objections to this state monopoly. For example, in 1967 a private bankers' lobby had fallen just short of ending it.[56] In the early 1980s, USAID and business community representatives began again to demand that private banks be allowed to compete on an even footing with the state banks. Their basic complaint was that the state system was "inefficient and corrupt"[57] and insufficient for building a modern economy.[58] Unlike the other two reforms studied here, domestic forces were as important, in not more so, in the fight for bank denationalization. Those who wanted to create a viable private banking sector knew exactly what they wanted and how to get it. They borrowed what leverage they could from USAID but did not need international technical expertise to design and implement the reform.

Those supporting the notion of putting private banks on an equal footing with the state system included virtually the entire business community (including the Association of Costa Rican Bankers [ABC], the Union of Business Chambers [UCCR], the Chamber of Commerce [CCCR], and the Chamber of Industry [CICR]), the opposition PUSC party, top PLN technocrats, the conservative think tank ANFE, the leading daily *La Nación*, and USAID. Opposed were the management and labor unions of the state banks, other public-sector unions (the Confederation of Workers [CUT], the Confederation of Costa Rica Workers [CTC], the Costa Rican Confederation of Democratic Workers [CCTD], and two teachers' unions) and the traditional wing of the PLN.[59] But whether the legislation would be passed in the PLN-controlled legislature depended fundamentally on the intraparty split between PLN "neoliberals" and "socialdemocrats." Again, the most dedicated opposition to the reform came from within the decision-making apparatus, in this case the Legislative Assembly.

The problem that precipitated bank reform in the early 1980s was that USAID was prepared to grant and loan a large amount of money to nascent private banks but Costa Rican law made that illegal.[60] Costa Rican members of the alliance also sought to change other aspects of the law in order to make the operation of private banks profitable. So USAID conditioned disbursement of aid in 1983 and 1984 on legislative action changing articles contained in the *Ley de la Moneda* and the *Ley Orgánica del Banco Central*. The main modifications required were: (1) to have the Central Bank open direct rediscount lines to private banks; (2) to allow private banks to accept term deposits of 180 days or more; and (3) to permit private banks to borrow from foreign creditors directly without intermediation from the BCCR.

Again, President Monge did not lead the reform effort so much as allow events to unfold. The executive branch did introduce the relevant legislation into debate but the president gave the impression that he had been forced to do so by USAID conditionality. *La Nación* ran editorials in favor of bank denationalization, business groups took out paid announcements and telegrammed legislators on its behalf, cabinet officers testified as to its importance, and supportive members of the PLN apparently met with the USAID director in a Turkish bath on Fridays to strategize.[61] By the spring of 1984, USAID had suspended aid disbursements in order to pressure the Legislative Assembly into passing the bills. It is well-known that while on a European tour in May, President Monge telephoned Ronald Reagan and asked him to release the aid even though the bank reforms had not yet passed. In June, USAID did release the funds on the condition that it be kept secret. The legislation finally passed after twenty-three straight hours of debate on August 19, 1984. Many of the legislators apparently felt that they had to vote for the reforms because the country was so dependent on external aid.[62]

After the traumatic 1984 vote and under the leadership of Central Bank president Eduardo Lizano (1984–1990), the state banks deregulated their own practices by largely eliminating *topes* and subsidized credit and by maintaining real interest rates. At the same time, the private banking lobby, more by virtue of its own influence than by external leverage, won further legislative modifications that have expanded the sector. For instance, in 1988, the Legislative Assembly passed the *Ley de Modernización del Sistema Financiero* which, among other things, extended state insurance coverage to individual deposits in private banks. The process continued into the 1990s and the private banks won the right to offer current accounts beginning in September 1996, for the first time making national savings fully available to them. They also now legally rely on the Central Bank for lender of last resort services. In exchange for these gains, the private banks will have to make some contribution to development objectives by opening more rural branches.[63]

By the mid-1990s, these changes had created a mixed banking system in Costa Rica. Between 1979 and 1995, the number of private banks grew from five to twenty-five with private finance companies increasing from thirteen to twenty-three in the same period.[64] In 1996, the total lending of private banks was slightly larger than that of their public counterparts.[65] But the three state banks have hardly withered away.[66] Instead, they are undertaking efficiency measures in order to better compete with the private sector. State banks have been ordered to lower administrative costs, reduce bad debts, and cut their spreads on loans.[67] The state banking system is also introducing more enticing services to consumers such as interest-bearing checking accounts. These measures may be working. Seven months after the private banks began offering current accounts, they had only gained 5.9 percent of the market.[68]

Two key points should be drawn from this description of the rapid changes in Costa Rica's banking industry during the last fifteen years. The first is that USAID formed a strong alliance with a very motivated and self-interested business lobby that overcame real political resistance to its proposals and that pushed for further policy modifications later in the decade without the aid of foreign assistance. The second aspect of this lobby that made for success was that it concentrated on the only politically viable option—allowing the private sector to sell the same services as state banks—instead of insisting on the outright divestiture of valued public institutions. In addition, competition from the private sector is clearly driving efficiency gains among the three state banks, particularly the largest of them (Banco Nacional),[69] although industry experts are not convinced that they will be able to survive in the longer run.

Opening Domestic Markets: Cases 4 and 5

The late 1980s saw the initiation of two reforms specifically aimed at opening Costa Rica to international competition: the elimination of agricultural subsidies and the liberalization of import tariffs. Intellectual alliances between domestic economists, particularly Central Bank President Eduardo Lizano, and World Bank officials drove the assault on protective barriers forward. These measures did provoke societal resistance, particularly from peasants, but they were still more easily accomplished than the state reforms discussed in the next chapter. The removal of crop subsidies and import tariffs did not require approval from the Legislative Assembly, enormous financial or technical resources, or new institutional structures and competencies. Rather, the executive branch had the power to decree an end to basic grains subsidies and to reduce import tariffs.

Elimination of Basic Grains Subsidies

The Costa Rican government began subsidizing domestic growers of basic grains (beans, rice, corn, sorghum) in the 1940s through the Consejo Nacional de Producción (National Production Council or CNP). The price supports met an important goal: to help peasants remain on their land and thus maintain rural social stability. The CNP acted as a state marketing board by monopolizing the purchasing, wholesaling, importing and exporting of these basic foodstuffs as well as imports of other grains such as wheat and oats. But because the CNP was buying dear and selling cheap, it ran debts with the Central Bank; USAID estimated that by 1980 CNP losses equaled 40 percent of the national budget deficit.[70] Like CODESA, the CNP became a target of efforts to reduce government spending, a campaign waged by international donors as well as domestic critics, chiefly Central Bank President Eduardo Lizano.[71]

USAID attempted to pressure the Monge administration into dropping agricultural support prices. In the 1984 and 1985 assistance agreements between the United States and Costa Rica, the Central Bank agreed not to authorize additional loans to the CNP to cover losses incurred through basic grains subsidies. But the Central Bank failed to comply. At that point, USAID pushed the CNP issue down several notches among its own priorities and the World Bank took over as the lead donor in this area. Both structural adjustment loans (SALs) I and II, signed by the World Bank and Costa Rica in 1985 and 1988, required the elimination of subsidies to basic grains growers.

The Arias administration moved to comply with the World Bank agreements. In 1986, the CNP removed itself entirely from the buying and selling of rice, and began to reduce subsidies to growers of beans and white and yellow corn. In addition, the state banking system sharply reduced the credit available for growers of these staples. These changes dramatically altered the outlook for some of Costa Rica's least well-off landholders as most beans and corn had been grown by peasants, although large farms dominated the production of rice.[72]

As is the case all over the world, eliminating agricultural subsidies drew a storm of political protest in Costa Rica. Unprecedented levels of rural political protest followed on the heels of price reductions. During 1986–87, peasant unions voiced their opposition by blocking roads and leading marches to the capital. In September 1987, for example, peasants marched to San José and occupied the Metropolitan Cathedral for two weeks. They demanded that Costa Rica maintain food self-sufficiency and that the government return to the previous subsidy and credit levels for basic grains.[73] The government handled the protest by forming public-private commissions to study the problem, through extensive negotiations, and by slowing the process. The peasants had little choice but to enter into negotiations with the government, for they had no legal avenues for blocking the executive branch's decisions. As a result of the compromises reached, the protest marches quickly subsided and price supports for growers of beans and corn were not completely eliminated until 1994.[74] The Figueres administration subsequently secured passage of legislation which created a "reconversion" fund to help small and medium farmers adjust to international markets.

The CNP no longer buys, imports, or distributes any grain. With all of the CNP's old functions eliminated, it appeared for a while that the institution would close. But the CNP found new life after 1994 when the director reorganized the institution to meet the emerging needs of its former clientele. The CNP is now an agency which helps small and medium farmers form cooperatives and other types of businesses by providing technical advice, marketing data, and agronomic studies.

Tariff Reform

Costa Rica initiated its own import-substitution industrialization (ISI) program shortly before joining the Central American Common Market (CACM) in 1963 and so domestic and regional industrialization policy grew completely intertwined. As a member of the CACM, Costa Rica adhered to its common external tariff (CET), a system through which the five member countries standardized external tariffs on all imported goods. These nominal tariffs combined with non-tariff barriers and surcharges drove effective rates of protection to over 200 percent for some products.[75] Although they continued to protect producers of basic agricultural foodstuffs, the Central American countries dropped tariffs on manufactures traded among themselves. Industrialists were also awarded exemptions from taxes on imported inputs as well as other incentives that were standardized across the Central American countries. As noted in chapter 2, Costa Rica's participation in the Central American Common Market peaked in 1980, when 28 percent of its total exports went to other CACM countries.

Beginning in 1963 then, Costa Rica's import tariffs were strictly tied to CACM policy. This fact would seem to make unilateral import liberalization nearly impossible. But by the mid-1980s, the CACM was near collapse and its internal payments system suspended because of the wars and economic crises raging throughout the region. The temporary failure of the CACM helped convince Costa Rican industrialists that alternative international markets would have to be found and made the other Central American countries more amenable to policy change. In addition, both the World Bank and USAID made clear that they intended to help Costa Rica integrate itself more fully with the world economy, not to revive the CACM in its current form.[76]

Beyond vetoing any possibility of helping to reinvigorate the CACM, USAID remained completely uninvolved with import tariff reform. Perhaps the United States avoided confronting the Costa Rican government on this issue because several business allies in the private banking and export promotion lobbies were working simultaneously against tariff reductions. Or perhaps it was because the generous incentives provided to nontraditional exporters and real depreciation in the exchange rate were enough to balance the antiexport bias of protectionist policies, at least in the short run. No matter what the case, tariff reductions were not necessary for USAID's private-sector promotion efforts or for reactivating the economy. Instead the World Bank, again in alliance with a small group of state technocrats, took the lead in pushing for import liberalization.

The Costa Rican government took preliminary steps toward import tariff liberalization under the auspices of the first structural adjustment loan (SAL I), signed with the World Bank in 1985 and put into affect on January 1, 1986. Costa Rican officials not only succeeded in winning a slower schedule of tariff reductions than the World Bank had wanted, but also worked to convince the other CACM members that this first round of tariff reform be taken simultaneously by all within a regional framework.[77] Because average tariffs were reduced very little, Costa Rican industrialists did not offer much resistance to the first round of reforms.[78] In 1986, the CACM switched its tariff nomenclature to that of the Brussels code, converted tariffs to ad valorem rates, removed all tariff exemptions for industrialists, eliminated surcharges, brought down nominal tariffs to a maximum of 100 percent, and reduced tariff dispersion.[79]

Negotiations for further tariff reductions under SAL II began in 1987, and the Costa Rican government began to implement a second round of tariff reform in 1988, independently of the other CACM countries. This round brought Costa Rica's tariffs down to a maximum of 40 percent for finished goods and a minimum of 5 percent for imported inputs by 1990. Costa Rican industrialists had at first resisted when real tariff reduction began to be discussed in 1987. But realizing that the government was serious and that the executive could change import taxes by decree, industrialists quickly switched to a strategy of bargaining over the terms of tariff reduction.[80] The Chamber of Industry demanded that tariff reduction take place slowly, that some sectors be granted extra time to adjust, and funding for a program to help domestic industry prepare for the expected flood of imports.[81]

In 1989, the government met the industrialists' demands by setting up the Industrial Reconversion program (*Reconversión Industrial*) designed to help firms make the adjustment to the higher standards of international competition. Five industries were targeted for assistance: leather goods, textiles, processed foods, metal-mechanic goods, and pharmaceuticals. But the program had few results as it only lasted for one year before being dropped by the incoming Calderón administration in 1990. In addition, reductions in tariffs on textiles and leather goods were delayed (on average two years per round) so that these industries would have more time to adjust to international competition.

The beginning of the 1990s saw the winding down of regional wars and a desire on the part of all of the Central American countries to renew the CACM. But it would be a different CACM as years of pressure from the IFIs, the processes involved in joining the GATT, and a concern to be included in the Enterprise for the Americas Initiative pressed toward convergence on a very low Common External Tariff.[82] In 1991, the Central American presidents declared that the maximum CET would be reduced to 20 percent, something Costa Rica accomplished in 1993. In 1996, import tariffs on capital goods dropped from 5 to 3 percent, and were eliminated entirely on January 1, 1999. Tariffs on raw materials were eliminated on January 1, 1998. After a meeting in June 1996, the Central American countries agreed to further reduce the CET on finished goods to 15 percent on January 1, 2000.

It is widely believed in Costa Rica that the footwear and textile industries have been hard hit by liberalization, despite the extensions granted to them. But there is little research on the effects of trade liberalization in Costa Rica and so no way to substantiate this claim.[83] In agriculture, as in the other Central American countries, some domestic producers still benefit from extra levels of protection.[84] The other uncertainty is how successful the industrialist lobby will be in extracting government concessions in exchange for cooperation in further tariff reductions. During the 1990s, the Chamber of Industry began to demand that government authorities cut the fiscal deficit, shrink the size of the state, and grant concessions to private contractors for physical infrastructure projects. Chapter 4 will examine the extent of state reform in Costa Rica.

Conclusion

During the 1980s, economic adjustment was easy compared to the challenges of the 1990s. One reason for this is that an extraordinary quantity of foreign aid was available to fund the reforms themselves and to provide balance of payments support while the country's economy stabilized. But the quality of Costa Rica's interaction with external donors was equally central. Representatives of the IFIs, Costa Rican public officials, and private businessmen found several areas of agreement and adequate incentive to work together toward common goals. In fact, the demonopolization of banking and promotion of nontraditional exports proved extremely profitable and quickly produced groups of "winners" who would defend the new development strategy in the following decade.

The economic reforms of the 1980s were also technically and politically easier than those of 1990s. Policymakers did annoy some state agencies and legislators but they did not antagonize the managers or unions of the largest ministries. USAID coffers were sufficiently deep to circumvent the myriad obstacles and veto players dwelling in public institutions by building extragovernmental entities. Finally, the executive branch slashed agricultural subsidies and lowered import tariffs by administrative fiat, although the effected groups forced a more gradual pacing on the reforms.

In the latter part of the decade, the Arias administration, USAID, and the World Bank considered pushing measures, such as privatizing the power and telecommunications company ICE (Instituto Costarricense de Electricidad) and reducing the number of state employees, that would have struck at the heart of the public sector. All three quickly suspended such efforts citing insurmountable political opposition.[85] But by the 1990s, second-stage reforms could no longer by avoided. The next chapter focuses on the consequent attempts to transform key components of the welfare state.

4

Reforming the Welfare State: The 1990s

During the 1980s, Costa Rican policymakers managed to table serious consideration of the more complex economic policy changes. But in the following decade they would attempt a number of second-stage reforms intended to shrink state responsibilities and modernize public services. In marked contrast to the 1980s, none of these initiatives have produced clear results. This chapter first explains how changing international and domestic conditions pushed Rafael Calderón's PUSC administration (1990–94) and José Figueres' PLN government (1994–98) toward the more complex economic reforms. The following five case studies then illustrate the many obstacles to completing the reforms.

The International Environment of the 1990s

The most important change in Costa Rica's relationship with the external realm between the 1980s and 1990s was the loss of a large source of fungible foreign aid. Table 3.1 shows that U.S. economic aid to Costa Rica dropped from a peak of $219.1 million in 1985 to $6.1 million ten years later. Balance of payment support funds (ESF grants) begin to decline sharply in 1988 and ended after 1993. USAID's Costa Rican headquarters closed its doors in 1996, although the remnants of U.S. assistance live on in two trust funds, the Fundación de Cooperación Estatal (FUCE) and the Fundación Costa Rica-USA (CRUSA). As will be seen below, FUCE became an important "silent partner" in supplying the funding and technical assistance necessary to move forward several state reform initiatives during 1991–96.

To some extent, this loss was offset by new external flows brought in by the nontraditional export and tourism industries and by loans from the IMF, World Bank, and Inter-American Development Bank (IDB).[1] Costa Rica also reduced its debt overhang in 1989 by using the Brady Plan to retire nearly one billion dollars of its foreign debt.[2] Whatever the net differences in the quantity of external assistance received by Costa Rica in the 1980s and 1990s, changes in the quality of the aid are just as relevant to the reforms discussed below. On paper, the aid conditionality of the 1980s looked no less stringent than that of the 1990s. But in fact, Costa Rica's geopolitical situation meant that bilateral and multilateral donors observed greater leniency in the face of missed targets during the first period. During the 1990s, all three multilateral banks strictly policed limits on the budget deficit. Accordingly, they became more focused with how revenue is spent within the central government and whether public services are delivered efficiently. These concerns have translated into greater pressure to reduce the government work force and to accept sector loans to make improvements in the health and education ministries.

Domestic Support for Shrinking the State

The successful adjustment measures of the 1980s empowered the private sector to demand greater fiscal discipline as well as more efficient services and a broader scope of investment opportunities from the state. These forces, based in the PUSC, the business chambers, the right wing think tank ANFE, and the daily *La Nación*, rode herd on economic reform in the 1990s. The best example of how these groups flexed their muscles to limit public spending came in 1995. By April of that year, PUSC deputies had so successfully delayed passage of PLN President Figueres' tax package in the Legislative Assembly that he had to temporarily raise import tariffs to meet government obligations. The IMF also refused to close an agreement on a new and badly needed standby loan until the tax package passed. The IDB announced suspension of disbursements from the third structural adjustment loan until the IMF deal was signed. President Figueres had little choice but to negotiate a pact with the PUSC (and in effect with the Unión Costarricense de Cámaras y Asociaciones de la Empresa Privada [UCCAEP] which made the same demands as the PUSC) to allow tax increases to pass the Legislature by September.[3] Under the

Reforming the Welfare State: The 1990s

terms of this informal agreement, Figueres committed to more privatization, and to introducing legislation for a new constitutional amendment of "economic guarantees." The amendment would prohibit fiscal deficits of more than 1 percent of GDP and require that current expenses be financed only with current revenue. President Figueres did push slowly forward on privatization but the Legislative Assembly failed to pass the economic guarantees amendment before the end of his term.

Government authorities also found incentives to examine the efficiency of public spending. During the 1980s, the reduction of agricultural subsidies and the partial privatization of CODESA had helped to rein in the budget deficit. But in the early 1990s, the public wage bill remained high and runaway costs appeared in three other areas: pensions, higher education, and, most importantly, interest payments on the internal debt.[4] The Calderón and Figueres governments had floated increasing numbers of government bonds to finance public spending as U.S. aid levels dropped. As a result, by 1996, interest payments on the internal debt equaled 30 percent of government spending and 5 percent of the GDP.[5] This budget item, combined with allocations for pensions, salaries, and higher education, accounted for 72 percent of public spending in mid-1996.[6] The Figueres administration, in particular, felt the full weight of this budget crunch, a problem which helped to motivate efforts to cut public employment, reduce government spending on pensions, and privatize state-owned enterprises.

Not surprisingly, the PUSC and its conservative predecessors have always been more interested in economic liberalization than the PLN. But a third domestic factor which favored continued structural adjustment was the PLN's decision to come to terms with economic liberalization and state reform. This is not surprising given that leftist, social democratic, and labor parties in countries as diverse as Jamaica, El Salvador, Brazil, and Argentina have embraced structural adjustment. What is interesting about the PLN's reaction to changing times is its discourse about constructing a "third way" for economic adjustment, something between the status quo ante and the Chilean model. In September 1995, the PLN changed its ideological charter to allow for private-sector participation in former public monopolies and the decentralization of the state.

The PLN still experiences a good deal of infighting over how far away the party should move from the institutions it has helped to build since 1948. A few prominent members of the party object to what they see as a betrayal of traditional PLN principles. But over time, fiscal problems, the need for external assistance, and the low quality of many public services have encouraged a new emphasis on efficient administration and private-sector participation. Prominent members of the party, particularly cabinet members of the Arias and Figueres administrations, came to embrace partial liberalization and state reform. This group includes Carlos Manuel Castillo and Eduardo Lizano, both former presidents of the Central Bank, former Ministers of Finance Fernando Naranjo and Francisco de Paula Gutiérrez, and Leonardo Garnier, Eduardo Doryan, and José Manuel Salazar, who served as the Ministers of Planning, Education, and Trade, respectively, during 1994–98. It was the Figueres administration's stated intention to create an efficient and capable state and to lead a modern social democratic party. As we will see below, however, President Figueres' "New Democrat" approach could not modernize state institutions in four short years.

Streamlining the State: Cases 1 and 2

Campaign pledges to reengineer public institutions and privatize state companies have often resulted in broken promises as the reforms either stalled or progressed at a glacial pace. Some combination of political cycles, vested interests, setbacks at veto points, public opinion, and high costs caused delays in both areas. The small number of successful state reforms were led by visionary domestic leaders or transnational alliances.

In Costa Rica, the passage of controversial bills is often held hostage in executive-legislative standoffs or brought to a standstill in the sluggish last half of the four-year electoral cycle when the Assembly is less willing to tackle contentious proposals or the complex enabling laws required for much of institutional reform. Even if legislation is passed, it may face challenges from other levels of government. For instance, in one case, the Comptroller General effectively struck down a reform for technical reasons. Of course, those who stand to lose from the reforms have used public protests and civil service statutes to defend their interests.

In addition, Presidents Calderón and Figueres both had difficulty in generating support for the demonopolization of state control over energy and telecommunications, oil refining, and insurance. These institutes have fairly good track records and opinion polls show significant public support for them. Finally, neither

Rafael Calderón nor José Figueres could stomach large-scale layoffs of public employees. Without generous external funding for severance packages, the potential political costs discouraged such action.

Public-Sector Layoffs and Institutional Redesign

Effective reform in the area of public-sector employment eluded both the PLN and the PUSC in the 1990s. The idea of permanently reducing the public-sector wage bill had been kicked around since the late 1980s, but Rafael Calderón's administration was the first to try it. President Calderón's Minister of State Reform, Johnny Meoño, developed the first *movilidad laboral* (literally, labor mobility) program. Initial efforts to move public-sector employees out of their jobs in 1990 failed in the face of union opposition and delays by a cash-starved government unable to give workers the severance pay legally owed them.[7] In early 1991, the USAID mission in Costa Rica volunteered to assist the *movilidad laboral* program by funding and administering severance packages. Toward that end, USAID contributed $12 million and a new organization called FUCE (Fundación de Cooperación Estatal).[8]

Sources vary wildly over the outcome of *movilidad laboral* under the Calderón administration, but most consider it to have been a failure. The number of public-sector jobs eliminated by the Calderón government between 1990–93 was reported in different documents by various ministries to be 13,000, 9,719, 8,149, and 6,200.[9] Because the layoffs were mostly voluntary and there was no overarching strategy of institutional reform, employee departures paralyzed some agencies. As no central authority monitored *movilidad laboral*, these ministries and institutes often rehired their own or other laidoff workers just to accomplish basic tasks. In addition, the program excluded the ministries of health, education, and security, areas in which employment actually grew. Hence, there is also debate over the net number of state workers gained or lost during the Calderón administration. For example, President Calderón's Finance Ministry reported that the program achieved a net reduction of 542 public workers between 1990–93,[10] however, a Figueres administration document claims that the number of state employees rose from 173,083 to 176,615 during the same period.[11] An evaluation of FUCE concludes that the program was unsuccessful in terms of the numbers of public-sector workers laid off but useful in stopping the growth of state employment.[12]

Even though Calderón's PUSC administration could not carry

out effective labor reductions, it pressured incoming President Figueres to attempt much larger layoffs. The ensuing controversy sprang from President Calderón's negotiation of a third structural adjustment loan with the World Bank and the IDB. The three parties signed an accord and the president sent the deal to the Legislative Assembly for approval in 1993. But the PLN deputies managed to stall the bill in the Assembly while then-presidential candidate Figueres strongly criticized one of the loan's terms. The condition in question called for dismissing 25,000 public-sector workers, or about 15 percent of the state labor force, for whom PUSC officials would supply severance packages paid for with a $100 million World Bank loan. With approval of the third structural adjustment loan still pending when he took office in 1994, José Figueres felt sandwiched between private sector and external bank pressure to cut public-sector workers and a campaign pledge to lay off far fewer than 25,000.

In short time, President Figueres' renegotiated the terms of the loan and succeeded in eliminating the 25,000 worker layoff. But PUSC deputies in the Legislative Assembly retaliated by maneuvering to block the new version's approval. Hence, the president reverted to the original agreement, including the clause calling for the dismissal of almost 15 percent of the government's work force. The PUSC-led Assembly passed the original version in October 1994. Although many believed that the president would negotiate side agreements with the banks to avoid a political crisis over the labor shedding and privatization clauses, public-sector unions held several strikes during the next six months to make sure Figueres understood the stakes involved.

As it turned out, the potentially explosive 25,000 worker layoff plan disappeared after March 1, 1995. Costa Rican macroeconomic indicators failed to meet the World Bank's previous conditions for the first disbursement and the Bank canceled its entire portion ($100 million) of the third structural adjustment loan. What remained of the package ($180 million) was lent by the IDB without a requirement to fire 25,000 workers. Nevertheless, the Figueres administration always thought to reduce the budget deficit by releasing some state employees and settled on the goal of laying off 5,000 workers in another mostly voluntary *movilidad laboral* program.

Under the Figueres administration, the buyout offered workers was even more generous than the previous one, as it included the equivalent of four extra month's salary over the legal requirement.[13] FUCE again paid for and administrated the severance packages, reducing the former employee's waiting time from months to weeks. This time, the administration and FUCE implemented controls designed to avoid rehiring separated workers. But like the previous effort, there was no strategy involved in who took the buyouts, the idea was just to eliminate employees. And again, ambiguity exists as to the net number of public-sector jobs eliminated. In January 1996, the Ministry of State Reform announced that, under the Figueres administration, 4,000 government workers left voluntarily, 2,000 more were dismissed, and that 5,700 new jobs had been added in areas of ever-expanding public service (health, education, and police).[14] But administration officials later told the IMF that they eliminated 5,240 net public positions in 1995–96.[15] The *movilidad laboral* program closed in June 1996 when FUCE ended its participation and the Figueres administration became wary of negative political fallout from public layoffs.[16]

The logical next step would be to reform the regulations governing public-sector employment in order to make the size and the composition of the work force more flexible and to enhance performance. During interviews, several public officials complained about civil service regulations which they felt made the need for reform obvious. One agency director told a story that illustrated the disarticulation between pay incentives and worker performance. Upon following the president's orders to reduce the size and budget of his institution to nearly nothing (a very difficult political accomplishment), this director received a letter from the state workers' union to the effect that he had been demoted with a salary cut because the size of his agency had shrunk. With FUCE's help, the Figueres administration did write proposed legislation for a new civil service law but the bill failed to reach the floor of the Legislative Assembly for a vote before the 1998 elections.

Under President Figueres, ministerial reengineering was supposed to be something more than laying off public-sector workers. His administration made much of its commitment to also modernize and improve state capacity in functions as diverse as tax collection, budgeting, energy regulation, and postal services. Two things motivated this approach: real recognition of the need to improve the quality of public services and a strategy of preempting the PUSC's harsher approach to reform. By the mid-1990s, the debate within the PLN was about how to improve government institutions rather than whether the state needed any restructuring at all.

Halfway through Figueres' term, the government announced

that it had overhauled fifteen ministries and institutes and that state reform was about done.[17] All of these cases involved worker layoffs and reduced budgets, but to what extent have state institutions modernized their missions and improved administrative capacity? The results are not impressive. One former advisor to the state reform program even called institutional reengineering "bullshit."[18] On the other hand, pockets of reform do exist.

One example of true reengineering occurred in the Consejo Nacional de Producción (CNP), where Figueres appointees eliminated 468 employees but also changed the entire focus of the institute. The CNP was a state marketing board which monopolized the purchasing and wholesaling, importing and exporting of basic grains. It is now a government agency which supports small farmers' initiatives to form cooperatives and other business ventures. In 1994, a new director and deputy director came into office and implemented a shared vision for the CNP based on their experiences in the private sector and the agricultural economics department of the University of Kansas, respectively. Because most of the CNP's prior tasks had been eliminated, it had appeared that the institution would be closed. But the incoming directors defined a new mission and succeeded in convincing the remaining employees and the administration of its importance.[19]

A great deal of reform has also occurred in the Ministry of Finance where a loose transnational alliance between FUCE and several government officials spanning the Calderón and Figueres administrations designed and implemented the new ideas. The most dramatic improvement occurred in the ministry's customs administration. The idea to reform Costa Rica's notoriously corrupt and inefficient customs agency grew from discussions between FUCE's director and the Vice-Minister of Finance in 1991.[20] More than any other area in which FUCE participated in state reform, it took the lead in overhauling the customs administration.[21] FUCE spent $989,000, assigned fifteen full-time people, and hired numerous consultants over several years to restructure it.[22] FUCE and its consultants redesigned and streamlined the customs process by installing a computer system, writing a software package for it, and training workers in the new process. The result reduced the average time of transit for imported goods between the docks and the retailer from days to hours. After the new Minister of Finance absorbed a six-hour presentation from FUCE on this project in May 1994, he came on board the project and two months later fired 255 customs workers, many of whom had been accused of corruption.

Reforming the Welfare State: The 1990s 77

Passage of a new law governing customs (and drafted by FUCE's lawyers) in 1995 culminated the process of administrative reform.

Consultants paid for by FUCE also helped design a general reorganization for the Ministry of Finance, launched in 1995, which will modernize tax collection and accounting systems as well as decentralize the public budgeting process. The decentralization project will shift responsibility for payroll and procurement budgets to each public ministry and institute. The director of the program estimated that the Ministry of Finance would complete about one-half of its overhaul by the end of the Figueres administration.[23]

Projects to reform public institutions face three types of delays in Costa Rica. The first is that many of the changes (such as when an institute adopts new functions, decides to impose different rules on its clientele, or in the case of budget decentralization) require new legislation. Years often pass between the lawyers' first drafts of enabling legislation, their movement through congress, and enactment of the new laws. The gridlock created by interparty rivalries often stops the movement of bills through the Assembly, and, in any case, Costa Rica's short electoral cycle and single-term presidency provides a small window of opportunity to get important laws passed.

Second, in addition to affording public workers a certain level of job security, civil service statues slow down the removal of corrupt employees as well as the reassignment of others. The frustrated director of the postal system (CORTEL) explained that:

> I am in a very bad position here . . . I am aware of several employees who have been stealing, but because of the Civil Service Statute I cannot dismiss them without going through a very long process first. So I have to send them to what I call "Siberia," which means I put them in a job where they don't have access to the mail. This is a waste of my time and CORTEL's money.[24]

Finally, as is the case in the areas of health and education examined below, the project leaders with whom I spoke felt that passive resistance from line workers constituted a important obstacle to reform.

In terms of what is required for institutional reform to work, a minister or executive director with a clear vision of the change to be carried out and the willingness to undergo the political battles to get there seem to be indispensable. Many state managers are now working earnestly and energetically on improving the functioning of their institutions. But others reject change, lack a vision of what could be achieved, are unwilling to take political risks, or fall short of the resources to do so. As the involvement of FUCE indicates, external donors can provide critical assistance for second-stage reforms if they form partnerships with like-minded domestic technocrats and supply the sort of resources needed.

In addition to these slow and complex institutional reforms, the Figueres administration attempted to reduce the size and scope of the state by merging, shedding, or closing government offices. The results of these efforts were mixed. The ministries of government and security were merged and CENPRO, the Free Zone Corporation, and the National Investment Council were folded into one entity: PROCOMER (Promotora del Comercio Exterior de Costa Rica). Several agricultural boards that had enjoyed at least partial government support were turned over to the private sector.[25] But legislation to close two other government institutes, CONICIT (Consejo Nacional de Investigaciones Científicas y Tecnológicas) and INCOFER (Instituto Costarricense de Ferrocarriles), failed because of protests from employees and others who depended on their services.

Complex Privatizations

Presidents Calderón and Figueres made small advances in second-stage privatizations but they passed the bulk of the job to Miguel Angel Rodríguez (PUSC, 1998–2002). The demonopolization of state enterprises and the opening of bidding on public works to private companies have progressed exactly as we might expect, that is, at a snail's pace. The state companies are profitable, symbols of the post-1948 development model, and strongholds of organized labor. In addition, Costa Rica's decentralized state acts like a series of hurdles over which any complex privatization must pass.

President Calderón promised to privatize the state's monopolies on insurance (INS or Instituto Nacional de Seguros),[26] electricity and telecommunications (ICE or Instituto Costarricense de Electricidad) petroleum refining (RECOPE or Refinadora Costarricense de Petróleo) and drinking alcohol production (FANAL or Fábrica Nacional de Licores). In fact, he made all of these steps conditions of the third structural adjustment loan agreement signed with the World Bank and IDB. But Rafael Calderón underestimated the political difficulty of getting PLN legislators to let the structural adjustment agreement pass, and he failed to fully meet any of these promises.

Nevertheless, President Calderón did convince the legislature to pass a law allowing private firms to construct and operate power plants. They are still required to sell the electricity thus generated to ICE because it maintains a monopoly on energy distribution. Private firms now generate about 30 percent of Costa Rica's energy.[27] President Calderón also pushed through the *ley de contratación administrativa* which would allow the outsourcing of some government administrative needs, and the *ley de concesión de obra pública*, which makes it possible for private companies to bid on public works projects. In 1995, Calderón, as leader of the PUSC, made President Figueres promise to privatize FANAL and a small institute known as DINADECO (Dirección Nacional de Desarrollo Comunal) as a condition of their pact over taxes.

The new president followed through on his pact with Rafael Calderón by submitting bills to the Legislative Assembly which would have allowed the sale of FANAL and the closure of DINADECO, but they failed to pass. President Figueres did start preparing the INS for competition in 1996 by allowing its employees to begin selling INS-underwritten policies as independent agents. The executive had planned to introduce legislation which would have sold 40 percent of INS to the private sector but discovered that it would be necessary to first amend the Constitution to do so. Constitutional amendments must be made by the Legislative Assembly during ordinary sessions. The Figueres administration did not rank the INS issue highly enough to win it legislative consideration before the 1998 elections.

President Figueres was also unsuccessful at opening ICE's monopoly on electricity distribution and telecommunications. ICE is relatively efficient, but by the mid-1990s it was clear that the state could not afford to make the investments necessary to keep up with demand and technological changes. Allowing the private sector to provide some services seemed an obvious way to meet the deficits. For instance, in 1994 ICE's board of directors leased the rights to sell cellular phone packages to Millicom, a private firm. But the deal was blocked in 1995 when the Supreme Court declared it unconstitutional. New legislation would be required to privatize any of ICE's functions and so President Figueres introduced a bill to allow private (including international) investors to invest in energy and telecommunications provision in 1996. Under this plan, ICE would survive but would have to compete with private companies in an open market.

To garner support for the changes in ICE, the company held forums open to its unions and to the public so that all could ask questions and express opinions about the proposals. The president also addressed the public about this issue during his appearances around the country. Unsurprisingly, the plan to open the ICE monopoly confronted strong opposition. ICE's unions struck against it,[28] and some in the PLN remain opposed on ideological grounds.[29] Opponents have formed an organization (Consejo Nacional de Defensa a la Institucionalidad) composed of ICE's unions, a former president of Costa Rica, former deputies to the Legislative Assembly, a former president of ICE, and a former government minister.[30] President Figueres also faced substantial opposition to his proposal to demonopolize ICE from some of his own PLN deputies in the Legislative Assembly. In fact, the assemblyman who led anti-privatization forces within the PLN chaired the special commission considering privatization measures.

Whatsmore, a nationwide survey commissioned by *La Nación* in 1996 discovered that public opinion offered only lukewarm support for opening these monopolies.[31] The poll found that 90 percent of respondents were happy with ICE's electrical service and 82 percent were satisfied with telephone service.[32] A similar nationwide survey taken nineteen months later determined that 90 percent of respondents were still satisfied with ICE's services and that among Costa Rican institutions (including the Catholic Church), ICE scored highest in citizen confidence (87 percent).[33] Outright opposition to demonopolizing ICE as well as the public's positive feelings for the institution undermined all possibility for further privatization of its functions during Figueres' term. The President's bill never reached the floor of the Legislature for a vote.

President Figueres met with more success in strengthening the state's role as a regulator of public services by creating the Autoridad Reguladora de Servicios Públicos (ARESEP) in 1996. This Authority acts much as a state-level public service commission in the United States by evaluating rate hike requests from providers of electricity, heating fuels, sewerage and water, transportation, and telecommunications. Although questions have been raised as to whether appointments to the ARESEP's board ought to coincide with elections and whether the Authority has an adequate budget, its decisions have been considered to be independent and technically appropriate.

The last area which the Figueres administration attempted to open to private competition was in the construction, administration, and staffing of the country's docks and highways, two areas of the transportation infrastructure badly in need of investments the state could not afford. The *ley de concesión de obra pública* served as the legal basis for inviting private capital into these areas. But great obstacles have fallen in the way. First, the privatization of dock work has been a delicate political matter as the two main ports, Limón on the Atlantic and Caldera on the Pacific, are located in areas of relatively high unemployment, poverty, crime, and radical union organization. It has been understood that part of the purpose of the state agencies which oversee these ports, JAPDEVA (Junta de Administración Portuaria y de Desarrollo Económico de la Vertiente Atlántica) in the Atlantic and INCOP (Instituto Costarricense de Puertos del Pacífico) in the Pacific, is to provide public assistance through employment opportunities. Thus, explosive social protest met efforts to modify the arrangements local unions enjoy with these two agencies.

For example, in 1996 JAPDEVA announced that it would allow nonunion companies to compete for contracts for the loading and unloading of ships in Limón, Costa Rica's largest port. The stevedores' unions feared that nonunion labor would drive down their wages. Because stevedoring is the backbone of Limón's economy, a movement composed of fifty-nine labor unions and community organizations shut down the docks in August and settled in for a ten-day confrontation with the government. The conflict left three people dead but in the end the government ordered JAPDEVA to suspend efforts to open stevedore contracting.[34]

A second step toward using the new public works law shipwrecked on the rocks of Costa Rica's system of checks and balances. After an international consortium won the right to construct a badly needed highway in June 1996, the Comptroller nullified the contract a year later saying that it had been improperly awarded. The Comptroller found that the law contained flaws that made it impossible to administer the bidding system without breaking other Costa Rican laws. The Figueres administration then rewrote the law on public works concessions taking these problems into account as well as the objections of the dockworkers. A new *ley de concesión de obra pública* passed the legislature in April 1998 with a clause excluding existing ports from concessions to the private sector.

The private sector will likely gain the right to provide insurance policies, basic utilities, and public works only very slowly. And President Figueres did not even open a dialogue about the possibility of privatizing petroleum refining. It appears that instead of selling off publicly owned companies, as was the case with CODESA's subsidiaries in the 1980s, the state will gradually demonopolize certain activities, more along the lines of banking deregulation. This strategy may not bring the immediate positive impact on the government budget that true privatization would. But it carries the political advantages of deferring public-employee layoffs and minimizing disruption by allowing private firms to slowly build expertise in providing services to the Costa Rican market.

Tinkering with Social Policy: Cases 3–5

Costa Rica entered the 1980s in good standing as a welfare state. Quality social security, health, and educational coverage had been extended to virtually the entire population. As Table 4.1 illustrates, Costa Rica did and still does score impressively on basic development indicators. But by the end of the decade, pressing problems had developed that, although not yet visible in standard indicators of well-being, captured the attention of Costa Ricans and the multilateral development banks.

First, given expectations about population growth and aging, it became clear that the fiscal price tag of the welfare state would rapidly grow out of control. This was particularly worrisome to the administrators of the pension system. Second, after a decade of little public investment in health and educational facilities, they had deteriorated badly. Third and relatedly, health and education services had suffered alarming declines in quality, evidenced by long waiting lists for particular treatments, doctors' demands for bribes to move patients up on the schedule for procedures, increasing student dropout rates, and lowered test scores. By the 1990s, social security and education ministry services were underfunded for a variety of reasons. Most were negatively impacted by the economic crisis of the 1980s and subsequent macroeconomic conditionalities (especially budget deficit restrictions) agreed to by the Costa Rican government and external donors. Then, in each area: pensions, health care, and education, a specific combination of factors conspired to create problems. These include population aging, tax evasion, program inequities, poor resource allocation, epidemiological changes, technological advances, and the impact of Nicaraguan refugees. The interaction of these factors in each policy area is discussed subsequently.

Table 4.1
Basic Development Indicators for Costa Rica

	Before Economic Crisis [a]	After Economic Crisis [b]
GNP/Capita (in U.S. $)	1730	2610
Life Expectancy at Birth (years)	70	77
Infant Mortality Rate (per 1000 live births)	20	13
Percent of Population with Access to Safe Water	77	100
Percent of Adult Population Literate	90	95
School Enrollment as a Percentage of Age Group		
Primary female	104	105
male	106	106
Secondary female	51	49
male	44	45
Tertiary total	21	30

SOURCE: World Bank, *World Development Report*.
a. All figures based on 1980 data except for access to safe water (1975) and literacy (1977).
b. All figures based on 1995 data except for school enrollment (1994).

Addressing problems of costs, quality, efficiency, and equity in social programs has been somewhat more successful than privatization and institutional streamlining. But compared to the structural adjustments of the 1980s, changes in social policy are definitely second-stage reforms. Like the first set of state reforms studied here, attempts to tinker with, as opposed to remove, the state's involvement in pension coverage, health, and education have met with problems. To a greater or lesser degree, the proposed changes faced strong public attachment to the status quo, protests from those would lose from the new rules, an electoral cycle which offers a short window within which controversial or complex legislation has a chance to pass, and impediments in the form of civil service statutes and other state institutions.

In as much as the externally funded reforms in public health and education involve large-scale changes in the standard operating procedures and job descriptions within the effected ministries, the obstacles have been even more complex. And in both cases, there is some evidence that IMF conditionality works at cross purposes with the programs backed by the IDB and World Bank. But the education ministry's initiatives have performed better than those in health. Three main factors explain the greater difficulties experienced by the latter: (1) weak leadership and passive resistance from within the health institutions; (2) poor relations between the IFIs and their domestic counterparts; and (3) the demand for large changes in the most complex administrative units: hospitals.

Pensions

The Costa Rican Social Security Fund (CCSS), a government institution, covers virtually the entire population. Most citizens contribute to and draw pensions from the general fund (named IVM or Invalidez, Vejez, y Muerte). But until recently, nineteen separate public funds existed for teachers, judicial workers, legislators, and other state workers, all of which provided preferential terms of retirement. In addition, some state agencies offer supplemental funds to which employees may contribute. There are no programs operated by the private sector that could be considered strictly retirement funds. Hence, the state completely dominates social security insurance in Costa Rica.

Costa Rica's pension funds have not yet sunk to the depth of crisis reached by Uruguay, Argentina, and Chile because its population and social security system are younger. Nonetheless, in the early 1990s, two factors forced alterations in the pension schemes. First, the Costa Rican population is aging faster than any of its neighbors and officials began to see that to keep the cost of the pension funds manageable in the future, they had to switch to less-generous payouts. Second, and more importantly, these funds were already running deficits, forcing the central government to transfer money into them to help the CCSS meet obligations.

As in many other developing countries, we can locate the causes of the underfunded pension system in the state's shortsighted treatment of it. Costa Rican law obligates the central government to pay a quota for each worker into the fund as well as to transfer certain percentages of particular tax collections to the

CCSS. Beginning in the 1970s, the state often did not meet these requirements.[35] Not only has the state not kept pace with its obligations but over half of the CCSS general fund holdings were invested in short-term government bonds in the 1980s.[36] During that decade, the earnings on these bonds fell well behind inflation; the CCSS general fund showed a negative −10.5 investment return for 1980–87.[37]

In sum, the state's financial difficulties have forced it to undermine the long-term health of the pension system through indirect borrowing. These patterns resulted in rapidly rising central government expenditures on state pension funds,[38] whose deficit as a proportion of GDP is expected to rise from 2.5 percent in 1995 to over 7 percent in 2010.[39] To address the problem, the Calderón and Figueres administrations tinkered with retirement guidelines and contributor quotas, and reduced the number of special funds. Designs for a new system of private complementary funds are in the planning stages.

All Costa Ricans working in the private sector as well as those who became state employees after 1992 belong to the CCSS's general pension program. To this program workers contribute 2.5 percent of their salary, employers put in 4.75 percent and the state 0.25 percent. Full pensions equal 60 to 65 percent of the average of an employee's salary during the last twenty years of work. The last modifications to the general program, made in 1991, increased retirement ages to fifty-nine years and eleven months for women and sixty-one years and eleven months for men.[40] In 1996, the CCSS announced that the retirement age for the general fund would be increased to sixty-five for men and women. But public protest led the CCSS to suspend the new retirement ages indefinitely.

Until 1992, there were nineteen additional special funds covering public-sector workers. The special funds granted more liberal entitlement conditions and larger pensions to retired civil servants, thus creating significant inequalities. Carmelo Mesa-Lago reports, for instance, that in 1987, 42 percent of pension payouts went to the 20 percent of retirees who belonged to the special funds while the rest went to beneficiaries of the regular CCSS fund.[41] A law passed by the Legislative Assembly in 1992 unified sixteen of the special funds and sent all new state employees to the CCSS general fund. For those falling under the unified scheme (as opposed to the general fund), the retirement age is set at sixty or sixty-five, depending on the length of service and both the state and the employees pay 7 percent of the worker's salary into the pension fund.

These changes were passed relatively easily. But real controversy erupted when the Figueres administration attempted to modify the teacher's special fund.[42] Costa Rica's school teachers started the first pension fund in the country in 1886. Until 1995, the state contributed 14 percent of each contributor's salary to the pension fund (7 percent as the employer and a separate 7 percent as the state) and the teacher paid 7 percent.[43] But the fund was nearly bankrupt by the early 1990s because of unsustainable payout policies (i.e. awarding pensions equal to 100 percent of salary, allowing those with 25 to 30 years of service to retire at any age) and unpaid state contributions. With the state having to transfer money to the fund to meet pension obligations, the Figueres administration decided to close the teacher's pension fund.

This move ignited the largest protest marches ever seen in Costa Rica because it involved either forcing teachers to pay much higher pension contributions or transferring them to the CCSS general fund, a substantially less generous regime. Throughout 1995, teachers held twenty-four-hour strikes as the government negotiated with them over a new scheme that would reduce state contributions to the pension fund. But the two sides did not reach agreement. In July 1995, the executive used arguments about equity within the public pension system to persuade the Legislative Assembly to pass a bill to close the teacher's pension fund. In its place, all teachers would have the option of transferring to the CCSS general fund or joining an alternative scheme into which they would have to pay 11 to 15 percent of their salaries, agree to smaller contributions from the state, and accept a minimum retirement age of sixty-two.[44] The well-unionized teachers went on nationwide strike for exactly one month, at one point bringing eighty thousand people to downtown San José in a protest march.[45] The strike only ended after President Figueres offered to talk over the matter. Further negotiations occurred but the president won the stand off and the teachers' fund was closed.

Figueres administration officials also put together a set of initiatives to overhaul Costa Rica's entire pension system.[46] Technocrats in the vice president's office pushed forward two types of changes. First, they sought to shore up the financial standing of the current IVM, or general fund, and make the payout system more equitable via several modifications. In 1996–97, the CCSS tightened requirements for disability pensions (an area of abuse) and recalculated the formula used to determine old-age pensions. The latter modification should shrink the gap between the best and the worst-paid workers.[47] The pension reform team and CCSS officials also attempted to effectively raise retirement ages. The first attempt to do so in 1996 drew a public outcry. Thereafter, the reform team plotted a rule change which would have the same effect but be presented to the public in the guise of personal choice. The new rule would raise the age required to earn a full pension but allow people to choose whether to retire earlier with a smaller pension or work even longer than required to get a larger one. This change had not yet been enacted by election time in mid-1998. Finally, in 1997, President Figueres sent a bill to the Legislative Assembly which would make it a crime for contributors to evade payment of CCSS taxes. This controversial law was clearly aimed at employers. Unsurprisingly, it failed to reach the floor for a vote before the 1998 elections.

The second and more dramatic change envisioned by the planning team involved setting up a complementary fund system overseen but not invested by the state. Under this scenario, the current state scheme would change to mixed system in which contributors would receive a minimum pension from the state and a supplementary pension from the complementary fund. Although the level of government pensions would probably be reduced, the plan differs from the Chilean system in that the state fund would remain open. Planners forecast that in the future, the state system will provide about two-thirds of a retiree's pension with the rest coming from the complementary funds. The CCSS would collect the extra and obligatory contributions for the complementary fund but somehow turn this money over to private companies which would invest them. Workers would be able to choose the private firm in which they wished to invest their supplementary retirement fund.

Costa Rica has lagged far behind the other Latin American welfare states in bringing market mechanisms into the pension system. This is because of the relative youth of Costa Rica's pension system, the underdevelopment of its stock market, and strong support among political parties, the public bureaucracies, and the citizenry for a dominant state role in social security. But the Figueres administration took incremental steps preparing the way for a mixed, public-private pension system. There are several things left to be done. Establishing complementary funds will require the passage of several pieces of enabling legislation aimed at the pension system itself as well as others meant to adapt financial markets and insurance regulations for these purposes. And technical consultants will have to continue working with CCSS officials to modernize the institute's information technologies so that taxes and checks can be transferred electronically and contributors can access individual accounts by telephone. The Figueres administration simply ran out of time before accomplishing structural changes that required complicated legislation and significant modification in the functioning of the CCSS.

Health

The same institute that administers the pension system, the CCSS, also provides the only health insurance plan and most curative services in Costa Rica. As we saw in chapter 2, almost the entire Costa Rican population is covered by CCSS health insurance. The CCSS shares responsibility for the health sector with the Ministry of Health. The Ministry formulates policy, coordinates health care provision, and conducts all disease eradication efforts. The Ministry transferred all of its hospitals to the CCSS in 1973 but in the same year started a program providing preventative and primary health care to low-income rural populations and to people in marginal urban zones (at the time not yet fully covered by CCSS insurance). Because each of these two institutes operates hundreds of health posts, areas of overlapping services have arisen, and this is one of the objects of reform, to be discussed below.

Well over 90 percent of Costa Rica's doctors work for the state, most in one of the CCSS's twenty-nine hospitals. The CCSS hospitals and clinics have 6,819 beds available and twenty-five thousand people are employed in its health care facilities.[48] The CCSS also manufactures a significant portion of Costa Rica's medical supplies, including drugs. There is a private health sector in Costa Rica which includes five small hospitals in the capital (with a total of 146 beds) and accounts for about one-quarter of total health spending.[49] Some 34 percent of Costa Rican doctors have private practices.[50]

The public health care system is clearly the crown jewel of Costa Rica's welfare state as it provides the same level of medical services to all, even the unemployed. Rural dwellers obtain the same quality of health coverage as the urban population, an achievement only matched by Cuba in Latin America. But since the 1980s, health officials have become concerned about symptoms of declining quality and unmet demand within their system. These can be summarized as follows:

... long waiting lists that increasingly limit access to outpatient services, alarmingly long waiting periods for specialized medical services, shorter patient consultations, slow laboratory and diagnostic services, and a lack of CCSS pharmacological supplies.[51]

Everyday one hears stories of patients waiting months for desperately needed operations or being asked by a doctor to pay a large extra (and illegal) fee for preferential treatment (usually scheduling an operation ahead of others). Emergency rooms and regular wards of public hospitals spill over with the sick for whom there is no room.

There are multiple causes for these problems but they fit into three general categories. The first involves changes in the population's average age and epidemiological profile. Health agencies have done a marvelous job of wiping out the infectious diseases and infant diarrhea once responsible for high mortality rates in a young population. It turns out that these interventions were relatively cheap compared to current demands. The aging population now presents health officials with a relatively greater proportion of the expensive, chronic, and degenerative diseases common in advanced industrialized countries. These changes have driven up demand for advanced medical technology and increased the cost and the length of hospital stays as well as out-patient drug and physical therapies.

Various types of inefficiency constitute the second and most controversial reason for the problems of the public health sector. These problems result from a suboptimal use of the main human resource, doctors, and from antiquated managerial systems. The only quantitative evidence of a drop in doctors' efficiency is the decline in the number of consultations per doctor between 1983–1995.[52] More serious is the sense of disincentive and demoralization that many CCSS system doctors feel and the consequent professional apathy this causes. CCSS doctors have little opportunity to form personal relationships with patients or to choose their cases. Rather, in the clinics, patients are randomly assigned a doctor for each appointment and doctors work on a rough quota system. The same is true in the hospitals. Doctors are simply required to complete a minimum number of appointments or procedures and are not evaluated (or rewarded) according to the outcomes of their care. The result of this "assembly-line" process is that doctors search for shortcuts to reduce the amount of time and effort they expend in their offices, lose competitive desire to discover new and better treatments, and often fail to keep up in their fields.[53]

The CCSS itself is notoriously bureaucratic, overcentralized, and riddled with outdated allocative and accounting practices.[54] For example, the CCSS headquarters in San José assigns hospitals their budgets based on the previous year's expenditures. Thus, hospital directors have minimal incentive to economize. The CCSS collects little in the way of outcomes data. Without this information, physicians and administrators lack feedback about the quality of their work, nor can they be held accountable for it. The CCSS's accounting procedures are also insufficient for tracking and controlling costs. For instance, since patients are not billed for services at all, the CCSS literally does not know how much many of them cost in per-unit terms. There is also no method for tracking and controlling patients' hospital visits. Currently, citizens from every corner of Costa Rica simply choose to bypass the regional care system and present themselves at one of the national hospitals in San José. This fact alone is responsible for a large part of the congestion in the national hospitals. Finally, the CCSS system cannot send an invoice to or enter a payment from a third party.

A final problem is funding. Despite rising per-unit costs caused by the factors treated above, real public spending on health care as a proportion of GDP declined between 1985–1995.[55] Deteriorating service in the regional hospitals, unmet demand in the national hospitals, long lags in the acquisition of new technologies, and a halt to maintenance of the physical infrastructure all resulted from insufficient resources. The resource deficit was further aggravated by the strain that Central American immigrants, almost entirely Nicaraguans, placed on the system. Waves of Nicaraguan immigrants have flooded Costa Rican in the last twenty years, fleeing first political strife and then economic disintegration in their country. In 1999, conservative estimates put the number of Nicaraguans living in Costa Rica at 340,000 to 360,000, or 10 percent of the country's population. [56] Most of them are undocumented and therefore neither they nor their employers pay social security taxes. The CCSS estimates that the difference between what Nicaraguans pay into the public health system and the value of the services they receive equals 3.5 percent of the institute's budget.[57]

During the 1980s, a lot of discussion took place within the CCSS regarding these problems, in addition, its officials were well aware of the worldwide trend toward decentralization and preventative care in public health systems. [58] In 1988, the CCSS opened negotiations with the IDB for a loan to fix these problems. The talks dragged on for years, with the World Bank joining the process in 1992. Finally, in 1994, Costa Rica obtained a loan package including $42 million from the IDB and $22 million from the World Bank to fund an overhaul of the public health system. The banks began disbursing the loans in 1995 and the project runs through the year 2000. Three main components make up the improvement plan: (1) the building and repair of the physical infrastructure, (2) the formation of preventative health care teams to work in rural and marginal urban environments, and (3) institutional reform. The progress made in each area is examined below.

Under the first component, the principal goals are to construct a new hospital in Alajuela (in the Central Valley) and build the health posts to be used by the preventative health teams. In mid-1998 not a brick of the new hospital had been laid and the project was far behind schedule. Many new health posts had been built, but that task was behind schedule as well.

As for the second area of reform, about one-half (nearly 400) of the total number of planned preventative health teams or EBAIS (Equipos Básicos de Atención Integral de Salud) are now in operation and located almost entirely in rural areas. Each is composed of a doctor, a nurse, and two or more technicians. The teams make visits to communities, educate residents about health and hygiene issues, and refer patients to clinics and hospitals when necessary. But both the doctors' association (Colégio de Médicos) and CCSS officials acknowledge that the shift from a curative to a preventative model of health care on the primary level has been harder than was imagined. For Costa Rican doctors, employment in the EBAIS is extremely undesirable as the physicians do not have the opportunity to put most of their training to work and tend to feel isolated from their peers and profession. As one doctor told me about the EBAIS, "this is public health, not medicine." Consequently, the EBAIS mostly attract recent medical school graduates who have no other options. Apparently, the rural population is not entirely accepting of the new innovation either. In a country where most have had access to decent curative medicine for decades and feel that this is their right, citizens seem to prefer visits to doctors in clinics and hospitals to talks on personal hygiene.

The third component of reform is institutional reform, another area in which change has proceeded at a snail's pace. Most of the reform team's time and effort has been spent trying to implement improvements in the administration of the public health care system. Institutional reform comprises a number of changes in CCSS accounting and information systems meant to speed them up and make bureaucrats more result than process-oriented. But the central component involves decentralizing responsibility for hospital outcomes and budgeting. This is to be done through performance contracts (*compromisos de gestión*),[59] whereby the CCSS gives a hospital a finite budget with which its officials must meet agreed-upon goals, including filling quotas for the quantity and quality of service. Exactly what services will be provided and how personnel will be organized to deliver them is left up to the hospital to decide. And, after meeting the goals, the hospitals will be allowed to retain any unused portion of the budget to use however they see fit. It is hoped that this combination of freedom and accountability will encourage a more efficient use of resources.

In January 1997, the CCSS began piloting the new budget system in seven of the largest hospitals. While it is too early to evaluate this experiment, officials report that implementation of the new system is moving along more slowly than desired, both in the hospitals and in the CCSS central administration.[60] The major impediments seem to be a lack of managerial training among hospital administrators and foot-dragging among employees. The plan is to extend decentralized budgeting to all hospitals and clinics by 2000.

A second major component of institutional reform requires the elimination of overlapping functions between the CCSS and the Ministry of Health. Specifically, all curative programs and personnel will be consolidated under the CCSS while the Ministry will retain responsibility for policy formation and public health campaigns. This shift was to take place before the World Bank loan started dispensing in 1995 but, three years later, two hundred of the total 1,200 Ministry of Health employees had yet to be transferred. The Ministry employees have not wanted to move for a combination of reasons involving fear of being laid off (officials vehemently deny this possibility), reluctance to blend into a new system, and the clash of professional cultures between the two organizations. Many of the workers involved have been able to use Costa Rican labor legislation to delay or refuse the transfer.

A number of factors have conspired to frustrate the progress of the reform program. First, although the director of the CCSS and the Minister of Health officially endorsed the program during 1994–98, those in charge of implementation felt that their superiors were not doing everything possible to support the planned changes. In addition, the office in charge of organizing and carrying out the new ideas is hierarchically situated below the ministerial level and outside the chain of command. This undoubtedly lends the reform team members a certain degree of independence from bureaucratic pressures, but it also robs them of the authority to carry out politically controversial tasks, especially in the absence of full ministerial backing.

Second, relations between Costa Rican officials and the international financial institutions have also hamstrung the health reform package. Specifically, CCSS, World Bank, and IDB officials display distrust for each other. The World Bank and IDB task managers assigned to the project are extremely critical of what they see as the bureaucratic bumbling of the CCSS and the latter believe that the IFIs do not understand the political problems involved in proceeding too fast. In addition, because of strict inflation and government spending limits set by the IMF, the Ministry of Finance will only release loan money for health reform (which is counted as fiscal spending) in small amounts. Slow disbursement of loan funds has slowed reform implementation.

Resistance from within the CCSS constitutes a third type of obstacle to the reform plans. This resistance is mostly passive (as opposed to organized by labor unions) and seems to come from the layers of management within the CCSS. Many CCSS officials simply do not want to loosen their centralized control over the administration of health care.[61] In addition, middle managers have not been offered positive incentives to learn the new skills and duties assigned to them. The doctors constitute the single most organized source of resistance to the reforms. As discussed above, the doctors have strongly voiced their dislike of the EBAIS and the Colegio de Médicos has effectively blocked plans to link physicians' pay to performance goals under the decentralization program.

The final impediment to the rapid implementation of the health reform program is legal. Costa Rican law governs the rights and responsibilities of public entities in minute detail, and so, again, enabling legislation will have to be passed before the reform process in complete. The Ministry of Health has only begun the lengthy process of drafting and lobbying through the legislature language that will solidify its role as regulator of the public health system. Until that legislation is approved, the Ministry of Health will not have the legal authority to enforce performance contracts in CCSS hospitals.

The Future of Health Care in Costa Rica

Given the enormity of the CCSS's problems and the snail's pace of reform, we might wonder about the prospects for the growth of Costa Rica's private health care entities. Private health care provision will continue to grow in Costa Rica but the public system will dominate the sector for some time to come. Tampering with the mandatory nature of public health insurance quotas paid by employers and employees would be politically unpopular, so much so that no important politician has suggested it. And the mandatory payment system makes it difficult to develop private health insurance plans in Costa Rica. To date, none exist.

What about the possibility of public-private ventures? The CCSS experimented with three mixed medicine models in the 1980s. Under one program, private firms agree to hire a CCSS doctor and provide him or her with an office and a nurse. This person becomes the primary physician for all of the company's employees while the CCSS pays laboratory, diagnostic, and pharmacy costs. By 1995, about one thousand firms had CCSS company doctors.[62] Under another plan, individuals have been allowed to select a personal physician from a preapproved group of CCSS candidates, and pay for the office visit themselves while the state continues to provide all the tests and drugs the doctor may order. CCSS officials found that the success of this program was limited by the ability of citizen's to pay doctors' fees and the desire of some to avoid the slowness of CCSS laboratory procedures.

The most interesting experiment took place in 1988 when the CCSS contracted a local cooperative to take over a clinic in a crowded capital-city suburb. Under the agreement, the CCSS transferred a fully equipped clinic to the coop, which itself was responsible for hiring health care professionals and maintaining the premises. The CCSS and the Ministry of Health gave the coop a finite budget with which to run the clinic. The coop did manage to provide quality services at costs below the average for CCSS clinics. There are now five such cooperative clinics in San José. But the model was not incorporated into the reform program because the CCSS's board of directors decided to allow no new similar projects. Opponents of the coop clinics argued that the economies of scale they achieved by virtue of being located in densely populated areas cannot be replicated outside of San José. In addition, many of the applications received from other coops were apparently not well-thought-out and the CCSS board of directors was concerned about maintaining full control over services provided under the CCSS's name.[63]

Whatever the case, it appears that reforms in the public health care system will concentrate on making it "the same but better" instead of embracing a mixed-medicine model. At the same time, there is every reason to expect the middle and upper classes to continue using disposable income to purchase better quality clinical consultations, lab tests, and out-patient procedures from private sources. Of course, in the absence of private health insurance plans, only a very small percentage of the population will be able to afford private hospitalization. The new Hospital San José, a private facility set to open in 1999, expects to mainly serve foreigners engaged in health tourism. In sum, we should expect to see creeping privatization in Costa Rica's health sector. Whether or not the well-to-do completely abandon the state system will depend on the outcome of the current reform and success of a nascent private sector in establishing integrated physician-hospital networks and alternative insurance schemes.

Education

Costa Rica's educational achievements shine in comparison to those of its Central American neighbors. Adult literacy stands at nearly 100 percent of the population, almost a third of young adults attend university, and, as with health, the opportunity to receive a public education is now equally available in rural and urban areas. But in comparison to other Latin American countries, Costa Rica's educational system does not top the rankings in the same way that its health indicators do. For example, the percentage of age-appropriate Costa Rican children enrolled in high school lags far behind that in Chile, Argentina, and Uruguay.[64] Thus, the Costa Rican educational system still faces substantial unmet needs.

The Ministry of Public Education (MEP) centralizes all decisions and program implementation regarding personnel and training, curricula and classroom material development, and planning and policy for the K–12 levels in Costa Rica. The National Council of Deans (CONARE) oversees planning for the four autonomous state universities. There are private alternatives to public education at all grades but, as tables 4.2 and 4.3 show, these are most important at the preschool and secondary levels.

In addition, there has been an explosion in the number of students attending private universities with their matriculation jump-

Table 4.2
Distribution of K–12 Students in Costa Rica, 1996
(by level and type of school)

	Preschool[a]	Primary	Secondary
Percent of Matriculated Students Enrolled in:			
Public School	79	93	86
Private School	19	5	8
Semi-Public School	2	2	6

SOURCE: Ministerio de Educación Pública, "Estadísticas del sistema educativo costarricense, 1980–1996."

a. Includes kindergarten, nursery school, and programs for younger children.

Table 4.3
K–12 Educational Institutions, 1996

	Preschool	Primary	Secondary
Percentage of Schools which are:			
Public	76	95	70
Private	22	5	25
Semi-Public	1	0.5	6

SOURCE: Ministerio de Educación Pública, "Estadísticas del sistema educativo costarricense."

ing from 6 percent of total students enrolled in institutions of higher education in 1980 to 29 percent in 1996.[65]

The high percentage of preschoolers in private institutions reflects the newness of preschool education in Costa Rica and the fact that only in 1997 did the Legislative Assembly amend the Constitution to obligate the state to provide free and public preschool facilities nationwide. Free and public primary and secondary education is also available across the land and very low university tuitions are meant to provide access to higher education regardless of social class. Nevertheless, as in most Latin American countries, we see in Costa Rica that poorer children make up a disproportionate number of pupils at public primary schools but that the wealthiest students are overrepresented at the state universities. In 1992, children from the lowest income quintile accounted for almost 35 percent of those in public primary schools while the offspring of households from the top income quintile made up nearly 40 percent of state university students.[66] The fact of the matter is that students from the private high schools are better prepared for university admissions exams and more able to put off full-time employment in order to attend. Because the public universities charge tuition far below cost, the system disproportionately subsidizes wealthier families.

As in health, the 1980s brought a decline in the quality of basic education and a growing public awareness of the same. The Ministry of Education applied national achievement tests in basic subjects for the first time in 1986 and found that the majority of children failed to meet minimum standards in Spanish and math.[67] Grade repetition rose as did high school dropout rates.[68] *La Nación* and other news media regularly reported these and other findings on the state of Costa Rica's educational system. In addition, very little infrastructural building or maintenance had been done during the decade. By 1991, one-quarter of elementary schools were in urgent need of repair and 98 percent of schools operated two shifts.[69] Schools also lacked educational materials. For example, 45 percent of elementary students had no textbooks in 1991.[70]

The causes of these shortfalls are all derived from MEP budget problems. During the 1980s, spending by the Ministry of Education fell in relation to the GDP, as a percentage of total government expenditure, and in per-student terms.[71] Whatsmore, the spending cuts fell disproportionately on primary and secondary level schooling, where the bulk of the students are. Between 1980 and 1990, the government increased spending on preschools from 2.1 to 3.7 percent of its educational budget and outlays for the state universities from 25.2 to 35.3 percent, but decreased spending on primary education from 38.9 to 38.4 percent and pushed down funding to secondary schools from 29.4 percent of the total to 22.9.[72] Again, although there are no statistics quantifying the problem, it is thought that Nicaraguan immigrants are placing a strain on the public education system in the San José metropolitan area and in the northern zones of the country. The impact of illegal immigration is believed to be most pronounced in primary grade levels.[73]

While an increase in preschool spending seems to be overdue considering popular expectations of such support, the inequality in spending on university and lower-level education is a constant irritant. The budget for the state universities does not actually come directly from the MEP, rather the government maintains a special fund from which public institutions of higher education receive support. Costa Rica's constitution guarantees state funding for the public universities, the existence of a special fund for doing so, and increases at least equivalent to the rate of inflation. Every five years, state university representatives renew funding commitments via direct negotiations with the executive. Thus, during the 1980s, governments were not able to force the universities to help the lower levels of the educational system shoulder the burden of the financial crisis.

These budgetary problems are also believed to be in good part responsible for the declining quality of teaching in primary and secondary schools. During the 1980s, the number of unqualified teachers (those without the required academic certification) rose; in 1989, 24 percent of primary and secondary school teachers fell into this category.[74] Despite the fact that almost the entire MEP budget is eaten up by ministry salaries, teachers' work incentives were eroded by plummeting real wages and sharp inequalities between two different groups: full-time teachers who have job security and good pension plans and part-time teachers who do not have stable positions or access to the special social security regulations for educators. Such a situation can hardly be expected to attract talented university graduates. The salary gap and the lack of incentives for administrative personnel to pursue efficient management practices points to problems with the MEP's internal allocation of resources as well as the need to obtain a larger global budget.

President Arias recognized the seriousness of Costa Rica's educational problems and took preliminary steps toward resolving them. With an $8 million contribution from USAID, President Arias decided to modernize Costa Rica's public school system by following through on a campaign promise to put a computer in every school. His goal was to prepare the country's children to work in a modern economy. In 1988, a private foundation established with the U.S. donation set out to build computer laboratories in schools around the country. By 1993, 160 labs had been established serving about 30 percent of public school students.[75] Because there is at least one lab in every *cantón* (approximately county), it appears that the foundation is making good on its promise not to exclude poor and rural children.

In order to make broader improvements in primary and secondary education, the Arias government began and the Calderón administration concluded negotiations for a joint World Bank-IDB loan package. In 1993, the Costa Rican Legislative Assembly approved the loan package including $23 million from the World Bank and $28 million from the IDB. The project, called "PROMECE" (Programa de Mejoramiento de la Calidad de la Educación General Básica or Program to Improve the Quality of Basic Education), only got under way in 1995 and will extend until 1999. Precisely like the loan package for health, the funding is to enable institutional reform and new capital investments. The project is run from an office inside of the Ministry of Education and is charged with building and repairing schools all over the country, improving curricula, arranging for and purchasing new classroom materials such as books, teacher training, and institutional reform. All of these changes are targeted toward the kindergarten through tenth-grade levels.[76]

PROMECE's progress outshines that of the health reform project. Before the end of 1997, PROMECE had built twenty new computer laboratories, progressed in curricular reform, repaired eight hundred classrooms (as well as hundreds of school bathrooms, kitchens, and offices), and supplied over eighty thousand new desks.[77] By 1998, the project had spent more than one-half of the loan money and finished most of the reforms that did not require capital investments. These tasks included the purchase of new classroom materials and the instruction of teachers in the use of the same, training of teachers and MEP functionaries in evaluation techniques, and the completion of teacher certificate programs by over 3,500 teachers.

What is left to be done are several of the proposed institutional reforms and about half of the physical infrastructure projects. In terms of administration, improvement has occurred in speeding up the arrival of paychecks to teachers (who in the past have gone as long as six months without being paid) and in reducing from months to days the time that students must wait for things like degree certificates. But the new computer system and organizational structure are not yet in place. The main obstacles to completing institutional reform are a combination of technical glitches and passive resistance within the central bureaucracy.[78] Because the physical infrastructure projects are the most expensive of all the tasks listed, the same fiscal limits set by the IMF and Ministry of Finance that are limiting payout of the loans to the health project are inhibiting their completion.

There are four main reasons why PROMECE had more success in meeting its goals than the CCSS project during 1994–98. One is that, unlike the case of health reform, PROMECE received concerted support from President Figueres and Minister of Education Doryan. Hierarchically, PROMECE is located outside of the MEP's chain of command but, in fact, it operates like a special program of the Minister's office. The MEP effectively "owns" the reform project. Independent of PROMECE, the Figueres administration launched its own education initiative, EDU-2005, which in 1997 succeeded in convincing the Legislative Assembly to amend the Constitution and compel the government to allot the equivalent of at least 6 percent of GDP to public education. In addition, Minister Doryan appeared in a series of television spots to highlight the link between public education and Costa Rica's future and to tell parents what they could do to ensure their children's success in school.

Second, my interviews made clear that the PROMECE and multinational bank representatives respect each other and have much more similar ambitions for the reform project than is the case in health. Third, as will be discussed further, the PROMECE project has not attacked the most politically divisive area of Costa Rica's public education system: the universities. Fourth and relatedly, neglecting the university system also makes the educational reform project less managerially demanding than its counterpart in health.

Prospects for Educational Reform

In July 1997, Costa Rican and IDB officials agreed to terms for a new $28 million loan to improve preschool and secondary education in similar form to what is already being done through PROMECE. The completion of both loans and the new constitutional funding guarantee for public education are expected to bring considerable benefits to K–12 students. But there are large unresolved problems in higher education which have been left unaddressed by domestic and international reformers.

Much as the CCSS hospitals compose the most complex units in the health system, the four state universities are the most organizationally multifarious in public education. Like the hospitals, the universities employ the most highly trained professionals in the field, comprise numerous departments specializing in rarefied knowledge, and function out of enormous physical units in which thousands of clients can be found on site at any one time. Another similarity is that university expenditures in per student terms much exceed those of lower levels of education,[79] much as hospital per patient costs are higher than those in the clinics. But unlike their medical counterparts, educational reformers have steered clear of proposing efficiency-related changes in the university system. Although they are dependent on the state for financing, the constitutional guarantee of such funding and the legal autonomy that the universities enjoy in deciding how to use it impedes outside interference.

Conclusion

Costa Rica is not pursuing the rapid privatization of state-owned industries, insurance markets, or provision of social services. Instead, all evidence points toward the slow demonopolization of energy generation and distribution, telecommunications, insurance (except for health), and pensions. If the pattern established with bank demonopolization holds up, private firms, national and foreign, will gradually be awarded equal status with public entities. No privatization is planned for public education or health, where the goal of reform initiatives is to make public agencies operate more efficiently. Nevertheless, in these areas we are witnessing creeping privatization, or the erosion of state capacity to provide quality health care and education and the slow flight of upper and middle-class citizens to market solutions.[80]

Several factors resulting from Costa Rica's political institutions made for slowness and difficulty in almost all of the second-stage reforms attempted. The electoral cycle produces a small window of opportunity in which to introduce controversial legislation and complex reforms, thereby restricting the number of policy changes an administration can hope to see through the Legislative Assembly. And controversial proposals tend to get bogged down in legislative-executive gridlock especially when, as was the case during 1994–98, the president's party does not hold a majority in congress. In addition, decisions by other branches and institutions of government, such as the Comptroller and the constitutional court (Sala IV), can also nullify legislated reforms.

And then there is the matter of who might oppose or support a reform. Second-stage reforms often pit large numbers of concentrated, vested interests against taxpayers and the general population, especially the young and the poor who rely disproportionately on state services. The potential losers tend to see very well exactly how a proposed reform will affect them and have the autonomy to oppose it, either through organized protest by public-sector unions or individualized passive resistance. But collective action problems inhibit the organization of potential winners. They are disperse, often poor, and divided by class, geography, and other factors. In addition, as we see in the case of attempts to privatize ICE, Costa Rican public opinion strongly supports some state monopolies. Many state institutions remain popular in Costa Rica because they have performed so well in the last several decades.

Given the institutional and political barriers to second-stage reforms in Costa Rica, not to mention the cost of funding severance packages for public workers, presidents (and parties) who attempt them run great risks. They must implement painful reforms and weather the damage, all the while hoping to take credit for some positive outcomes before the next elections. Under these conditions, it should not be surprising that President Figueres halted public employee dismissals, institutional reform, and unpopular changes in pension regulations halfway into his term. Of course, politicians must weigh these risks against the size of the expected benefits and the possibility that continuing with the status quo will bring even greater unpopularity.

Two additional considerations relate to measures which demand the transformation of large public bureaucracies, particularly in the health and education ministries in Costa Rica. First, the quality of leadership for such changes matters. As the leader of a complex organization, the minister can help implementation by making the reforms a top priority, ordering departments to cooperate with the effort, directing resources toward the project, and making public appearances on its behalf. In this sense, we have seen that Costa Rica's education minister performed better than health officials. A second factor is the quality of a ministry's relationship with external donors. The more the internal reform team feels that it owns the project, that is, the more that they see their own contribution to the design and implementation of the plan as well as the possibility for taking credit for the results, the better. In Costa Rica, mutual respect and similar visions of future outcomes between the MEP's team and its international counterparts contributed to higher morale, greater risk taking, and smoother execution of the reform program. The health reform program has not benefited from this kind of alliance.

Finally, the case studies examined in this chapter offer little

Reforming the Welfare State: The 1990s 103

evidence that either the PUSC or the PLN have been able to drive forward a new public policy agenda based on a clear set of goals for the future. The lack of a comprehensive national vision on this level must have contributed to the rather weak and variable quality of leadership for state reform among the government ministries. Given the conservative forces present in the PUSC, President Calderón appeared ideologically aligned with many of the neoliberal policy solutions favored by international institutions and the private sector. But President Calderón never articulated a vision of how this orientation would fit with the other major current in his party: the Christian Democratic concern for the poor and commitment to welfare state universal programs. Indeed, he had campaigned on the claim that his father, the prewar president, had been the true founder of the Costa Rican welfare state and on promises of housing grants and agricultural subsidies aimed at low-income citizens who perceived themselves to have been hurt by the PLN's structural adjustment policies.[81] Calderón's administration never struck a balance between these two currents. For example, in 1991, the government was rocked by Vice President German Serrano's accusation that its budget proposal paid insufficient attention to social needs. Yet later the same year, the government suffered the resignation of Finance Minister Thelmo Vargas, whose quest to reduce university funding President Calderón refused to support.

In similar fashion, President Figueres and the PLN were unsuccessful in developing a coherent, third-way model for Costa Rica. José Figueres had used the discourse of a "New Democrat" dedicated to economic efficiency, human capital development, and poverty alleviation. He spoke of creating a smaller, fiscally responsible, but modern and agile state which would adopt international best practices in social service delivery and be aggressive in helping business compete in the global economy. But the president fell short of delivering the third-way model in two senses. First, he failed to create an intangible but crucial good: an overarching vision of what the new, modern Costa Rican state would look like and how the outcome would differ from the neoliberal agenda of privatization and public-employment reduction. Second, of course, President Figueres ran into a great deal of difficulty in translating the various elements of state reform into practice. For this the president can thank the factors above (as can President Calderón) as well as the continual divisions within his own PLN. The PLN remains split between the New Democrats, who are willing to open state monopolies, introduce market mechanisms into public administration, and fire public employees, and an old guard who fear that such measures would intolerably erode the rights of social citizenship and the possibilities for social engineering via public power.

5

Costa Rican Outcomes

The debate over the relative merits of gradualism versus shock therapy will not be solved by examining a single case. But we can gain insight into the potential outcomes of the gradualist model by studying an important Latin American example. This chapter will illustrate and explain the economic, social, and political outcomes of the Costa Rican case to date. The first section examines the prospects for the industries created by the policy changes of the 1980s as well as the possibility that Costa Rica's piecemeal approach to reform is producing significant economic distortions. The second section considers how poverty and inequality have varied during the period of reform and why little social instability has accompanied structural adjustment in Costa Rica. The final section deals with the creation of political forces for and against the new economic policies. The conclusions emphasize that Costa Rica's gradualist program has led to generally positive results.

Economic Results

The policymakers who masterminded the reforms of the 1980s believed that economic revival depended on private sector expansion into new opportunities provided by a greater openness to the international economy. They thought that because Costa Rica already possessed a good physical infrastructure and a well-educated population, the new policies would bear fruit quickly.[1] The proponents of reform seem to have been right. Overall, the results of the new development strategy have been positive. Indeed, after two years of negative growth in 1981 and 1982, Costa Rica's GDP grew at an average of 4.1 percent between 1983–1996.[2] On the microeconomic level, the recovery period saw booms in tourism, nontraditional exports, and private banking. What are the prospects for the new industries?

The New Industries

We learned in chapter 3 that the value of Costa Rica's nontraditional exports jumped from $90 million in 1983 to $3.8 billion in 1998, or from 10 percent of total exports to 68 percent. Although not specifically promoted by the USAID coalition, tax breaks established by law in 1985 provided new incentives to the tourism industry as well. Soon after the export contract legislation was passed, an already existing hotel industry copied the concept. This lobby convinced the Legislative Assembly to establish tourism contracts granting exonerations on import, local, and income taxes to investors in hotels, transportation services (airlines, boats, and rent-a-car companies), travel agencies, and restaurants. The number of tourism contracts granted, as well as investment in the most expensive sort of tourist development, hotels, peaked in 1991–93.[3] In 1998, tourism dividends added up to $830 million dollars,[4] second only to computer chip exports.

Figure 5.1 shows the dramatic growth of tourism and the top four nontraditional exports: microprocessors, textile products, flowers and ornamental plants, and fish and seafood. These products and services not only represent a growing percentage of Costa Rica's foreign exchange earnings, but also an expanded contribution to the country's GDP. From under 10 percent in 1983, nontraditional exports and tourism grew to account for 16 percent of GDP in 1990 and 44 percent in 1998.[5] Thus, growth in these industries continued at a rapid pace throughout the 1990s; this indicates that the new model of integration with the global economy has sustained itself beyond the takeoff phase, that is, the foreign-aid rich 1980s.

The outlook for these industries portends brighter growth prospects in some than in others. In tourism, for example, visitor arrivals and the dollars spent by them grew steadily from the early 1980s, dipped in 1996, and rebounded strongly in 1997. A wealth of new business establishments grew up around tourism including hotels, restaurants, excursion services, and car rental agencies. Costa Rica has played on its comparative advantage in ecotourism. Its range of microclimates, national parks easily accessible from the capital, and nearby beaches have made the country a popular des-

Figure 5.1
Top Four Nontraditional Exports and Tourism

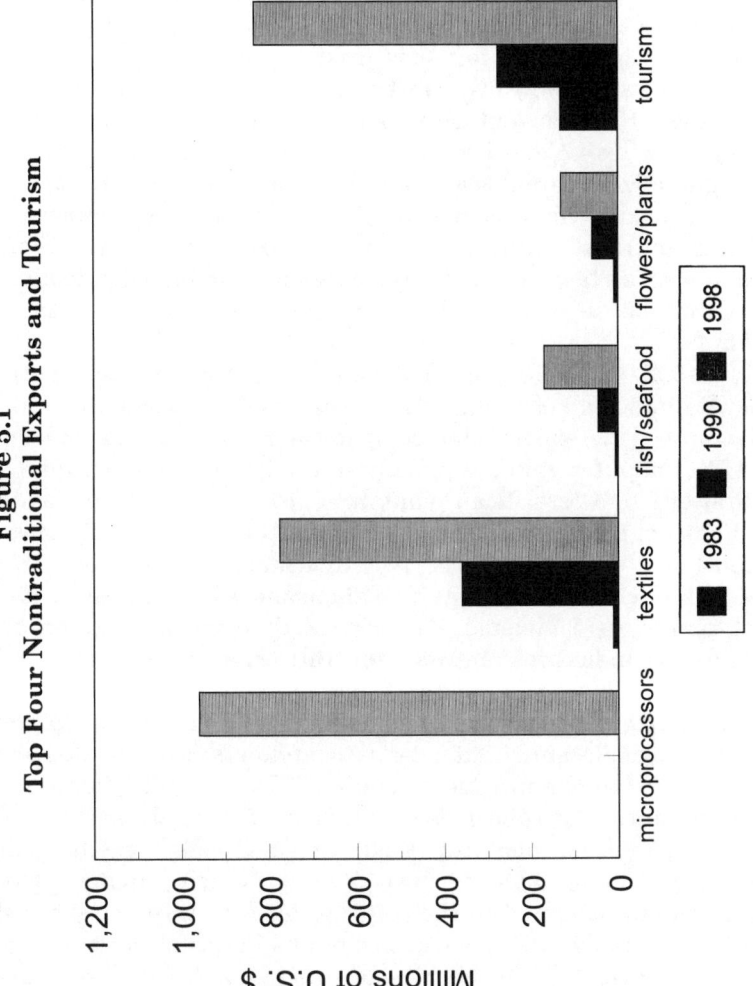

SOURCES: Data on textiles from U.S. Department of Commerce, all other data from PROCOMER.

tination. The medium to long-term outlook for the industry remains quite good, although several potential problems loom. One is that because of domestic prices and high airfares, the costs of Costa Rican vacations tend to exceed those found among competitors in Mexico and the Caribbean. Looking into the future, tour operators expect that U.S. citizens will soon be allowed easy access to cheap vacations in Cuba. Another problem involves the natural limits to ecotourism. Costa Rica's formerly pristine, deserted beaches and national parks are now overrun by visitors, especially during the high season. Some adventure seekers and nature lovers are now seeking more exotic and less-crowded destinations in neighboring Nicaragua and Panama. Investors are reacting to these trends by exploiting a niche market not yet developed in Central America: high-end tourists willing to patronize exclusive country club marina resorts. Rising crime rates (see below) and inadequate highway maintenance also threaten to limit the future growth of tourism.

In 1997, Costa Rica did not manufacture a single computer chip, yet by the end of 1998, microprocessors had become the country's number one export. One company accounts for this change. The U.S. computer chip manufacturer Intel began construction of the first of four Costa Rican plants in 1997. The first began shipping Pentium processors in April 1998 and the second in late 1999. Currently, Intel employs over two thousand workers,[6] but that number will climb as high as five thousand when the third and fourth plants are completed. Far more so than the other nontraditional export industries and tourism, Intel has created a demand for highly skilled workers and has made financial contributions to the University of Costa Rica and the Costa Rican Technological Institute to make sure that adequate numbers of graduates are equipped with the knowledge it requires.[7] The one potential drawback to the Intel export boom is that it depends entirely on the decisions of one multinational firm. Costa Rican officials hope that this dependence will be lessened over time as other computer-sector companies are attracted to the country. Already three U.S.-based firms which supply Intel have opened plants in Costa Rica,[8] and the company is also thought to be encouraging a nascent software industry.[9]

The trend line in the flowers and plants sector shows slow but steady growth. Exporters of cut flowers, ornamental plants, and foliage engage in a capital and labor-intensive, extremely competitive agricultural business. This sector came to symbolize nontraditional exports in the mid-1980s as many Costa Ricans hoped to profit from small, domestic companies venturing into the new high technology field. But the whole sector, especially the cut flower industry, suffered growing pains and temporary periods of stagnant growth at the hands of various production and marketing problems, worst of all the U.S. International Trade Commission decision against Costa Rica in a flower dumping case in 1987.

These problems drove many smaller Costa Rican companies to bankruptcy. But the difficulties also encouraged a healthy trend toward growing newer and more diversified varieties, a strategy useful for taking on established companies from other countries. Firms exporting from Costa Rica have diversified away from the three traditional flowers (roses, carnations, and chrysanthemums) and standard ornamental plants toward more exotic tropical varieties and the leather leaf fern, all of which grow well in the country's wet microclimates. The extraordinary competition to develop ever newer varieties will continue to make flower, plant, and foliage export businesses high risk ventures. Yet the surviving companies have developed agility and international marketing expertise.

The fish and seafood industry has been anything but stable. After a rapid takeoff in the 1980s, fish and shrimp exporters, most of them domestic, ran into serious supply problems due to overfishing and the effects of the *El Niño* current in the early 1990s. The industry has also been plagued by corruption; in 1993 the government closed nine companies for overinvoicing (the purpose of which was to obtain higher export subsidies or to launder drug money). But since 1995, fish and seafood exports have climbed spectacularly as shrimp farms came on-line and investors with larger boats exploited resources farther offshore.

Costa Rica ranks among the top exporters of textile goods, mostly assembled garments, to the United States, where it sends nearly 100 percent of the product. But, like other Central American and Caribbean countries, Costa Rica has been concerned about NAFTA's potential for diverting investment in this industry toward Mexico, where garment exporters now need not worry about U.S. import quotas. The original fears seem to have been overblown. Costa Rican textile exports to the United States dipped for the first time in 1996, but they rebounded strongly in 1997.[10] This peaceful Central American nation continues to be an appealing production site because of its political stability, efficient factories, and quality workmanship. Multinational garment manufacturers also like to spread their risk by maintaining plants in several countries.[11] In addition, the World Trade Organization seems disposed to offer some defense against other forms of trade discrimination practiced by the United States. In late 1996, the WTO ordered the United States to drop a quota on imports of Costa Rican underwear, a top apparel export.

Still, there is uncertainty about the longer term viability of Costa Rica's textile exports. For instance, although Costa Rica has joined other CBI beneficiary countries in lobbying the U.S. Congress to grant them some sort of parity with Mexico regarding the treatment of textile imports, these proposals have been voted down by Congressional committees four times since 1993. In 1998, the U.S. International Trade Representative made it clear that the Clinton administration would not support another attempt to award NAFTA-type privileges to CBI textile exports.[12] In addition, Costa Rica's high wages, relative to neighboring countries, may have had more impact on the firms that decided to leave than did NAFTA. In my interviews, though, economic officials seemed relatively unperturbed by the latter possibility. They usually responded by saying that as long as unemployment remained low, it should be taken as a positive sign that firms looking for the cheapest labor left the country.

Finally, the outlook for private banking in Costa Rica remains very positive. Although their entry into the market has been subject to the gradual pace of financial deregulation, chapter 3 noted that by 1996, the private banks loaned more money than their public-sector competitors. At this point, private banks can legally offer all of the same services as their public counterparts. But there are now a great many private banks competing and vying for market share in a very small country, this cutthroat competition is behind the current spate of mergers. Nevertheless, President Rodríguez came into office talking about privatizing one or two more of the remaining state banks and so future opportunities for expansion may exist.

Policy reforms intended to restart the economy after the crisis of the early 1980s have worked well as the private sector has capitalized on the new opportunities. The export, tourism, and banking industries have grown dramatically and appear to have reasonably positive prospects for future stability and expansion. But those who prefer more radical change would say that the slow forward progress of structural adjustment as a whole still leaves much to be desired from the economic viewpoint. Detractors of gradualism would argue that persistent inefficiencies—particularly outdated state services—have made economic growth slower than it would have been otherwise.

Economic Distortions

A key argument made by shock therapists is that opportunities for economic growth are forgone as long as needed reforms remain undone. In 1997, a study cited by the Inter-American Development Bank estimated that Costa Rica could gain an additional two percentage points of GDP growth if within five years it caught up to the rate of policy change occurring in the leading Latin American reformers.[13] While econometric investigations of this claim lie far beyond the scope of this book, it is easy to point out areas of incomplete policy change which may constitute a drag on growth opportunities.

The most obvious pockets of inadequacy lie in public services. For example, in Costa Rica it is hardly debatable to say that the state insurance monopoly INS and postal system lag far behind international standards. And although the well-managed public energy and telecommunications monopoly ICE operates in the black, beginning in the 1980s, the state has not been able to afford infrastructural upgrades. Outside of a percentage of power generation, the private sector is barred from investing in the sector. Thus, to date, Costa Rica has forgone the benefits of modernizing these services.

Delays in implementing economic reforms have been even more costly in the area of physical infrastructure (highways, airports, sea ports). During the 1990s, private sector complaints have been most often directed at the country's decaying and overtaxed physical infrastructure. The export and tourist industries especially feel that this area constitutes a major bottleneck in their operations. As we saw in chapter 4, the *ley de concesión de obra pública* was supposed to ease these problems by allowing private-sector bidding on public works. But legal flaws delayed its implementation. A revised law was only passed in April 1998 and, thanks to protests put up by the Limón stevedores (see chapter 4), it contains an exemption for existing seaports. We can now expect private domestic and international companies to win contracts to construct and administer public works, but only fifteen years after structural adjustment began.

In purely economic terms, allowing some inefficient and underfunded state monopolies to linger is probably less costly than a scenario in which no adjustments were made but more taxing than one in which they were quickly privatized. Nevertheless, this consideration should not obscure the fact that the economic contribution, and, it will be argued below, the employment impact of the new industries has been very large in Costa Rica. The problem of lingering distortions should also not distract our attention from the social and political impact of the form and pace of Costa Rica's adjustment model. As we shall see, Costa Rica has managed to avoid the increased poverty and inequality associated with structural adjustment in so many Latin American countries.

Social Indicators: Poverty and Inequality

Among social scientists and politicians, there is no small amount of concern that should a rise in poverty and inequality accompany a shift in development strategy, people may revolt and demand the rollback of the new policies. The history of revolutionary activities in Latin America's poorest countries, urban riots in Venezuela, and recent peasant uprisings in Mexico all seem to indicate a connection between poverty and political instability in the region. Clearly the link is not always direct. Intervening variables (e.g. radical ideologies, availability of outside political leadership) may have to come into play to spark political violence. And direct attacks on the interests of the middle class may ignite more conflict than those on the poorest. In addition, those left impoverished may express their anger not through political organizing but through crime and other forms of social anomie. Finally, nonadjustment might be more impoverishing and thus more dangerous than the dislocation experienced during economic reform. Nonetheless, no one is arguing that increased poverty and inequality are good for political stability. Economists also believe that they can be detrimental to growth itself.[14]

In the 1980s, many Costa Ricans worried that economic liberalization would increase poverty and inequality rates in their country and somehow ruin the political stability achieved after 1948. In particular, because Costa Rica is a country where the majority of the population still resides in rural areas,[15] concern arose about the potential social consequences of eliminating basic grains subsidies. Some imagined a scenario in which thousands of *campesinos* would be pushed off their land and migrate to the Central Valley where, unable to acquire sufficient employment, they would live in shantytowns ringing the capital. Economic authorities painted a brighter picture in which the industries recently created by outward-oriented policies would generate enough jobs to drain off redundant rural laborers, maintain low unemployment rates, and provide a bridge between the disintegration of the old development model and the construction of the new one.[16] Policymakers did not claim that inequality levels would remain exactly the same but did appear confidant that large increases in poverty rates would be avoidable. Below I examine Costa Rica's record regarding economic crisis, adjustment, poverty, and inequality to determine which scenario better matches reality.

Data

Economists agree that Costa Rican poverty increased during the 1980s but returned to precrisis levels by the mid-1990s. There are disagreements over the percentage of Costa Rican households below the poverty line at any one time and over when poverty figures dropped, but each study tells a similar story. The Economic Commission for Latin America and the Caribbean (ECLAC) offers statistics from 1981, 1988, 1990, 1992, and 1994. ECLAC reports that the percentage of total households that were poor or indigent did not drop below 1981 levels until 1994.[17] Other reliable studies found that poverty had dropped to precrisis levels by the end of the 1980s. For instance, a study by Samuel Morley, using government household survey data, displays a marked decline in poverty from 25.4 percent of the population in 1981 to 10.2 percent in 1989.[18] A comparison of poverty studies conducted under the auspices of a Costa Rican economics institute concludes that they all show a jump in the percentage of poor households between 1981–85 and then a return to late 1970s or 1980 levels by 1988.[19]

Finally, the work on the subject most respected by Costa Rican social scientists, *La pobreza en Costa Rica* (1995), concurs with these analyses. Authors Victor Céspedes and Ronulfo Jiménez show that the percentage of poor households in Costa Rica peaked at 48.1 in 1982, and then fell to 19.8 percent in 1990, slightly below the 20.8 figure for 1980.[20] Figure 5.2 charts the ECLAC, Morley, and Céspedes and Jiménez data for comparison. The Céspedes and Jiménez series extends the furthest into the 1990s where the trend points to record low levels of poverty well under 20 percent.[21]

The data on income inequality offer a murkier picture of how Costa Rica has changed since the early 1980s. One study finds a decrease in income inequality between 1981–89, using both a Gini coefficient and a standardized Theil index.[22] Another frequently cited analysis concurs.[23] These outcomes were culled from incomes data for the entire country. ECLAC's data on urban households,

Figure 5.2
Households in Poverty in Costa Rica, 1980–1994

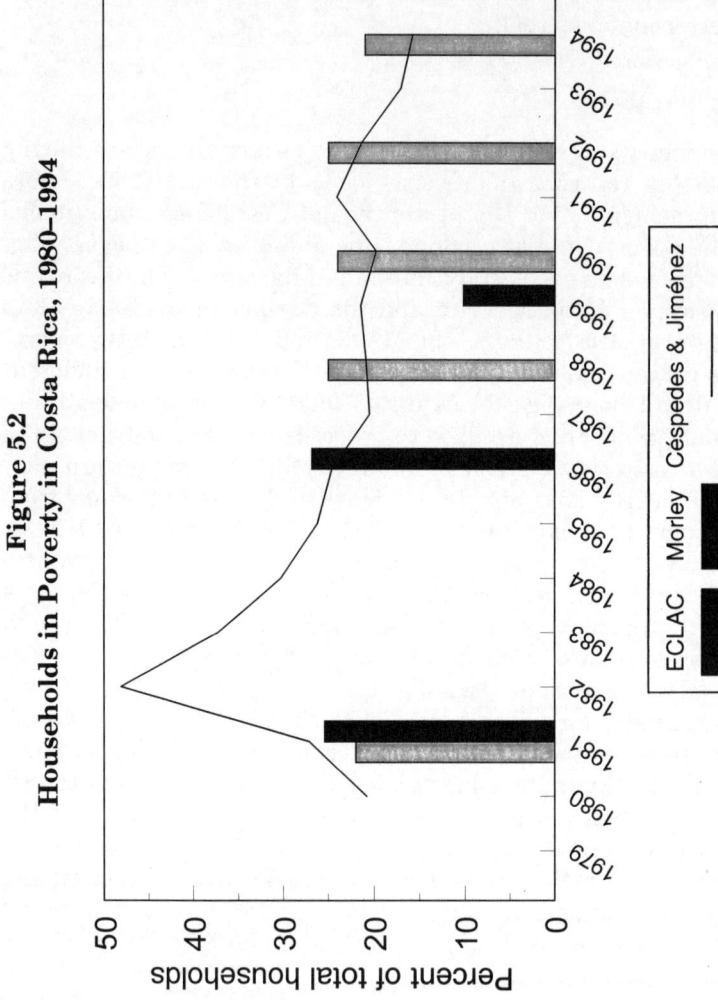

SOURCES: ECLAC, *Statistical Yearbook for Latin America*; Morley, *Poverty and Inequality*, pp. 139–141; Céspedes and Jiménez, *Pobreza en Costa Rica*, p. 85.

however, tell a different story. Displayed in table 5.1, the data show an increase in inequality between 1981–1994. The other sources do not offer comparable data, so we cannot yet know whether the roots of their divergence lie in methodology or rural/urban differences. But the suggestion that metropolitan San José is experiencing a growing gap between the poorest and the richest is strongly supported by the author's impressions during multiple visits spanning an eighteen-year period. Clearly these findings call for more detailed demographic investigation.

Whatever the real direction of change in income inequality, a perusal of comparative data on poverty in Latin America in the 1980s and 1990s shows that Costa Rica holds one of the region's best records. In his 1994 and 1995 volumes, Morley correctly argues that the principal explanation for Costa Rica's success lies in the ways that macroeconomic recovery, led by outward-oriented growth, has reached the poorest and has helped to pull them into better circumstances. But credit is also due to government wage policy and the social safety net.

Macroeconomic Recovery

Despite disagreements among the various measures of Costa Rican poverty, all concur that it shot up during the early 1980s and tended to drop toward the end of the decade and into the mid-1990s. As figures 5.3 and 5.4 show, drops and recoveries in the GDP growth rate and in real wages roughly mimic this pattern while

Table 5.1
Income Distribution among
Urban Households in Costa Rica
(Percentage of households in each quintile)

	1981	1988	1990	1992	1994
Income Quintiles					
Q1 (poorest)	6.8	6.4	5.7	5.7	5.8
Q2	12.1	10.8	12.1	11.4	11.6
Q3	16.7	16.2	17.0	17.0	16.4
Q4	24.5	23.3	24.5	23.5	22.7
Q5	40.1	43.3	40.7	42.5	43.5

SOURCE: ECLAC, *Statistical Yearbook for Latin America and the Caribbean* (1997).
NOTE: The 1981 and 1992 totals do not equal 100 because of rounding.

Figure 5.3
Costa Rica: GDP and Real Minimum Wages, 1978–1996

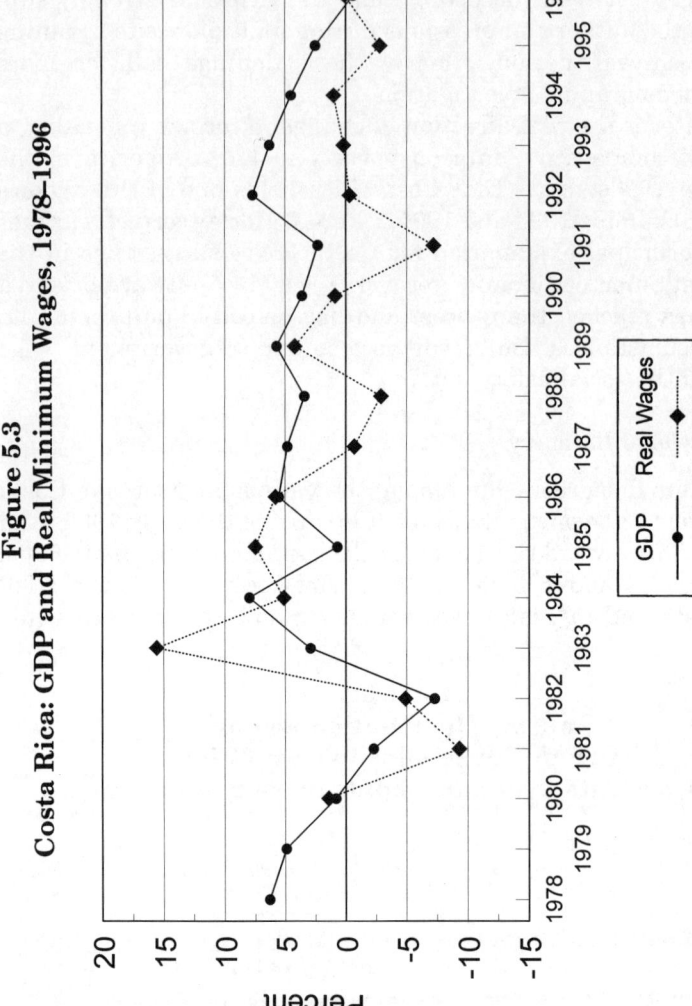

SOURCES: GDP growth rate from Inter-American Development Bank, *Economic and Social Progress in Latin America*, annual variation in urban real minimum wage from James W. Wilke, *Statistical Abstract of Latin America*.

Figure 5.4
Costa Rica: Inflation and Unemployment, 1978–1996

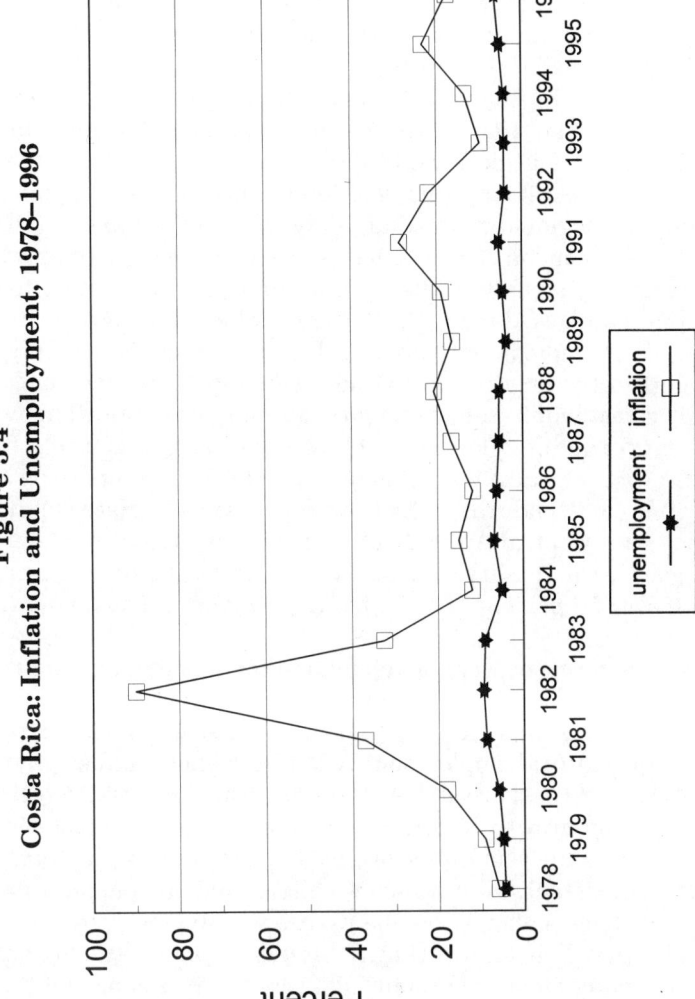

SOURCES: National unemployment rate from International Labour Office, *Yearbook of Labour Statistics*, annual growth of the consumer price index from Inter-American Development Bank, *Economic and Social Progress in Latin America*.

unemployment and inflation vary inversely to it. The similarity in the shape of the data strongly suggests that the economic crisis of the early 1980s caused the increase in poverty while the relatively quick recovery from it, spurred by stabilization and at least some aspects of structural adjustment, brought increased employment and real wages to the poor. Costa Rica's relatively quick macroeconomic recovery is the chief reason why poverty rates had dropped to precrisis levels by 1990.

A second striking point of agreement among the major poverty studies covering the 1980s is that poverty, unemployment, and underemployment fell more rapidly in rural than in urban areas. Taking a closer look at why this is so lends considerable support to the optimistic argument postulated by the policymakers cited above. Two phenomena helped avert a greater crisis in the rural economy during the 1980s. One is that currency devaluation and other policy changes during the decade helped the agricultural traded goods sector expand rapidly, thus providing new employment opportunities in the countryside. During the second half of the 1980s, direct employment in nontraditional agricultural activities grew at a rate of 2,000 to 2,500 jobs per year, accounting for 7 percent of agricultural employment by 1989.[24] In comparison to the situation in Honduras, which occupies second place behind Costa Rica as a Central American exporter of nontraditional agricultural goods, the quality of the new jobs in Costa Rica is quite good, with over 53 percent of them being permanent instead of seasonal.[25]

But these new jobs were not enough to cover population growth in the countryside or the loss of employment created by the desubsidization of basic grains growers.[26] There was also an overall migration out of agricultural employment (whether or not families physically moved out of rural areas).[27] At the same time, the service sector expanded, led by growth in tourism and the *maquila* industries.[28] Although data on the geographic origins of employees in the service sector are nonexistent, most scholars believe that the *maquila* and tourism industries siphoned off the excess working-age population from rural areas. It is known that the *maquila* plants employ predominantly young females without high school educations and that because of labor market constraints in the Central Valley, such firms began to locate in semirural areas in the 1990s.[29] Tourism establishments are also located in urban and rural settings.[30]

In sum, it appears from available data that the loss of traditional agricultural jobs and the need for employment for a growing rural population has been adequately met by new service-sector opportunities. This information lends support to policymakers' arguments about the way that the new development model would soak up unemployment caused by the disappearance of the old one. In this sense, Costa Rica was fortunate to be able to attract assembly industries and tourists at precisely the moment that they were needed. But Costa Rica's success is not based just on luck or on the "magic of the marketplace." Prior public investments in education, physical infrastructure, the national park system, as well as generous incentive packages (see table 5.2) made Costa Rica a very desirable location relative to the other Central American and Caribbean nations with whom it competed for direct foreign investment, subcontracts, and travelers. Finally, it should be added that all of the CINDE representatives and government authorities I talked to were well aware of the shortcomings of these types of employment, particularly the garment assembly jobs, and said that they expected more sophisticated industries to arrive in the medium term. The arrival of Intel and other high technology firms, discussed previously, makes that a credible expectation.

More worrisome are the social ills that have sprung up along with the postcrisis development model in Costa Rica. Gaggles of unlicensed teenage prostitutes have appeared in San José,[31] and the country has suffered a spectacular increase in all crime, especially that involving violence. Measured in terms of crimes per 100,000 inhabitants, most types of offenses rose steeply between 1987–1995, including burglary, robbery, and kidnapping (up 57 percent), as well as assault, homicide, and rape.[32] The crime wave may be a sign of frustration among those excluded from the new economic model, the result of the appearance of tourists who make easy marks for thieves, or the outcome of unrelated phenomena.[33] Unfortunately, criminologists have yet to specify the roots of this problem.

Government Policy

Government policies comprise a complementary explanation for Costa Rica's positive record with poverty in the aftermath of the economic crisis. President Monge, himself a labor leader in early adulthood, engineered an important change in the calculation of minimum wages. Throughout the 1970s, annual negotiations determined private and public-sector wages. Although talks became more frequent during 1980–82, real wages deteriorated with devaluation and inflation. In September 1982, to make good on a campaign pledge to halt the erosion of real wages, President Monge indexed them to the *canasta básica*, a basket of basic foodstuffs and other items thought to represent minimum household necessities, and permanently increased the pace of wage adjustments to every six months.[34] Rapid increases in minimum wages (one for each of sixty-five different job categories) ensued. During the recovery years of the mid-1980s, wages rose more rapidly than the GDP per capita,[35] and real earnings went up fastest in the bottom income deciles.[36] Although as figure 5.3 shows, growth in the real minimum wage was reduced after 1987 and negatively effected by the recession of 1991, it has not been allowed to erode seriously.

Progressive wage policy and the universal health, education and pension systems provided for the needs of most Costa Rican citizens in the aftermath of the economic crisis. In addition, a web of government welfare programs was available to those who fell through the cracks. Forty assistance programs target the poor and indigent with health, nutrition, and educational aid as well as housing and old-age pension subsidies. Poor mothers, children, and rural people depend disproportionately on these programs. An entity named FODESAF (Fondo de Desarrollo Social y Asignaciones Familiares or Fund for Social Development and Family Allowances), administered from an office in the Ministry of Labor, finances the welfare programs. Created in 1974, FODESAF does not manage any welfare organization directly, rather it channels resources to the ministries and government institutes running individual programs.

The FODESAF system is far from perfect. Although outcomes data are not collected, fragmentary evidence suggests that a wide variance exists between several programs which seem to affect a small number of families (mostly in agricultural support services and occupational training), health posts serving thousands of people, projects successful in targeting poor recipients (child care and housing), and those notorious for leakage of services to higher-income populations (the pension for indigents and school lunch).[37] There has also been concern about FODESAF's ability to respond to the rise in human needs during times of economic crisis. Its own funding derives from payroll and sales taxes, making the financial capabilities of targeted welfare programs procyclical, falling during recession at exactly the moment when they need to be stepped up. Funding for FODESAF dipped sharply in 1981–87 but then returned to precrisis levels. In 1994, spending on FODESAF represented 1.7 percent of the gross domestic product.[38]

Despite FODESAF's imperfections, Costa Rica's social welfare system as a whole works well enough that it was one of the few countries in the region not to implement a social investment fund in the last fifteen years to fill the gap between the needs of the population and the shortcomings of the social service ministries.[39] Costa Rica also stands out for its continued and overwhelming reliance on the public sector to deliver social welfare services. In addition, in marked contrast to most other Latin American countries, these social policies have aimed to reduce urban bias in economic development patterns.[40] This helps explain why Costa Rica did not experience agrarian-based revolutionary activities in the 1980s or 1990s.

Since the beginning of the economic crisis, Costa Rican presidents have also sought to use FODESAF resources and other funding to design ad hoc compensation packages to address particular problems and meet campaign promises. President Monge implemented several emergency compensation programs for the poor during the worst of the economic crisis. These included temporary employment and food aid programs, and increased state bank credit for the urban informal sector and peasants. The work and low-income credit programs were financed with domestic resources. USAID apparently paid for most of the temporary nutritional assistance program which distributed food on a monthly basis to somewhere between 25,000 to 40,000 needy families.[41]

During his campaign, presidential candidate Oscar Arias promised to find a solution to the growing shortage of decent shelter for low-income people by building eighty thousand houses. To meet this goal, the president received assistance from USAID. At Arias' request, USAID decided in 1987 to contribute to the housing program, so long as the government bypassed the myriad of public institutions already existent in the sector.[42] Thus, the new National Housing Mortgage Bank (BANHVI) was created to channel funds[43] to state and private banks for direct lending for low-income housing. USAID provided BANHVI with a seed grant from ESR local currency accounts equivalent to $15 million, and projected that its contribution to the Bank would reach $50 million by the early 1990s. Forty percent of "housing solutions" achieved between 1986–1990 were attributable to financing overseen by BANHVI.[44] The Arias government complemented BANHVI's activity with a family housing subsidy (*bono de vivienda*), funded by FODESAF and other internal sources, which provided subsidized credit to very low-income families.

During the next election period, presidential candidate Rafael Calderón accused the Arias administration and the PLN of not doing enough about the poverty wrought from the economic crisis. When he took office, Calderón turned the housing subsidy into a grant. He also directed FODESAF to develop two new schemes, the *cupón alimentario* (food stamp) program and the *bono escolar* (school subsidy). The food stamp program targeted extremely poor households. By 1993, 131,000 families had been served.[45] While this is an impressive level of coverage, the plan duplicated the efforts of a preexisting FODESAF program. Unlike most Costa Rican welfare programs, the school subsidy provided cash payments, instead of aid in kind, for very poor parents of school age children. The program began in 1993 and in that year almost sixty-two thousand families received between 1–3 subsidies (cash stipends were available for up to three children) aimed at helping the parents afford school uniforms and supplies.[46]

But the Figueres administration decided to discontinue this program in favor of a the more broadly based *salario escolar* (school salary or wage). The objective was the same: help families meet the costs of uniforms and supplies to ensure that all children get to school. To public-sector workers, the government paid an additional amount, the *salario escolar*, equal to 2 percent of their annual salary, each January. The private sector strongly resisted meeting the same kind of obligation and in January 1996 won the right to offer the *salario escolar* only to minimum wage workers.

Overall then, gradual reform seems to have alleviated crisis-related poverty in Costa Rica. The way that macroeconomic recovery reached all strata of society is the main reason for this, but government wage policy, preexisting social welfare programs, and ad hoc relief efforts helped as well. Now we must consider the political consequences of Costa Rica's slow, piecemeal approach to structural adjustment. Supporters of gradualism hypothesize that, over time, coalitions of "winners" will build and come to outweigh "losers" and even insist on further reforms to secure favorable conditions for their businesses. Shock therapists, on the other hand, fear that slow change allows opponents ample time to organize and stall or even reverse reforms. They also worry that politicians and citizens will tire of market-oriented economic policy change, either because partial reforms worked well enough to produce complacency or because each reform is so disruptive that no one is willing to push the agenda forward.

Costa Rican Outcomes 123

Political Constituencies

Again, Costa Rica's experience strongly supports the gradualist camp. Those who have benefited from Costa Rica's greater integration in the international economy, particularly exporters of nontraditional products and operators of tourism companies, have formed powerful new lobbying organizations. And the last four administrations used several techniques to preempt dissent and thus smooth the way for policy change. The groups which lost protected markets and subsidies have not mounted effective counter campaigns for a variety of reasons explored here. Although we do know that second-stage reforms have been met with more impressive protest than the earlier adjustments, public-sector unions are not uniformly opposed to them nor is organized labor the only political obstacle to these policy changes.

New Policy Coalitions

The sustainability of an economic development model depends on continued political commitment to supporting policies. As described in chapter 3, during the 1980s the CINDE coalition acted in lieu of a yet-to-be-formed group of beneficiaries to lobby for policies designed to promote nontraditional exports. But because of shifting priorities in the organization and then a reduction in U.S. funding for CINDE, it became necessary for the beneficiaries of these policies themselves to form effective interest groups. As the new industries grew, so did the number and the political strength of their representatives. Members of this new beneficiary group founded the Chamber of Exporters (Cámara de Exportadores or CADEXCO) in 1984. In addition, nontraditional exporters, including many manufacturing companies which diversified markets or products, have thoroughly infiltrated the Chamber of Industry (Cámara de Industrias). The tourism sector developed more slowly and more autonomously. Two organizations represent the business: CANATUR (Cámara Nacional de Turismo), and ACHA (Asociación Nacional de Hoteles y Afines). In addition, Presidents Arias, Calderón, Figueres, and Rodríguez pledged their support for the new outward orientation.

Private and public-sector interests have generally made good on their pledges to defend the macroeconomic and sectoral policies put into place on behalf of the new industries. Chief among these is the exchange rate, the key macroeconomic policy of concern to exporters and a variable of importance to tourism operators as well. From their viewpoint, undervaluation of the exchange rate would be the most favorable policy course unless it increased exports of a sensitive product so much that an importing nation put up protectionist barriers and applied pressure for revaluation. This backlash scenario would be most likely to occur in textile exports to the United States. In the past, the United States has limited East Asian textile imports through quotas and pressured those countries to revalue their currencies. Nevertheless, in the short term, undervaluation would seem to have the advantage of making up for the current phaseout of the main nontraditional export subsidy by providing a more subtle form of subsidization, one less likely to provoke protectionist measures from importing countries. A depreciating exchange rate also probably does more good than harm for the tourism industry as Costa Rican vacations become more attractive for potential visitors.

As figure 5.5 shows, Costa Rica's real effective exchange rate depreciated after Central Bank officials instituted the mini-devaluation system (1985), and has not been greatly overvalued or undervalued since then. Exporters would undoubtedly prefer and even faster pace of depreciation. On the other hand, consumers and importers would presumably opt for a stronger currency, thus encouraging a higher level of import consumption as well as reducing inflation. The internationalists have thus far been the winners in this contest, however, not only because of the their political strength, but also because Costa Rica conducts almost constant loan negotiations with the IMF and IDB, both of which would object to a revalued exchange rate.

Representatives of the nontraditional export and tourism industries have also been reasonably successful at maintaining favorable sectoral policies, although state agencies have been able to modify some incentives for the public good. Table 5.2 displays the benefit packages available to the nontraditional export and tourism industries. Over the last ten years, government officials have made the free zones relatively more attractive to manufacturing-sector exporters, because they noticed that they tended to lure companies involved in higher value-added production than the garment-assembly plants concentrated in the drawback regime. In addition, concerns about regional development and the scarcity of low-wage workers in the Central Valley led officials to establish special incentives for companies locating in free zones in outlying zones in 1990. Discrimination in favor of the free zones appears to be working as

Figure 5.5
Costa Rica: Real Effective Exchange Rate, 1979–1996
(1990=100; Below 100=Real Depreciation)

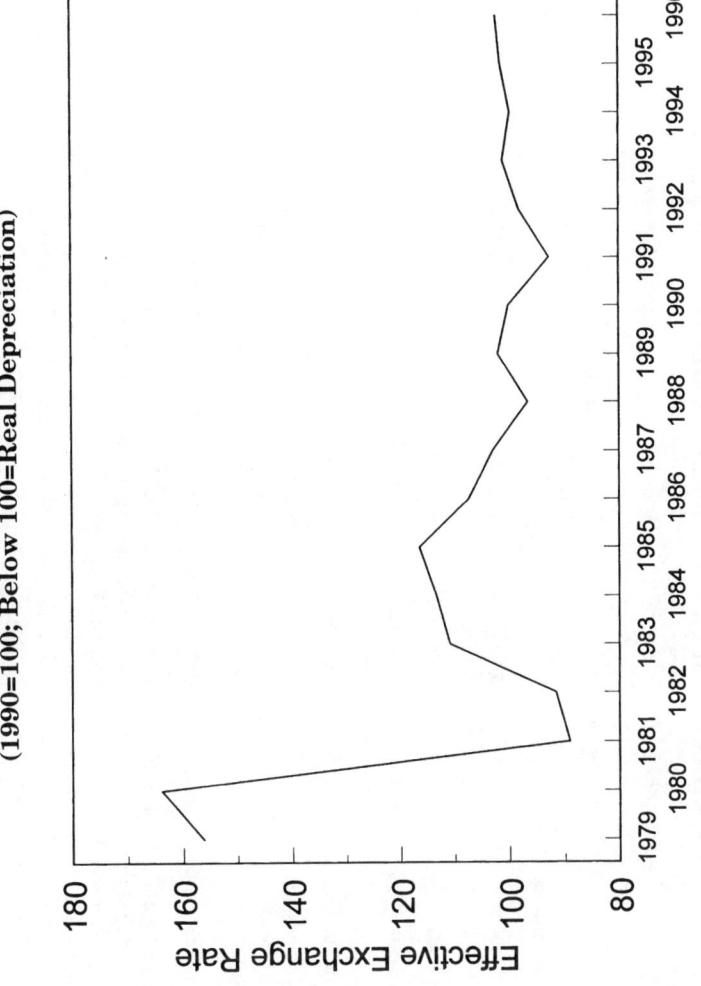

SOURCE: IMF, *International Statistics Yearbook*.

Table 5.2
Costa Rican Nontraditional Export and Tourism Regimes

	Free Trade Zones	Drawback	Export Contract	Tourism Contract
Tax Exemptions				
Machinery and Intermediate Inputs	100%	100%	100%	Up to 100%
Profits	100% (8 years) 50% (4 years)[a]	None	None	None
Tax Rebates	Up to 15% of payroll[b]	None	0–20% of FOB value[c]	None
Local Market Sales	Up to 40%, subject to approval	None allowed	No restrictions[d]	n/a
Customs Benefits	On-site inspection[e]	None	None	n/a
National Value Added, Local Content, & Ownership Requirements	None	None	35% minimum national value added	51% local ownership

SOURCES: Information provided by PROCOMER and the Costa Rican Tourism Institute.

a. Schedule for plants located in the Central Valley. In December 1990, new legislation awarded a 100 percent tax break on profits for the first twelve years and 50 percent for the next six years of a firm's operation if located in an "underdeveloped area" (the provinces of Limón, Guanacaste, and Puntarenas).
b. Applies only to industrial parks located in underdeveloped areas. Plants in these parks can receive a five-year tax rebate which is worth 15 percent of the company's payroll in the first year and then declines 2 percent per year until reaching 7 percent.
c. See discussion of CATs in text for explanation.
d. Tax benefits awarded for portion of production exported only.
e. This is a significant timesaving benefit given that all other exports must pass customs at the airport or docks where twenty-four-hour delays and problems warehousing goods awaiting inspection are common.

the total added-value produced within them surpassed that coming from the drawback industries for the first time in 1995.[47]

The most contentious change in nontraditional export incentives involved the lucrative tax rebate known as the CAT (*Certificado de Abono Tributario*) and offered only under the export contract. CATs are tax credit certificates worth up to 20 percent of a firm's nontraditional export sales and negotiable on the national stock exchange. Over three-fourths of Costa Rica's nontraditional export firms were eligible for the export contract in 1985 (almost all the agricultural and agroindustrial firms as well as manufacturers that can meet the 35 percent national value added requirement). And until the government stopped awarding new CATs in 1992, almost all of these received them. For the state, the cost of the CATs rose rapidly out of control. According to unpublished government data shown to the author, the cost of the CATs peaked in 1990 at the equivalent of 8 percent of central government tax income and 6 percent of central government expenditures. An IMF study calculated that the direct cost of the CAT subsidy was $2.27 per each dollar of additional net exports.[48]

Besides the cost of the CAT program, government officials worried about the distribution of the benefits. A small group of large companies received the majority of CAT payments. For example, unpublished data produced by the Ministry of Foreign Trade at the end of 1989 showed that, in an eighteen-month period during 1988–89, Del Monte's pineapple subsidiary PINDECO (Pineapple Development Corporation) received approximately 10 percent of all CATs awarded. The same data revealed that the top eight CAT earners (1.5 percent of companies receiving CATs) got 27 percent of the total. Three of these top eight fell below the required minimum of 35 percent national value-added on their exported products. Fifty-one percent of CAT expenditures went to only twenty-six firms (5 percent of all companies in the program).[49] Corruption was also a constant issue as government officials were aware that some companies obtained unduly high CAT benefits through overinvoicing.[50]

The Arias administration initiated negotiations with nontraditional exporters for reductions in the skyrocketing CATs costs. Resistance by the exporters and the consensual style of policymaking traditional in Costa Rica's democracy meant that the following five years witnessed an excruciatingly complex process of negotiating reductions in the benefits of a newly powerful sector. The outcome of the negotiations consisted of three successive schedules reducing the maximum level of CATs awarded to new export contract applicants. These schedules began on January 1, 1990; each reduces the CATs awarded to firms at a rate dependent on the national value-added of the product exported.[51] The government stopped issuing new CAT contracts in late 1992. Most export contracts ended in 1996, although some will extend to 1999.[52]

Public officials succeeded in reducing the fiscal burden of the CAT, although they were not effective in meeting equity concerns. In 1996, thirty companies still garnered nearly one-half of CAT payments and PINDECO retained its top-earner status throughout the decade.[53] The nontraditional exporters themselves have continued to prosper despite earlier claims that the elimination of the CAT would be catastrophic for the sector. Their lobby succeeded in forcing a slow phaseout of the CAT, thus allowing firms the time to make adjustments.[54]

In 1992, the Ministry of Finance began to target subsidies to the tourist industry as a source of cost reduction. The government eliminated an incentive that offered a 50 percent break on the income tax charged on a person's or company's ownership of stock in a firm with a tourism contract as well as all benefits for restaurants. In addition, car rental firms saw their tax exonerations on imported cars reduced from 100 to 50 percent. Nevertheless, as the tourism industry has grown so has its economic weight and organizational abilities. The private tourism lobby has engaged in an impressive show of strength on the Costa Rican political scene since 1996.

First, CANATUR and ACHA persuaded the president to introduce a bill removing the 3 percent hotel room tax, a measure they saw as necessary to survive a fall in tourist arrivals in 1996.[55] Then the tourism lobby launched a campaign to take over a large chunk of the ICT (Instituto Costarricense de Turismo), a semiautonomous public institution. The ICT performs two main functions: administration of the tourism contracts which secure tax exemptions for businesses, and the promotion of Costa Rican vacations in international markets. The private sector wants to leave administrative matters to the government but take the ICT's public relations functions (as well as 40 percent of its budget) into its own hands. Tour operators feel that Costa Rica's image abroad and the advertisement of its vacation opportunities greatly influence the choices of prospective customers. They also believe that a privately controlled public relations organization would better serve the industry. These matters were tabled during the 1998 election season but the Rodríguez administration is thought to favor the private sector's proposals.

Techniques for Introducing Reform

Some of the techniques Costa Rican leaders used to introduce economic policy changes greatly enhanced the population's acceptance of them and thus have reduced the possibility that they will be rolled back. The last four administrations' use of dialogue, pacing, and compensation conformed to the norms of Costa Rican political culture. While staying within these norms made for slow, piecemeal policy change, I will argue that the outcomes are highly sustainable.

Few Costa Rican officials would think of initiating a policy change without consulting all interested parties. Such dialogue may lead to compromise about the shape and timing of the measure or it may not result in any real government concessions. In either case, the government goes to great lengths to offer explanations for the proposed changes. This is accomplished through presidential speeches around the country, bipartisan roundtables with business and labor representatives, and debate via television, radio, and newspaper media. The length and depth of the debate often has the effect of making all sides feel that they have participated and have been heard.

Of course, this consensual style slows the pace of economic policy change and fosters a sequencing of reform which favors the rapid adoption of less controversial steps and a slower shift toward unpopular measures. A critical, if unintended, outcome of pursuing easy changes before difficult ones in Costa Rica has been to produce the positive effects of reform before many of the negative consequences. As we saw earlier in this chapter, the appearance of positive economic outcomes and new beneficiaries has helped to sustain existing reforms and create a more aggressive and outspoken private sector (for better or worse). The Chamber of Industry is now demanding that the Rodríguez administration open the insurance and telecommunications monopolies,[56] opinions that were unheard of less than ten years ago.

Finally, in a move entirely consistent with past practice, the Costa Rican government has used compensatory measures to offset the losses of those hurt by policy change and to help society's poorest. Compensation has the effect of blunting opposition and of demonstrating a government's concern for the poor. The political impact of these actions can only be positive. As Alan Angell and Carol Graham point out, social support services are useful not only for providing actual economic help during difficult times, but also because: "The perception that the government is doing something to alleviate the social costs of adjustment may create popular support for the government—if not for adjustment *per se* . . ."[57] that will allow officials to continue with reforms.

The Other Side of the Coin

Let us look more closely at the groups who have or could be expected to protest the reforms already implemented, particularly peasants, public-sector unionists, and industrialists producing for the domestic market. We have seen that wage policy, social services, ad hoc compensation measures, and the employment offered by the new industries have helped poverty levels to fall after the economic crisis of the early 1980s. But these factors affect the groups mentioned above unequally and do not explain the political logic of their response to the new conditions.

To the extent that what motivates concern about opposition to structural adjustment is its potential for political destabilization, it is important to understand a fundamental quality of Costa Rican political culture. A reformist, as opposed to a radical or revolutionary ideology permeates Costa Rican political organization and helps to explain the lack of protest against the democratic regime during the economic crisis and structural adjustment. Though various groups may protest particular policy measures, they cannot be found calling for the overthrow of the state, something which attests to the basic legitimacy Costa Ricans bestow on their political institutions. In addition, as noted in chapter 2, Left parties are exceedingly weak in Costa Rica. Support for Left parties peaked in 1982 when they gathered 3.3 percent of the vote in the presidential race. But this support had dropped to 0.9 percent by 1992.[58] And in a survey, Mitchell A. Seligson and John Booth found that only 6 percent of Costa Ricans identified their political ideology as leftist.[59] Costa Rican political culture is in fact staunchly anticommunist,[60] and when the government wants to discredit a group it has simply to label the organization "communist." Finally, a recent investigation shows that those among the lowest wage earners themselves list the single greatest reason for poverty as "laziness."[61]

That being said, after decades of near invisibility, peasant unions expanded rapidly throughout the 1980s in Costa Rica and used protest measures to grab attention in the national media. They spoke on behalf of the small producers whose livelihoods were at risk because of reductions in subsidized prices and bank credit for basic grains, falling prices for vegetable crops, and the skyrocketing costs of agricultural inputs such as pesticides and fertilizers. These organizations invaded land, blocked highways, led marches to the capital, and obtained audiences with political leaders to press their demands. But peasants were also quite interested in trying their hands at producing nontraditional export products. They quickly discovered that some of the new crops—passion fruit, cassava, black pepper, plantain—could be grown profitably on a small scale. My visits to peasant settlements around the country in 1990–91 left the impression that their main demand was that the government respond to some serious transitional problems. For example, there had been cases in which groups of small farmers had been swindled by export companies or lost entire crops to pests and fungus. In these cases, the peasants demanded that government institutions provide adequate technical assistance, help in marketing, and forgive loans.

Costa Rica has distinguished itself from most of its Central American neighbors by refraining from the violent repression of peasant unions, instead accepting them as something like interest groups and allowing the expression of rural demands.[62] As we saw in chapter 3, peasant protests did not stop the elimination of basic grains subsidies, but they did win a more gradual timetable. We also saw that certain agriculture commodities typically produced on small plots of land in Costa Rica, such as potatoes and onions, remain protected by high import tariffs. Finally, in 1997, President Figueres made good on his campaign pledge to pass legislation providing for a reconversion fund to help small and medium farmers adjust to the new markets.[63]

A second group normally expected to resist structural adjustment, especially second-stage reforms, is organized labor and, in particular, public-sector unions. Indeed, we saw in chapter 4 that stevedores working for Costa Rican public institutions managed to stop efforts to demonopolize that service. And in 1995, teachers walked off the job for a full month to protest the closing of their pension fund, although they were ultimately unsuccessful in halting the decision. The problem is said to be particularly acute in social service ministries, where, according to a recent World Bank publication:

> Reducing waste, corruption, and inefficiencies will require major administrative, financial, and technical reforms. In many cases these have been opposed by public sector unions, which defend old privileges and refuse to become accountable.[64]

The evidence from Costa Rica only lends weak support to this statement. There has been some organized opposition from unionized employees in the health and education ministries, most notably from doctors. But the project coordinators I spoke with were more concerned with passive resistance at all levels, especially middle management, and a lack of support from clients themselves (in these cases, patients and parents of school children). The Costa Rican evidence better supports the notion that organized labor's reaction to proposals to reform social service ministries is more varied than had been assumed.[65]

The last potential source of political backlash would be the manufacturing sector where firms producing for domestic and regional markets suffered steep reductions in protectionist barriers because of tariff liberalization. Here we find little evidence of such protest from employers or employees. Why? One reason is that the set of opportunities facing industrialists improved a great deal during economic recovery. The Costa Rican manufacturing sector expanded in every year between 1985–1995,[66] as positive growth rates generated demand for almost all manufactured goods. In particular, industrialists exploited new opportunities to export to extraregional markets, and, during the 1990s, to a rejuvenated CACM. Local companies also supplied inputs such as cardboard boxes and plastic bags to exporters.

The Chamber of Industry has become a proponent of export-led growth and now supports further liberalization. The Chamber is now focused on making the most of opportunities born from free trade agreements with other Latin American countries. Costa Rica has entered into a web of international obligations which carries the effect of institutionalizing free trade policies. And like their public-sector counterparts, the industrialists want Costa Rica to be seen as a modern economy, as a player in the international arena. Costa Rica is a member of the new and improved CACM,[67] which recently negotiated free trade agreements (FTAs) with the Dominican Republic and the Caribbean trade group CARICOM. In 1994, Costa Rica become the first Central American country to sign an FTA with Mexico. Costa Rica is currently pressuring the United States for entrance into NAFTA and negotiating FTAs with Chile, Colombia, and Venezuela.

How do we explain the quiescence of wage workers in the manufacturing sector where a grand total of three strikes took place between 1987–1995?[68] Manufacturing did grow more slowly than other sectors of the economy during 1985–1995, shrinking its importance in proportional terms. Nevertheless, the absolute number of persons employed in manufacturing grew each year until 1995. In addition, Costa Rica's low unemployment rates, averaging 5.1 percent between 1985–1995,[69] and the availability of jobs in faster-growing sectors such as services would have helped displaced workers to find other jobs. It also relevant that Costa Rican labor law presents significant obstacles to calling legal strikes,[70] but the quality of labor organization is a more important explanation for the quiescence of the postcrisis period.

As noted in chapter 2, *solidarista* associations predominate in the private sector. These company unions attempt to foster cooperation between workers and management and discourage confrontational measures such as strikes. They were made even more attractive to employees with the 1984 Solidarity Law which allowed them to offer such benefits as profit sharing and low-interest loans. In addition, the CUT, the labor confederation representing communist unions, suffered a tremendous blow in 1984 from which it has yet to recover. The few communist unions surviving the 1948 war operated in the banana plantations of the Pacific and Atlantic coasts. In a terrible miscalculation, the Unión de Trabajadores de Golfito decided in July 1984 to strike against a Pacific-coast subsidiary of the United Brands company. After a two-month standoff, workers in dire need of a paycheck trickled back to the plantation. But losing the strike was not the least of the union's problems. Shortly afterwards, the company, one of the largest employers in Costa Rica, announced that it would be forced to abandon its operations in the country because of the banana exports lost during the strike. In addition, President Monge denounced the union and its parent confederation as extremists linked to foreign, communist forces.[71] This incident seriously damaged whatever attractions radical unions still held for private-sector workers.

Conclusion

This chapter demonstrates that the economic, social, and political effects of structural adjustment measures taken thus far in Costa Rica have been overwhelmingly positive. Costa Rica rapidly developed new areas of private-sector expertise while poverty rates dropped and the democratic regime remained unthreatened by social or political instability. There is now a high level of political support for extraregional export-led growth and free trade, something not seen fifteen years ago. It is also advantageous in a country where over one-half of the population lives outside of cities that rural areas benefited disproportionately from the economic recovery. Indirect data indicate that the new export industries and tourism soaked up those displaced by fading agricultural support prices.

The rapid and sustained recovery that followed the economic crisis of the early 1980s is primarily responsible for these positive effects. But government wage policy and social welfare programs cushioned the impact of the economic crisis and subsequent transitional costs to a certain extent. In addition, Costa Rica's conservative political culture discouraged the development of antiregime movements and anticapitalist ideologies. Finally, consecutive administrations used dialogue and compensation as tools to ease structural adjustment forward, even if that meant moving in a slow and piecemeal fashion.

Thus, gradualism would seem to have much to recommend it, especially where it is possible to build coalitions of beneficiaries before attempting more controversial second-stage reforms. The chief danger in this approach is that the most difficult policy changes, usually everything that comes under the rubric of state reform, will just never get done. Many elements of state reform involve high political costs in return for gains which are too long-range, intangible, or disperse to look attractive to a sitting administration. In such cases, it is easy for reform fatigue to afflict proponents and potential allies. Institutional modernization and initiatives to reduce the public payroll may well succumb to reform fatigue in Costa Rica.

6

Conclusion

Summary of the Findings

This study shows that we can divide attempts at economic reform in Costa Rica between the "easy" adjustment phase during the 1980s and the subsequent "hard" period of the 1990s. In each stage, a combination of domestic and international factors pushed toward reform. The implementation of these reforms has occurred gradually, in stages, in almost all of the ten cases covered. But we can see that the changes proposed in the 1990s have been met with formidable political opposition and institutional barriers; several have stalled well short of their rather modest goals. Chapter 5 acknowledges the potential drag on the economy resulting from unenhanced state bureaucracies and monopolies but argues that, all in all, the outcomes of Costa Rica's gradualist model have been tremendously positive.

The early 1980s brought Costa Rican leaders and international donors together through a coincidence of interests. The foreign debt crisis and the collapse of the hybrid development model, combining traditional commodities exports with regional ISI, spurred the private and public sectors to seek financial assistance from outsiders. The changing conditions encouraged businesspeople and public-minded intellectuals to seek reforms, such as the privatization of CODESA, the demonopolization of banking, and the elimination of agricultural subsidies, which previously seemed politically impossible. At the same time, the United States, driven by the Reagan administration's Central American policy, offered Costa Rica enormous quantities of financial assistance and a willingness to cooperate with the business community's priorities. The

World Bank supplied Costa Rica with two structural adjustment loans and complemented the USAID-backed programs by focusing on eliminating protectionism. The free-market ideology of both institutions strengthened the position of the critics of the post-1948 development model.

As a result, by the 1990s, business elites were better able to perceive and articulate their interests in further privatization and a reduction in the size and scope of the state. In addition, even social democrats recognized that some revamping of the state was in order, particularly in the social services which had deteriorated (health and education) or were at risk (pensions). Again, the quality of available foreign assistance pushed Costa Rican policymakers to address these concerns. With the electoral defeat of the Sandinistas and the end of the Cold War, the United States quickly terminated large-scale concessional aid to Costa Rica. The IMF, World Bank, and IDB rode herd on fiscal spending limits and the latter two offered sector loans for health and education reform. Costa Rica thus embarked on a series of second-stage reforms in the 1990s.

Implementing the reforms of the 1980s was easier because the individual measures faced low institutional barriers and presented fewer managerial challenges. For example, the myriad veto points existent in Costa Rica's democracy did not have much relevance to the first-stage reforms. Agricultural subsidies and tariffs were reduced by executive decree and, while the other three reforms required enabling legislation, its passage was relatively simple and only created controversy in the case of banking. The reductions in domestic protection of industry and agriculture did adversely affect producers, particularly those growing basic grains. But farmers and industrialists had no legal avenue for blocking the measures and so their resistance served only as leverage in negotiations over the pacing of reform. The Arias administration defused tensions in these issue areas by using Costa Rica's tradition of compromise and offering mediation, gradualism, and compensatory gestures.

The reforms of the 1980s were also administratively simple and avoided attacks on vested welfare state interests. In no case did major government bureaucracies need to be overhauled. Where new administrative competencies had to be built, USAID paid for parallel agencies and expatriate expertise to handle the job. Thus, state workers found neither their routines nor their jobs threatened. Finally, the balance between winners and losers from these first-stage reforms tilted heavily toward the former. The reforms aimed at private-sector development in particular (privatization of

CODESA, nontraditional export promotion, and opening the banking monopoly) produced large payoffs rapidly while hurting virtually nobody. This incentive structure helped to produce groups of domestic interests willing to ally with foreign proponents of liberalization and internationalization. Transnational alliances occurred in all five cases.

During the Calderón and Figueres administrations of the 1990s, the management of structural adjustment was much more challenging. The incentive structures facing would-be reformers in the 1990s were more negative than those of the 1980s. Rather than expecting adjustment measures to result in rapid payoffs, politicians were aware that several of them (public-sector layoffs, privatization, and pension reform) would spark controversy and only generate positive and disperse benefits years down the line. Even those reforms expected to produce substantial and timely savings for the central government's budget were considered politically dangerous. Resources, particularly financial support and visionary leadership, were in short supply. For instance, external donors were not willing or able to provide sufficient funds for the lucrative severance packages that might have contributed to greater public employment reduction. And we saw that when it came to reforming the institutions overseeing public health and education, which are also Costa Rica's two largest employers, poor ministerial leadership and feelings of alienation from an internationally financed program undermined implementation in health.

Several qualities of Costa Rica's democracy also impeded the reforms. Welfare state retrenchment has not been popular either among public employees, who have expressed their opposition to layoffs and changes in job descriptions through organized unions and random, individualized resistance, or among the populace, who through public opinion polls have shown a continued attachment to state-run services and a disinterest in privatization. With the exception of a few cases like CODESA, there is little popular feeling in Costa Rica that government institutions and services are mistakes that ought to be dismantled. The country's political institutions also present barriers to proponents of rapid and radical adjustment. The president's weak decree power means that almost all state reform measures must be approved by the legislature. There they are often blocked for political reasons or fail because Costa Rica's short electoral cycles do not leave enough time to debate the ideas and work out compromise legislation. We have also seen that independent decisions by veto players, in particular the

Supreme Court and the Comptroller, have reversed privatization measures.

In sum, Costa Rica's model has been one of slow, piecemeal opening of the economy, retraction of the size and scope of state enterprises (in some cases replaced by public regulatory agencies), and modernization of key social services. Despite all of the obstacles to second-stage reforms illuminated here, Miguel Angel Rodríguez, the PUSC candidate elected president in mid-1998, is a businessman committed to continued retrenchment. We should expect the gradual model to continue forward however haltingly.

To understand the consequences of the gradual model, chapter 5 evaluates the outcomes of the last fifteen years of economic policy. The findings are overwhelmingly positive. Costa Rica has enjoyed positive GDP growth in every year since 1983 except for 1996. The new industries: nontraditional exports, tourism, and private banking, have boomed. The only dark spot on the economic ledger are the "procrastination costs" that unfinished reforms may levy on growth. In particular, the country's physical infrastructure has eroded as private-sector groups have been barred from financing and administering public works projects until very recently. On the social side, poverty peaked during the early 1980s and has since returned to precrisis levels, although there is disagreement over the direction of change in income inequality. The macroeconomic recovery after 1982 and government wage policies, welfare programs, and compensation packages have all benefited the poor, particularly in rural areas. It appears that the new industries helped to soak up unemployment, especially among those being pushed out of agriculture.

Finally, the political impact of Costa Rica's structural adjustment has unfolded as gradualist therapists predicted. The beneficiaries of the new policies have formed powerful new lobbies to protect their interests and to demand further reform. An unintended consequence of inducing so much change and growth in the private sector while putting off state reform may be to make market solutions to public-sector problems more likely in the long term, especially in areas such as social security, infrastructure development, and policing. Also, in great part because of the new economic opportunities, only limited political protest has accompanied policy changes, and certainly nothing regime threatening. The strategies used to affect change in Costa Rica—compromise, gradual pacing, compensation—are slow, messy and expensive, but they appear to have the advantage of sustainability.

Of course, the Costa Rican case is only one of many that will have to be examined in order to address the broader debate about whether gradualism or shock therapy is better recommended to countries attempting structural adjustment. While Costa Rica has performed surprisingly well for a small, poor country highly vulnerable to changes in the international economy, previously existing government investments and commitments undoubtedly helped make economic adjustment work. For example, the population already enjoyed high quality education, health care, and social welfare policies that were simply continued throughout the 1980s and helped smooth the transition to greater openness toward the international economy. These preexisting investments, in addition to a decent physical infrastructure and an organized national park system, also made Costa Rica very attractive to foreign investors. Larger studies will have to somehow factor in these sorts of national idiosyncrasies.

Comparative Perspectives

How does Costa Rica compare with other Latin American welfare states? Are other nations with similarly statist legacies able to conduct rapid economic reform or do they more closely resemble the Costa Rican case? First we must identify the other welfare states. Using the percent of the economically active population covered by each country's pension funds as a proxy, only five other nations have large welfare states (in which over 60 percent of said population benefits from social security): Uruguay, Brazil, Argentina, Chile, and Cuba.[1] I will exclude Chile and Cuba from the analysis because we are interested in structural adjustment conducted under democratic auspices. Most of the reforms in Chile took place during General Pinochet's authoritarian regime and Cuba is not a democracy. Of the remaining three, the Inter-American Development Bank rates Uruguay and Brazil, as well as Costa Rica, as slow or gradual reformers. Argentina is considered a rapid reformer.[2] The main question, then, is what separates the Costa Rican, Uruguayan, and Brazilian cases from that of Argentina.

Because we can assume that second-stage reforms will by nature present similar complexities and managerial requirements to all four countries, the distinctions between first and second-stage reforms in each cannot tell us very much about different implementation records across the set of nations. However, the quality of

140   *Gradual Economic Reform in Latin America*

each country's democracy can be expected to vary. Remember that the institutional design configuring the president's power composes a large part of what I defined as democratic quality. Conveniently, Scott Mainwaring and Matthew Shugart provide a table ranking executive authority for Latin American governments on two measures. From this table, I created an index with a single score for each.[3] Figure 6.1 displays Costa Rica, its peer welfare states, and ten other Latin American democracies in the process of carrying out economic reforms. Each has been charted by coordinates measuring executive authority (the president's legislative and partisan powers) and the size of its welfare state (percent of the economically active population covered by social security pension programs). In addition, each country is labeled a gradual (G) or rapid (R) reformer based on the IDB rankings.

Figure 6.1 shows that neither fragmented power nor a large welfare state alone are enough to prevent rapid reform from happening. In fact, the data suggest that one interesting area of further research would be the rapid reform accompanying right wing populism in a group of low-income, politically traumatized countries (Peru, El Salvador, Nicaragua, and Bolivia). When we compare the four large welfare states,[4] however, we see that the degree of executive authority does seem to divide the rapid reformer from the slower ones. Although we would need a larger number of cases to really test the significance of this variable, institutional differences appear to have strong explanatory value across cases. Below I will describe the ways in which Uruguayan and Brazilian institutions more closely resemble those of Costa Rica than Argentina. I will also argue that two less quantifiable qualities: interests capable of forming autonomous pockets of resistance to structural adjustment and elite preference for a continued welfare state, also separate Costa Rica, Uruguay, and Brazil from Argentina.

Like their Costa Rican counterparts, Uruguayan presidents cannot decree legislation, and so must rely on the congress to pass most structural adjustment measures. In this they would seem to share the advantage of a two-party system (thus limiting fragmentation). But just as a Costa Rican president's partisan powers are undermined by his instant lame duck status and legislative deputies who spend the second halves of their terms seeking future employment by cementing loyalties with party precandidates, Uruguayan parties' *lema* system undercuts incentives to cooperate with the executive. Under this system, a single party can run multiple lists (*sub-lemas*) for president, vice president, and governors.

Figure 6.1
The Quality of Democracy and the Speed of Reform in Latin America

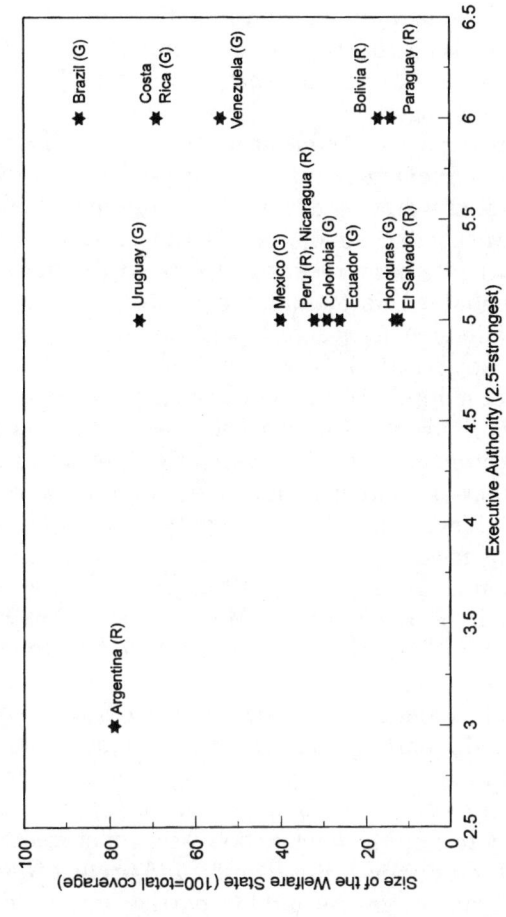

SOURCES: Pension data from Mesa-Lago, *Changing Social Security*, p. 22; data on executive authority from Mainwaring and Shugart, "Conclusion," p. 432; country rankings (G) and (R) from Inter-American Development Bank, *Economic and Social Progress in Latin America* (1997).

NOTES: Size of the welfare state represented by percent of the economically active population covered by pensions. The Costa Rican figure is lower than previously stated in the text because here pensions to indigents are not included. Executive authority is the combined score of the president's constitutional (legislative) and partisan powers.

The presidential candidate whose *sub-lema* garners the most votes from the party which earns the most votes overall, wins.

A common result is that presidents come to power after having won far less than the majority of votes and then face a legislature in which it is difficult to secure partisan cooperation because of the intraparty divisions created by competing *sub-lemas*. In both countries, then, the window of opportunity for passing complex, controversial legislation is minimal. And in both countries, neither the constitution nor the political culture allows the president to overcome gridlock by decree or some other power grab. Thus, presidents attempt to put together bipartisan coalitions or working agreements in order to pass the highest priority bills. While sometimes effective, such agreements almost always include concessions which have the effect of watering down the original proposals.[5]

Another institutional commonality is the existence of veto points. Uruguay's are less numerous than Costa Rica's, but its constitution allows a popular referendum, which must be held whenever 25 percent of eligible voters sign a petition opposing a law, to veto legislation already passed by Congress. As a result, Uruguay's major utilities (telecommunications, electricity, water, and petroleum refining) remain in state hands because a 1992 plebiscite overturned large sections of a 1991 privatization law and another restored the state power company's monopoly in 1998 after Congress passed a bill allowing private participation in electric power generation and transmission.

That labor organizations and the left coalition Frente Amplio (which had captured the mayoralty of Montevideo in 1989) were important in organizing these referenda[6] should alert us to another relevant similarity between Costa Rican and Uruguay. While left parties are not at all strong in Costa Rica, in neither case does the state or the two main parties control labor unions, community groups, or other political organizations, leaving them free to protest structural adjustment measures. Just as the Costa Rican groups used their autonomy to stop the demonopolization of stevedore contracting in Limón, limit public-sector layoffs, and protest the privatization of ICE, Uruguayan unions and left parties organized referenda to strike down neoliberal legislation and helped convince President Luis Lacalle (1990–94) to drop his original plan of firing twenty-five thousand state workers.[7]

A final commonality is that in both Costa Rica and Uruguay, political leaders would prefer to preserve the welfare state by making it the same—only better. José Figueres made much of his desire

Conclusion 143

to create a modern social democracy with a streamlined, but not minimal state, something between the status quo ante and the Chilean model. Recent Uruguayan president Julio Sanguinetti (1994–98) put it this way: "We don't want to change the welfare state. We just want to make it more rational and modernize it so it can remain viable."[8] Such goals indicate that Costa Ricans and Uruguayans desire to keep much of the past development model.

Brazil has advanced somewhat farther toward neoliberalism than Costa Rica and Uruguay, particularly in the area of privatization. But decentralized authority, actual opposition, and leaders' affinity for social democratic-like discourse have prevented a total embrace of market-oriented economic reform. Although the Brazilian executive is endowed with fairly strong constitutional powers over the legislature, robust federalism, rampant clientelism, and a notoriously fragmented party structure undermine presidential authority.[9] Congress rejected President José Sarney's (1985–1989) proposals for privatization and reducing state employment,[10] and dealt a similar fate to President Fernando Collor (1990–92), although he was able to initiate the sale of firms in the steel and petrochemical sectors.[11] Collor's Vice President Itamar Franco saw little progress on structural adjustment during his two years in office as interim president. Ironically, President Fernando Henrique Cardoso (1994 to present), a former leftist intellectual, has achieved the farthest reaching changes.

Privatization of some well-known companies has been the main accomplishment of Brazilian structural adjustment. The 1990s have seen the sale of many public firms, including the telecommunications giant Telebrás, yet one author explains that Brazil had only sold the equivalent of 12 percent of state-owned enterprise assets by 1996.[12] Independent labor unions utilized the court system as well as sabotage to slow but not stop the sales. More notably, the independent actions of other Brazilian politicians have caused President Cardoso a good deal of trouble in carrying out his agenda. Difficulty in corralling his six-party coalition into a useful legislative majority and representatives' disinterest in reducing a state program from which they can extract favors meant that President Cardoso needed five tries before he could convince Congress to pass a mild social security reform package in 1998. More intransigent has been state governors' refusal to follow federal directives to reduce budget deficits, fire public employees, and prepare state banks for privatization.

Led by former president Itamar Franco, now Governor of

Minas Gerais, a group of opposition governors has decried all forms of neoliberalism and refused to cooperate with federal authorities on many budget matters. In early 1999, it appeared that Franco had formed a loose coalition for these purposes with important figures in the Brazilian left, including Luiz Inácio Lula da Silva of the Workers' Party, Leonel Brizola of the Democratic Labor Party, and leaders of the Movement of Landless Workers and a large union confederation.[13] Thus, the political elite is not nearly unified behind market reform. President Cardoso himself is well-known for his New Democrat platform which supports a streamlined state but at the same time calls for increased public spending in areas such as basic health and education as well as antipoverty programs.[14]

Argentina's President Carlos Menem, on the other hand, with his relentless pursuit of neoliberal policies, provided unambiguous ideological leadership to those seeking to break the Argentine state away from its past form. In contrast to his counterparts in Costa Rica, Uruguay, and Brazil, Menem seems to have what Joe Wallis describes as a leadership style ". . . characterized by its commitment to reconstruct public policy on the basis of principles derived from a new and coherent policy paradigm."[15] These types of leaders have the "tunnel vision" necessary to set clear goals, the political will to take unpopular positions, and the skills to overcome resistance from within and without the government.[16] Indeed, President Menem moved forward particularly rapidly during his first term (1989–1994) when his government privatized much of the public enterprise sector including the national telephone, airline, and railroad companies, slashed federal and state budget deficits, rewrote labor legislation, and laid off over 200,000 civil servants.[17]

Besides the variable of presidential vision, Argentina differs from Costa Rica, Uruguay, and Brazil on the other two factors as well. President Menem took advantage of Argentina's institutional configuration to centralize power in the executive office. And he successfully reduced the disruptive capacity of organized labor, the interest group most likely to resist structural adjustment. Unlike the Costa Rican and Uruguayan cases, the constitutional powers of the Argentine president are extraordinary, particularly as Carlos Menem employed them before 1994. Menem used his decree authority to make new legislation extensively to pursue state reform, especially with the powers delegated to him by Congress through the Reform of the State and Economic Emergency Laws of 1989.[18] President Menem also reduced the balancing powers of what checks and balances exist on presidential authority by limiting the autonomy of the provinces and co-opting the Supreme Court.[19]

In addition, whereas societal groups were often able to produce effective protest against state reform in Costa Rica and Uruguay and at least slow down privatization in Brazil, President Menem seemed to simply run over Argentina's once impressive labor unions. Menem did this with a combination of decree authority, persuasion, and changes in the structures of political and economic incentives. In 1990, he limited the right to strike with a decree[20] and then persuaded the labor-linked Peronist Party to cooperate with much of his program.[21] That most Peronist labor leaders went along with Menem can be explained by a variety of factors including loyalty, opportunism, and similar analyses of the future of the Argentine welfare state.[22]

Implications

On the theoretical level, this brief comparative exploration reinforces the idea that institutions are a crucial variable in determining whether gradual or rapid structural adjustment is more likely in a given country. But it may not be the only one, and herein lies an interesting possibility for further research via a larger cross-national study. The contrast between Menem and the other presidents studied here points toward the role of leadership in making reforms happen. The presidents of Costa Rica, Uruguay, and Brazil appear to be not just responding to the institutional barriers of their political systems, but demonstrating ideological preferences quite distinct from Carlos Menem's. In addition, real resistance from opposition politicians, leftist movements, and civil groups not controlled by sitting administrations bear some responsibility for slowing down economic reforms

What do these observations mean on a practical level? One clear conclusion is that rapid and deep second-stage reforms are possible in Latin American welfare states, but under conditions that do not obtain in most of them. Given current trends toward decentralization, the growth of autonomous groups within civil society, and some leaders' willingness to reject radical market reform, it is perfectly logical that policy change will only happen incrementally if at all, especially where prior statist experiments spawned vested interests and public attachment to state enterprises. As the Costa Rican and Uruguayan examples demonstrate, this is as true in the smaller countries which we might expect to be more vulnerable to external donor and market pressures for faster liberalization as it is for Brazil.

On a policy level, it would be most helpful to develop some best practices for the gradual implementation of reforms for countries in which shock therapy is impractical. We can start the process by identifying the main components of successful gradualist experiments. For example, in the Costa Rican case, adjustment policies were implemented in such a way that coalitions of new beneficiaries developed long before the more difficult reforms were attempted. By the 1990s, these groups were lobbying for efficient improvements in state services. The employment generated by these new industries, plus tripartite agreements to preserve real wages and government welfare programs, provided a safety net for those in the lower income deciles and limited the possibility of social unrest. Finally, both PLN and PUSC administrations have adhered to Costa Rican cultural norms throughout the implementation process by using dialogue, compromise, and compensation to smooth the way for the reform measures that have succeeded.

It would also be helpful to acknowledge that the gradual reformers may not be traveling to the same destination as those pursuing rapid and deep liberalization; perhaps they have a better one in mind. José Figueres, Fernando Henrique Cardoso, Luis Lacalle, and Julio Sanguinetti have all sought a "third way" or "middle road" to reform, acknowledging the shortfalls in old statist models but seeking greater responsibility for the public sector than pure neoliberalism allows. The problem for these leaders has been to communicate a convincing vision of the alternative model and build a stable electoral coalition around it. Those seeking a third way or social-democratic alternative cannot rely on a coherent policy paradigm or blueprint in the same way that market reformers can look to neoclassical economics. The social-democratic parties in western Europe, who used to supply such examples, are themselves in flux and facing many of the same practical and ideological challenges as the Latin Americans. The international policy community could bolster third-way models by developing technical advice for achieving social-democratic goals.

Notes

Preface

1. John Williamson coined the term "Washington Consensus" in "What Washington Means by Policy Reform." The policy measures prescribed in his article include fiscal discipline, tax reform, competitive interest and exchange rates, trade liberalization, privatization, and government deregulation. For an excellent overview of how the "Washington Consensus" has evolved since Williamson's publication, see: Moisés Naím, "Washington Consensus or Washington Confusion?"

Chapter 1. The Gradual Road to Reform

1. For example, in a recent survey on democracy in Latin America, Marta Lagos found that by any measurement used, Costa Rica and Uruguay consistently ranked as the most democratic Latin American countries and that on a multivariable "degree of democracy" scale, Costa Rica scored highest. See Marta Lagos, "Latin America's Smiling Mask."

2. I am using the terms structural adjustment, economic reform, market-oriented reform, and neoliberal reform interchangeably. During the 1980s and 1990s in Latin America, these terms have been used as shorthand to refer to a large set of policies including: selling off public enterprises, eliminating subsidies to domestic producers, export promotion, trade and financial liberalization, tax reform, reducing state contributions to pension plans, shedding public workers and decreasing their legal rights vis-à-vis employers, and making state social service agencies more efficient via performance assessments, targeting benefits, and fee collection. The idea is to create a market-directed and outward-oriented economy which relies on national comparative advantages in the global economy and a small, efficient, fiscally disciplined state. The best overviews

describing the extent of these reforms in Latin America are: Inter-American Development Bank, *Economic and Social Progress in Latin America* (1996, 1997), and Sebastian Edwards, *Crisis and Reform in Latin America*.

3. The Inter-American Development Bank, an institution with every incentive to exaggerate accomplishments in this area, reports that the average completion rate of Latin American countries is 62 percent. See Inter-American Development Bank, *Economic and Social Progress* (1997), 86.

4. For explicit consideration of "dual transitions" (the simultaneous pursuit of economic restructuring and democratization) in Latin America and Europe, see: Joan M. Nelson, *Intricate Links: Democratization and Market Reforms in Latin America and Eastern Europe*, and Luiz Carlos Bresser Pereira, José María Maravall, and Adam Przeworski, *Economic Reforms in New Democracies*. Other works on new democracies and economic reform include: Adam Przeworski, *Sustainable Democracy*; Stephan Haggard and Steven B. Webb, *Voting for Reform: Democracy, Political Liberalization, and Economic Adjustment*; and Stephan Haggard and Robert R. Kaufman, *The Political Economy of Democratic Transitions*.

5. Important works by Costa Ricans include: Carlos Sojo, *La utopía del estado mínimo: influencia de AID en Costa Rica en los años ochenta*; Carlos Sojo, *La mano visible del mercado: la asistencia del Estados Unidos al sector privado costarricense en la década de los ochenta*; and Lidiette Brenes, *La nacionalización bancaria en Costa Rica*. A notable exception to the Costa Rican norm of treating the United States as a central player in economic policy change during the 1980s is: Eduardo Doryan Garrón, *De la abolición del ejército al premio nobel de la paz*. Doryan focuses exclusively on decisionmaking by state elites.

6. The best single work examining the connections between U.S. support of the Nicaraguan *contras* and foreign aid to Costa Rica is: Martha Honey, *Hostile Acts: U.S. Policy in Costa Rica in the 1980s*. Bruce Wilson, *Costa Rica: Politics, Economics, and Democracy* has excellent information on Costa Rican political institutions and on the some of the neoliberal policy changes of the 1980s.

7. One superb study comparing policymaking in Costa Rica to that of other small democracies in the 1980s is: Joan M. Nelson, "The Politics of Adjustment in Small Democracies: Costa Rica, the Dominican Republic, and Jamaica."

8. Adam Przeworski, *Democracy and the Market*, 136, and Nelson, *Intricate Links*, 9.

9. Gosta Esping-Andersen, "Positive-Sum Solutions in a World of Trade-Offs?" 265–66.

10. Susan C. Stoakes, "Public Opinion and Market Reforms: The Limits of Economic Voting."

11. Nelson, "Politics of Adjustment in Small Democracies," 206.

12. See: Nelson, *Economic Crisis and Policy Choice*; Karen L. Remmer, "Democracy and Economic Crisis: The Latin American Experience"; Stephan Haggard and Robert R. Kaufman, "The Political Economy of Inflation and Stabilization in Middle-Income Countries"; and Adam Przeworski and Fernando Limongi, "Political Regimes and Economic Growth."

13. For discussion of this and other problems thought to afflict presidentialist systems see the introduction to Juan J. Linz and Arturo Valenzuela, *The Failure of Presidential Democracy*.

14. Stephan Haggard and Robert R. Kaufman, "Introduction: Institutions and Economic Adjustment,"19, and Haggard and Kaufman, *Political Economy of Democratic Transitions*, 337. The authors are fully aware of the potential for abuse in countries where presidents wield strong powers. They stress that in the longer term, institutions which promote consensus building better ensure the sustainability of the reforms.

15. Scott Mainwaring and Matthew Soberg Shugart, "Presidentialism and Democracy in Latin America: Rethinking the Terms of Debate," 41–48, is the best discussion of these powers in Latin American countries.

16. Ibid., 44–5.

17. Scott Mainwaring and Matthew Soberg Shugart, "Conclusion: Presidentialism and the Party System," 432.

18. John M. Carey, "Strong Candidates for a Limited Office: Presidentialism and Political Parties in Costa Rica," 206.

19. I am drawing on concepts developed by George Tsebelis, "Decision Making in Political Systems"; and Jorge Vargas-Cullell, "Privatization in Costa Rica: Democratic Constraints to Institutional Reform." Tsebelis defines a veto player as ". . . an individual or collective actor whose agreement . . . is required for a change in policy." (301). He concentrates on branches of government and political parties. Vargas-Cullell broadens the definition of "veto gates" for Costa Rica to include other government agencies. I will argue in the conclusion that the popular referendum provided for by the Uruguayan Constitution should also be considered a veto point.

20. These themes run throughout Gosta Esping-Andersen, *Welfare States in Transition: National Adaptations in Global Economies*, and Paul Pierson, *Dismantling the Welfare State?*

21. Moisés Naím coined the term second-stage reforms in "Latin America: The Second Stage of Reform." My definition also draws on Inter-American Development Bank, *Economic and Social Progress* (1996), 81–82.

22. The concept of path dependence in relation to institutional evolution is discussed in Douglass C. North, *Institutions, Institutional Change and Economic Performance*, 98–99.

23. In *Dismantling the Welfare State?*, Pierson makes a similar argument about what he calls "policy feedback," or the institutions, interests, practices, and expectations produced by the emergence of welfare states, and how it constitutes an enormous obstacle to retrenchment.

24. Stephan Haggard, *Pathways from the Periphery: The Politics of Growth in the Newly Industrialized Countries*, 46.

25. The motivations of policy elites in responding to economic crisis are thoroughly explored in: Merilee S. Grindle and John W. Thomas, *Public Choices and Policy Change: The Political Economy of Reform in Developing Countries*.

26. Haggard, *Pathways from the Periphery*, and Robert Wade, *Governing the Market: Economic Theory and the Role of Government in East Asian Industrialization*.

27. Joe Wallis, "Understanding the Role of Leadership in Economic Policy Reform."

28. These could be seen as an internationalized version of Wallis' "policy conspiracies," or collectives whose members are committed to a common vision and who share the public positions and other resources necessary to overcome protest against their program. See "Understanding the Role of Leadership," passim.

29. See, for example: Robert D. Behn, *Leadership Counts: Lessons for Public Managers*; and Eugene B. McGregor, Jr., "Toward a Theory of Public Management Success."

30. Shock therapy, also known as the bitter pill, big bang, or radical reform, refers to market-oriented policy changes which are large and rapid. Exactly how this might be defined within specific policy areas is discussed in: Inter-American Development Bank, *Economic and Social Progress* (1996), 83–85.

31. Luiz Carlos Bresser Pereira and Jairo Abud, "Net and Total Transition Costs: The Timing of Economic Reform," 911.

32. Anders Aslund, "The Case for Radical Reform," 69–71.

33. Przeworski, *Democracy and the Market*, 162–64.

34. Padma Desai, "Beyond Shock Therapy," 105.

35. Dani Rodrik, "Promises, Promises: Credible Policy Reform via Signalling."

36. The most explicit economic arguments for gradualism have been made by Mathias Dewatripont and Gerard Roland. They have coauthored three articles on the subject: "The Virtues of Gradualism and Legitimacy in the Transition to a Market Economy," "Economic Reform and Dynamic Political Constraints," and "The Design of Reform Packages under Uncertainty."

37. Pierson, *Dismantling the Welfare State?*, suggests that obfuscation is one such strategy.

38. For example, he identifies Chile (a fast reformer) and Costa Rica (a slow reformer) as the two most successful adjusters. See: Samuel A. Morley, *Poverty and Inequality in Latin America: The Impact of Adjustment and Recovery in the 1980s*.

39. Dewatripont and Roland, "Virtues of Gradualism."

40. Ravi Ramamurti, "Why Haven't Developing Countries Privatized Deeper and Faster?"

41. For example, in *Free Markets and Food Riots: The Politics of Global Adjustment*, John Walton argues that economic adjustment has caused political instability in several Latin American countries.

42. Debates about the origins of pressures on Latin American countries to seek market-oriented reforms dominated related scholarship in the 1980s. Arguments between those who understood international forces, domestic interests, or the flow of ideas to be primarily responsible for the new policies are best summarized in Nelson, *Economic Crisis and Policy Choice*; Barbara Stallings, "International Influence on Economic Policy"; Miles Kahler, "External Influence, Conditionality, and the Politics of Adjustment"; Paul Mosley, Jane Harrigan, and John Toye, *Aid and Power: The World Bank and Policy-Based Lending*. Vol. 1; and Edwards, *Crisis and Reform*. Contrasting explanations for the origins of structural adjustment in Costa Rica in the 1980s can be found in: Sojo, *La utopía del estado mínimo* and *La mano visible del mercado*; Doryan Garrón, *De la abolición del ejército*; Wilson, *Costa Rica*; Honey, *Hostile Acts*; and Mary A. Clark, "Transnational Alliances and Development Policy in Latin America."

Chapter 2. The Legacies of 1948: Democratic Institutions, Social Welfare, and Economic Development

1. The classic statement of this thesis is Carlos Monge Alfaro, *Historia de Costa Rica*. In English, see: Charles Ameringer, *Democracy in Costa Rica*, and James L. Busey, *Notes on Costa Rican Democracy*.

2. Lowell Gudmundson, *Costa Rica before Coffee: Society and Economy on the Eve of the Export Boom.*

3. Mitchell A. Seligson, *Peasants of Costa Rica and the Development of Agrarian Capitalism.*

4. Robert G. Williams, *States and Social Evolution: Coffee and the Rise of National Governments in Central America*, 127.

5. Those who had been dispossessed by the transition to export cropping simply moved farther out into Costa Rica's vast agricultural frontier where it was easy to acquire land.

6. José Luis Vega Carballo, *Poder político y democracia en Costa Rica*, 28–30.

7. Ronald H. McDonald and J. Mark Ruhl, *Party Politics and Elections in Latin America*, 170. The authors admit that Costa Rica suffered an unpopular military dictatorship during 1917–1919.

8. Fabrice Edouard Lehoucq, "The Institutional Foundations of Democratic Cooperation in Costa Rica," 330.

9. Cynthia Chalker, "Elections and Democracy in Costa Rica," 102.

10. Lehoucq, "Institutional Foundations of Democratic Cooperation," 330.

11. Scholars still debate the causes of the 1948 war. A sample of the best sources on the subject include: John Patrick Bell, *Crisis in Costa Rica: The 1948 Revolution*; Manuel Bolaños Rojas, *Lucha social y guerra civil en Costa Rica: 1940–48*; Fabrice Lehoucq, "Class Conflict, Political Crisis and the Breakdown of Democratic Practices in Costa Rica: Reassessing the Origins of the 1948 Civil War"; Jacobo Schifter Sikora, "La democracia en Costa Rica como producto de la neutralización de clases"; and Deborah J. Yashar, "Civil War and Social Welfare: The Origins of Costa Rica's Competitive Party System."

12. Bolaños Rojas, *Lucha social y guerra civil*; Schifter Sikora, "La democracia en Costa Rica"; Yashar, "Civil War and Social Welfare."

13. Yashar, "Civil War and Social Welfare," 75.

14. Bell, *Crisis in Costa Rica*, and Yashar, "Civil War and Social Welfare," ft.18.

15. This description of the PSD, AD, and the Centro para el Estudio de los Problemas Nacionales relies heavily on Yasher, "Civil War and Social Welfare," 76–78, the best succinct discussion of the topic.

16. Yasher, "Civil War and Social Welfare," 79.

17. Ibid., 80. The tax was 10 percent on capital over fifty thousand colones.

18. Rafael Calderón did attempt a counterrevolutionary invasion from his land of exile, Nicaragua, in 1955. It was unsuccessful.

19. Yasher, "Civil War and Social Welfare," 80.

20. The Constitution was amended to this affect after José Figueres' third presidency (1970–74).

21. Political parties are to switch to open-list systems after the 1998 elections.

22. Carey, "Strong Candidates for a Limited Office," 203.

23. Ibid., 218.

24. Ibid., 206.

25. Andrew R. Nickson, *Local Government in Latin America*, 157–59.

26. Yashar, "Civil War and Social Welfare," 86–87.

27. Burt H. English, *Liberación Nacional in Costa Rica: The Development of a Political Party in a Transitional Society*, 132. Quote from the author's interview with Figueres, March 29, 1966.

28. Yashar, "Civil War and Social Welfare," 87.

29. Forrest Colburn, "Exceptions to Urban Bias in Latin America: Cuba and Costa Rica."

30. Yashar, "Civil War and Social Welfare," 88.

31. Ibid., 89.

32. These included the Partido Acción Democrático Popular (Popular Democratic Action Party) and the Partido Acción Socialista (Socialist Action Party).

33. Yashar, "Civil War and Social Welfare," 90, and McDonald and Ruhl, *Party Politics and Elections in Latin America*, 177.

34. Chalker, "Elections and Democracy in Costa Rica," 112.

35. Vargas-Cullell, "Privatization in Costa Rica." Vargas-Cullell actually argues that there are four additional veto gates, including the Ombudsman (Defensor de los Habitantes). But the ombudsman's office does not hold the same structural role within Costa Rican institutions as do the Supreme Court, Comptroller, or the semiautonomous institutions. These three share legal and administrative tools sufficient to block the implementation of new laws. The ombudsman has no legal authority to block or adjudicate laws, executive decrees, or contracts nor has this office

attempted to so since its creation in 1993. The ombudsman's office does have the mandate and moral authority to press public institutions to address citizen's complaints about the delivery of services and to offer an opinion when price hikes in utility charges are considered.

36. Wilson, *Costa Rica*, 154.

37. Vargas-Cullell, "Privatization in Costa Rica," 10.

38. Carlos Villalobos, "Anulan concesión de obra," *La Nación*, 27 June 1997. <http://www.nacion.co.cr/ln_ee/1997/junio/27/>

39. See Peter Katzenstein, *Small States in World Markets: Industrial Policy in Europe*. In "Politics of Adjustment in Small Democracies," Joan M. Nelson makes a similar comparison.

40. Katzenstein understands the ideology of social partnership in his cases to be the result of a shared sense of vulnerability to European conflicts. I see social solidarity in Costa Rica to be mainly a function of its universal welfare policies in the post-1948 era. Nevertheless, it could be argued that the Central American wars of the 1980s, particularly in Nicaragua, reinforced Costa Ricans' dedication to their capitalist welfare state and rejection of communism.

41. Claudio González-Vega and Víctor Hugo Céspedes, "Part I: Costa Rica," 82.

42. Mark Rosenberg, *Las luchas por el seguro social en Costa Rica*, 88.

43. Ibid., 149.

44. The only exception is a separate pension fund that the judicial system has been allowed to keep for its employees.

45. Juan Diego Trejos, et. al., "Enhancing Social Services in Costa Rica," 54.

46. Elderly people not eligible for the contributory programs may be granted a pension based on a means test. In 1992 it was estimated that 100 percent of senior citizens in need of these grants received the benefit. See: Juan Diego Trejos, "Costa Rica: The State's Response to Poverty," annex 1.

47. Trejos, "Enhancing Social Services," 55.

48. Carmelo Mesa-Lago, *Changing Social Security in Latin America*, 96.

49. Nancy Montiel, et. al., "La educación en Costa Rica: un solo sistema?" 3.

50. González-Vega and Céspedes, "Part I: Costa Rica," 92.

51. Figure for 1954 from Yashar, "Civil War and Social Welfare," 96. Data for 1985 come from United Nations Program for Development, *Estado de la nación*, 238–39. González-Vega and Céspedes, "Part I: Costa Rica," 39, cite similar growth in Costa Rican public-sector employment, from 6 percent of the labor force in 1950 to 20 percent in 1980.

52. These ideas came from economist Rodrigo Facio, perhaps the most influential intellectual force among the social democrats in the 1940s. Facio had a direct hand in putting these ideas into practice via his seat on the board of directors of the Central Bank during the 1950s. See Rodrigo Facio, *Obras de Rodrigo Facio*.

53. For a fascinating, detailed look at the development of this industry, see: Marc Edelman, "Land and Labor in an Expanding Economy: Agrarian Capitalism and the Hacienda System in Guanacaste Province, Costa Rica, 1880–1982."

54. Brenes, *La nacionalización bancaria en Costa Rica*, tables 3.1–3.6.

55. Ironically, this was the government of Otilio Ulate, a conservative representative of the coffee oligarchy who had allied with social democrats before 1948. Figueres maneuvered people in favor of the junta's program (such as Rodrigo Facio) into important positions on Ulate's cabinet and onto the directorate of the Central Bank.

56. For a detailed discussion of the origins and uses of the 1952 ad valorem tax, see Anthony Winson, "Confronting the Coffee Oligarchy: The Roots of Costa Rica's Middle Road."

57. Anthony Winson, *Coffee and Democracy in Modern Costa Rica*, 106–7.

58. Jorge Cornick Montero and Gladys González Rodríguez, "La política bananera costarricense, 1974–85," 21.

59. Ibid., pp.108–9.

60. First, in 1985, United Brands abandoned its Pacific coast plantations. Second, Standard Fruit continued to decrease its own exports because of financial problems in its parent company. Third, the remaining transnational subsidiary, BANDECO, took advantage of the situation to lobby the government for a reduction in tax rates. And finally, a hurricane destroyed thousands of hectares of bananas on the Atlantic coast in the same year. These events caused substantial drops in export earnings and an increase in the number of unemployed banana workers. The unattractive prospect of accelerating these trends is what probably led the state to reduce its demands on the industry.

61. Victor Bulmer-Thomas, *The Political Economy of Central America since 1920*, 119.

62. For more information on the struggle to pass the Industrial Promotion Law of 1959, see: Jorge Rovira Mas, *Estado y política económica en Costa Rica, 1948–1970*, 140–150.

63. President Kennedy discussed the matter with the Costa Ricans on a trip to San José during the same year. He made membership in the CACM a requirement for admittance into the Alliance for Progress. González-Vega and Céspedes, "Part I: Costa Rica," 91.

64. Ibid., 98.

65. Andrew Zimbalist, "Costa Rica," 24.

66. Tilman Altenburg, Wolfgang Hein, and Jürgen Weller, *El desafío económico de Costa Rica: desarrollo agroindustrial autocentrado como alternativa*, 72.

67. Zimbalist, "Costa Rica," 24.

68. Ibid., 27.

69. Bulmer-Thomas, *The Political Economy of Central America*, 194.

70. Claudio González-Vega, *Temor al ajuste: los costos sociales de las políticas económicas en Costa Rica durante la década de los 70*, 23.

71. González-Vega and Céspedes, "Part I: Costa Rica," 118.

72. Ibid., 101.

73. See Ana Sojo, *Estado empresario y lucha política en Costa Rica*, 185–241 for a full description of the polemics surrounding CODESA.

74. González-Vega and Céspedes, "Part I: Costa Rica," 119.

75. Calculated from data in González-Vega and Céspedes, "Part I: Costa Rica," 156–157.

76. Ibid., 44–45.

77. Bulmer-Thomas, *Political Economy of Central America*, 211.

78. See, for example: Robert Williams, *Export Agriculture and the Crisis in Central America*, chapter 8; John A. Booth, "Socioeconomic and Political Roots of National Revolts in Central America"; and Charles D. Brockett, "The Structure of Political Opportunities and Peasant Mobilization in Central America."

Chapter 3. "Easy" Structural Adjustment: The 1980s

1. For discussion of the causes of the economic crisis see: Helio Fallas Venegas, *Crisis económica en Costa Rica: un análisis económico de los*

últimos 20 años; Eugenio Rivera Urrutia, Ana Sojo, and José Roberto López, *Centroamérica: política económica y crisis* ; Jorge Rovira Mas, *Costa Rica en los años ochenta*; and Nelson, "Politics of Adjustment in Small Democracies."

2. Nelson, "Politics of Adjustment in Small Democracies," 184.

3. For details on the inconsistencies of President Carazo's economic policy see: Edgar Furst, "Estabilización vs. industrialización: crisis económica, medidas de estabilización y políticas industriales durante la administración Carazo: 1978–1982," and Eugenio Rivera Urrutia, "El Fondo Monetario Internacional y las políticas de estabilización en Costa Rica: 1978–82."

4. President Carazo expelled the IMF's representative from the country in January 1982 saying that the IMF was attempting to violate Costa Rica's sovereignty with its conditionality.

5. In 1982, inflation reached 90 percent while GDP growth fell 7.3 percent and real wages declined 4.9 percent (after dropping 9.3 percent over the previous annum). Data from figures 5.3 and 5.4.

6. Banana plantations on both coasts were the foci of these disputes. See Marielos Aguilar and Victoria Ramírez, "Crisis económica y acción sindical en Costa Rica (1980–87)."

7. Quoted in "Monge Seeks the Washington Vote of Approval," *Latin America Regional Reports: Mexico and Central America*, 5 June 1981, 5. Monge was referring to the supposed Cuban influence on Nicaragua and how the Sandinistas, and those Costa Ricans (especially labor unionists) ideologically allied with them, could benefit from Costa Rica's deteriorating economic situation to attract followers and further destabilize the country.

8. Quoted in Howard Banks, "Bankruptcy without Pain," 110.

9. See Honey, *Hostile Acts*, chapter 8, for the best account of the United States Central Intelligence Agency's involvement with the Southern Front.

10. Unfortunately, the CBI excludes many of the region's most important exports: textiles and apparel; petroleum; footwear and other leather goods; canned tuna; watches and watch parts; sugar; and beef. Partial compensation for these restrictions is available under U.S. Tariff Schedules 806 and 807, which allow firms operating in foreign countries to reexport articles assembled from U.S. components and only pay duty on the value added portion of the products. In 1991, Congress extended the CBI's benefits indefinitely.

11. At its peak in 1987–88, twenty-three career foreign service officers plus several times that many Costa Rican and U.S. contractees staffed

USAID's San José headquarters. Telephone interview with Cecil McFarland, USAID, Washington D.C., 1 March 1993.

12. USAID explicitly conditioned its disbursements on compliance with the terms of IMF agreements in 1982–1984. After passage of the 1984 Kemp-Kasten Act prohibiting explicit cross conditionality, USAID changed the wording of agreements with the government of Costa Rica (called Economic Stabilization and Recovery programs or ESRs) to require copies of reports filed with the Fund. The 1986, 1988, 1989, and 1990 ESRs contained specific macroeconomic targets and were meant to act as shadow IMF programs should no agreement with the IMF be reached within a given year.

13. Interview with former Arias administration official, Washington D.C., 22 October 1990.

14. According to USAID, "Costa Rica: Project Paper, Economic Stabilization and Recovery Program III," 6, the Central Bank revalued the free bank exchange rate from 43.60 to 42.60 colónes to the dollar, thereby violating a covenant obligating Costa Rica to maintain a competitive exchange rate policy.

15. The ambassador was originally quoted in a *Washington Post* article in 1984. Marc Edelman and Joanne Kenen, *The Costa Rican Reader*, 273.

16. This quotation comes from the court document, "U.S. Government Stipulation on Quid Pro Quos with Other Governments as Part of Contra Operations," cited in Honey, *Hostile Acts*, 63. The document was introduced on 6 April 1989 in the case of United States of America *v.* Oliver L. North, Defendant.

17. Ibid., 63.

18. Ibid, 59, and author interview with Oscar Arias, Madison, WI, 25 October 1992. The specific incidents of USAID holding up disbursements for such political reasons and related threats are: (1) suspension of $15 million in early 1986 immediately after President-elect Arias appeared on a Public Broadcasting Services (PBS) news program and told analyst John McLaughlin that he was against the $100 million *contra* aid package being considered by Congress; (2) delay of a $40 million disbursement in the fall of 1986 in reaction to Arias' plan to make public the existence of a clandestine airstrip in northern Costa Rica; (3) suspension of USAID funds between February and August 1987, the time period within which the President developed and achieved the signing of his Central American Peace Plan (Arias was finally able to get the money released by contacting democratic congressmen such as Senator Kerry, who threatened USAID with a scandal). In this last case, the United States also refused to help in debt negotiations with American commercial banks, as had been customary.

19. USAID, "Costa Rica: Economic Stabilization and Recovery III," 14.

20. These are former USAID/Costa Rica Director Daniel Chaij's own words. Author interview, Washington D.C., 18 October 1990.

21. Nelson, "Politics of Adjustment in Small Democracies, 184.

22. Ibid.

23. At its peak in 1982, CODESA absorbed 54 percent of state bank credit to the public sector or 21 percent of all state system lending. USAID, "Costa Rica: Economic Stabilization and Recovery IV," Annex III, 1.

24. The direct jobs (2,122) only accounted for 0.3 percent of Costa Rica's labor force. All figures from USAID, "Economic Stabilization and Recovery IV," 8.

25. Dennis Meléndez and Mauricio Meza, "CODESA: Origen y Consequencias," 38.

26. Brenes, *La nacionalización bancaria en Costa Rica*, 74.

27. USAID, Regional Inspector General for Audit, "Audit of Selected USAID/Costa Rica Local Currency Activities," Appendix 1, 11.

28. USAID, Regional Inspector General, "Audit of Selected USAID/Costa Rica," 20.

29. USAID, "Economic Stabilization and Recovery IV," 21.

30. USAID, "Economic Stabilization and Recovery V," 12.

31. USAID, Regional Inspector, "Audit of Selected USAID/Costa Rica," 19.

32. USAID, "Economic Stabilization and Recovery IV," 22.

33. Ibid., Annex III, 7.

34. USAID, Regional Inspector General, "Audit of Selected USAID/Costa Rica," Appendix 1.

35. Law 7330 of 1992 mandated that the shares be divided in the following manner: 30 percent to the employees of FERTICA and CEMPASA, 20 percent to small investors, 18 percent to unions and company unions (*asociaciones solidaristas*), and 8 percent each to cooperatives, groups of small agricultural producers, community development organizations, and business chambers.

36. Coopers and Lybrand L.L.P., "Evaluación del proceso de privatización de subsidiarias y liquidación de activos de CODESA y del programa de reforma de estado," chapter III, 27.

37. Interview with the Executive President of CODESA, San José, 30 July 1996.

38. Arthur D. Little International, Inc. "CENPRO: En el contexto de una estrategia para el desarrollo de las exportaciones de Costa Rica."

39. Author's interviews, San José, December 1990 and February 1991.

40. Arthur D. Little International, Inc., "Evaluation of the Private Sector Productivity Project as Implemented Through the Corporation Banex," 13.

41. Interviews with former members of CINDE's board of directors and with former USAID officials, San José, February and March 1991.

42. Minutes of the CINDE Board of Directors, 1983–84, and data provided by CINDE's budget office.

43. This attitude was apparent in both interviews and in CINDE Board of Directors minutes.

44. *Certificado de Abono Tributario* or Tax Credit Certificate. CATS are worth up to 20 percent of a firm's nontraditional export sales and are negotiable on the national stock exchange.

45. The export contract expanded some existing incentives, such as the CAT, added new ones, like the income tax exemption, and repackaged them all in a way that would be easier for the nontraditional exporter to use. The CAT first appeared as part of the Industrial Promotion Law of 1972 but was little used until 1984.

46. The data for 1983 come from José Salazar, et. al., "Precios, incentivos, y reformas de política." CENPRO provided the 1990 figures but they include the added value, as opposed to the gross export value, of garments and textiles. The 1990 figure would be larger if the latter measure of textile and garment exports were used. In Costa Rica, a nontraditional export is anything other than coffee, bananas, beef, sugar, cotton and a few other insignificant exports. Nontraditional exports are sold to "third markets" or those outside of Central America.

47. U.S. Department of Commerce figure for total Costa Rican textile and garment exports to the United States in 1990. The United States imports nearly all of Costa Rica's exports in this category.

48. Information on 1990 export levels of flowers and plants, seafood, and pineapple from CENPRO.

49. Data provided by CINDE Marketing Division, September, 1990.

50. Statement of James H. Michel, assistant administrator, Latin American and Caribbean Bureau, before the Subcommittee on Western Hemisphere Affairs, U.S. House of Representatives, 5 March 1991, Washington D.C.

51. PROCOMER, "Análisis de las estadísticas de exportación 1998."

52. Ibid.

53. Bruce Wilson, "When Social Democrats Choose Neoliberal Economic Policies: The Case of Costa Rica," 155.

54. Dr. Ottón Solís, ex-Minister of Planning (1986–88) and recent PLN deputy in the Legislative Assembly (1994–98) is the most articulate proponent of this viewpoint. He regularly publishes opinion pieces such as "Socialdemoracia y neoliberalismo," *La Nación*, 19 April 1990, 4A in which he defends the PLN's traditional principles.

55. Brenes, *La nacionalización bancaria en Costa Rica*, 82.

56. Wilson, "When Social Democrats Choose," 154.

57. These are the words of Vinzenz Smack, USAID/Costa Rica's then expert on banking. He said that the state banks required political connections to obtain loans and refused to collect on many bad debts, allegations the author heard often repeated by Costa Rican businesspeople. Interview, San José, 29 August 1990.

58. This was the opinion of Central Bank President Eduardo Lizano. Interview by Bruce Wilson for Ph.D. diss., Washington University, July 1990, cited in Honey, *Hostile Acts*, 79.

59. Wilson, "When Social Democrats Choose."

60. USAID apparently had transferred early loans to BANEX and other banks through offshore mechanisms that took advantage of loopholes in the law. Honey, *Hostile Acts*, 80.

61. These meetings are reported in Wilson, "When Social Democrats Choose," ft.50 and Brenes, *La nacionalización bancaria en Costa Rica*, 87.

62. Wilson, "When Social Democrats Choose," and Honey, *Hostile Acts*.

63. In addition to installing rural branches, the banks have to maintain 10 percent of current account holdings in programs to be defined by the executive branch. If a private bank does not want to do this, it may opt to deposit a minimum of 17 percent of its current account holdings in the state banking system, so that the latter can increase rural lending. Interview with Dr. Ronulfo Jimenez, Legislative Commission on Financial Reform, San José, 8 August 1996.

64. Honey, *Hostile Acts*, 90, and Patricia Leitón, "Prevén más alianzas y fusiones bancarias," *La Nación*, 24 August 1996. <http://www.nacion.co.cr/ln_ee/1996/agosto/24/>

65. Patricia Leitón, "Bancos nacionales duplicaran ganancias," *La Nación*, 7 February 1997. <http://www.nacion.co.cr/ln_ee/1997/febrero/7/>

66. The Banco Anglo was closed in 1994 in the aftermath of an unrelated corruption scandal.

67. Early data points to positive results in cost cutting. See Yanancy Noguera, "Avanzan reformas en bancos," *La Nación*, 6 August 1996, p.22–A.

68. Patricia Leitón, "Cuentas en expansión," *La Nación*, 26 July 1997, 18–A.

69. Per unit administrative costs in the Banco Nacional have been dropping rapidly in the 1990s. See Yanancy Noguera, "Nacional abrirá banco en Managua," *La Nación*, 1 August 1997, 22–A.

70. John Newton, *The Effectiveness and Economic Development Impact of Policy-Based Cash-Transfer Programs: The Case of Costa Rica*, B–3.

71. Dr. Eduardo Lizano lays out the case against agricultural protectionism in chapter eight of his *Desde el Banco Central*.

72. William Reuben Soto, "El potencial de la economía campesina en la reactivación económica y el desarrollo de Costa Rica," 216.

73. See "Marcha Campesina: cosecha de promesas," and "Entrevista con Carlos Campos de UPAGRA," in *Aportes* 38, October 1987.

74. The CNP also phased-out sorghum subsidies but the change went virtually unnoticed as it has always been a minor crop in Costa Rica.

75. Edgar Furst, "Liberalización comercial y promoción de exportaciones en Costa Rica (1985–1990)," 15.

76. During the 1980s, the World Bank pressured countries all over the globe to lower protectionist barriers and open themselves to international competition. As for USAID, besides the influence of Reagan-era free-market ideas on the organization, there was a geopolitical rational for turning Costa Rica away from the regional ISI scheme. Strengthening Costa Rica's participation in the CACM would have involved finding a way to help Nicaragua, Costa Rica's most important regional trading partner, pay the debt it owed to Costa Rica. The Reagan administration was not interested in indirectly helping Nicaragua revive its economy. Interview with Daniel Chaij.

77. Interview with World Bank official, Washington D.C., 18 October 1996. That Costa Rica led the rest of the CACM toward lower tariffs was one of the major goals for the World Bank in negotiating the first structural adjustment loan.

78. Furst, "Liberalización comercial," and Interview with José Manuel Salazar, former director of Costa Rica's Industrial Reconversion program, Miami, 5 December 1991.

Notes   163

79. Sylvia Saborio, "Central America," 293.

80. Interview with Marvin Rodríguez, Director of Research, Cámara de Indústrias, San José, 23 July 1996. Interview with Richard Beck, former president of the Cámara de Indústrias, San José, 23 July 1996. Interview with Samuel Yankelewitz, former president of the Cámara de Indústrias, San José, 8 August 1996.

81. Interviews with Yankelewitz and Beck, and Ciska Raventos, "The Construction of an Order: Structural Adjustment in Costa Rica (1985–1995)," 123–24.

82. Sylvia Saborio, "U.S.-Central America Free Trade," 202.

83. Arguing from the opposite viewpoint, the authors of one study conclude that Costa Rica's economic opening did not have substantial negative effects on the labor market between 1987–1993. See Víctor Hugo Céspedes and Ronulfo Jiménez, *Apertura comercial y mercado laboral en Costa Rica*.

84. For instance, the Costa Rican import tariff on chicken is 266 percent; on milk, 105 percent; on rice, 35 percent; on African palm oil, 30 percent; on sugar, 52 percent; on processed pork, 35 percent; on potatoes, 45 percent; and on onions, 52 percent.

85. In 1990, USAID judged that further privatization under President Arias was impossible due to the serious political protest provoked by the administration's talk of privatizing ICE. The Mission believed that such efforts would only be successful if the Costa Rican government led them, an event unlikely to occur during the president's last year in office. See: USAID, "Economic Stabilization and Recovery IX," Annex B, 4.

USAID had pressured the government to begin public-sector employment cuts and in 1988 began to use conditionality to cap the number of government jobs at 1987 levels (except in education and health). But President Arias resisted real cuts. And, according to USAID, the World Bank decided against including employment reduction targets in the second SAL, because it estimated that the expected political opposition to such a condition would make it unfeasible. See: USAID, "Costa Rica: Economic Stabilization and Recovery VIII," 32.

Chapter 4. Reforming the Welfare State: The 1990s

1. Costa Rica's stock market is not yet well enough developed to attract foreign portfolio investments.

2. Edwards, *Crisis and Reform*, 79.

3. The package included an increase in the sales tax to 15 percent, a 1 percent tax on businesses with assets greater than U.S.$160,000 dollars, and a uniform corporate income tax of 30 percent.

4. Mario Carvajal, "Transformación del Estado: Diagnostico y Metas," 17–18.

5. Yanancy Noguera, "Deuda del gobierno llegará a un billón de colones" *La Nación*, 18 November 1996. <http://www.nacion.co.cr/ln_ee/1996/noviembre/18/>

6. Ibid.

7. Under Costa Rican law, public workers who leave involuntarily or as part of an employment-reduction program must be paid one month's salary for each year they were on the government's payroll. In 1990, workers who left their government positions had to wait four to six months to receive severance pay.

8. Coopers and Lybrand, "Evaluación del proceso de privatización," V–4. Although legally independent, FUCE is really FINTRA (discussed in chapter 3). FUCE and FINTRA share identical offices and administrative personnel.

9. These sources are cited in Coopers and Lybrand, "Evaluación del proceso de privatización," V–5, and Carlos Sojo, *La gobernabilidad en Centroamérica: La sociedad después del ajuste*, 41.

10. Cited in Coopers and Lybrand, "Evaluación del proceso de privatización," V–5.

11. Carvajal, "Transformación del estado," 16.

12. Coopers and Lybrand, "Evaluación del proceso de privatización," V–10.

13. In ministries laying off large numbers of people, however, not all of the workers were allowed to benefit from the supplemental severance pay package.

14. "Mejorar servicios, próximo paso de reforma," *La Nación*, 29 January 1996. <http://www.nacion.co.cr/ln_ee/1996/enero/29/>

15. Patricia Leitón, "Superada meta de movilidad con FMI." *La Nación*, 10 July 1996, 22–A.

16. Several government officials whom I interviewed said that they thought the political cost of firing public-sector workers had put a stop to *movilidad laboral*.

17. Yanancy Noguera, "Gobierno dice que cumplió con reforma estatal," *La Nación*, 1 July 1996. <http://www.nacion.co.cr/ln_ee/1996/julio/01/>

18. Interview, Washington D.C., 15 October 1996.

19. Interview with William Barrantes, Deputy Director, CNP, San José, 8 August 1996.

20. Interview with Gonzalo Vega, Executive Director of FUCE, San José, 31 July 1996.

21. Coopers and Lybrand, "Evaluación del proceso de privatización," V–12.

22. Information on customs reform from here down comes from Coopers and Lybrand, "Evaluación del proceso de privatización," V–12–18 and interview with Gonzalo Vega. As was true of CINDE and FINTRA, FUCE's main advantage for the reform coalition was its independence from government labor and procurement regulations. FUCE could hire first-rate domestic and international consultants on short-term contracts and speed up the process of obtaining new equipment such as computer packages.

23. Interview with Adrian Vargas, Director of Reform in Finance Administration, Ministry of Finance, San José, 1 August 1997.

24. Christine Pratt, "Postal System in for Reform," *Tico Times*, 27 June 1997, their translation. <http://ticotimes.co.cr/briefs.html>

25. These are: ICAFE (coffee), OFIARROZ (rice), LAICA (sugar cane), CORBANA (bananas), INFOCOOP (producer cooperatives), Oficina Nacional de Semillas (seeds and genetic material), and the Junta de Tabaco (tobacco).

26. The INS has a monopoly on all kinds of insurance in Costa Rica except for health.

27. Jorge Vargas-Cullell, "Democratic Constraints to Reform," 34.

28. Carol Cordero, "Empieza foro sobre la conversión del ICE," *La Nación*, 15 July 1996, 6A.

29. José Guevara and William Méndez, "Crece debate sobre ICE en PLN," *La Nación*, 23 July 1996, 4A.

30. Cinthya Arias and José Mora, "Energía y telecomunicaciones: Tecnología demanda reformas," 75.

31. José Guevara, "Ticos fieles a Estado benefactor," *La Nación*, 9 October 1996. <http://www.nacion.co.cr/ln_ee/1996/octubre/09/> Researchers found that 49 percent of respondents wanted the Legislative Assembly to allow private investment in the electricity sector and 53 percent thought that telecommunications should be opened to competition.

32. Ibid.

33. "ICE, entidad más confiable," *La Nación*, 8 May 1998. <http://www.nacion.co.cr/ln_ee/1998/mayo/08/> The INS and RECOPE had confi-

dence ratings of 68 and 67 percent, respectively, also slightly outscoring the Catholic Church (66 percent).

34. "Limón Strike Ends," *Tico Times*, 6 September 1996. <http://ticotimes.co.cr/briefs.html>

35. Mesa-Lago, *Changing Social Security*, 98.

36. Francisco Ramírez, Jaime Lobo, and Marvin Acuña, "El estado de los regímenes: el caso del régimen de invalidez, vejez y muerte de la CCSS," 10.

37. World Bank, *Averting the Old Age Crisis*, 128.

38. Carvajal, "Transformación del estado," 17.

39. Economist Intelligence Unit, *Country Report: Costa Rica, Second Quarter 1995*, 20.

40. Average retirement age is actually closer to 64. This is because to draw a pension, a person must complete a minimum of thirty-eight units (years) of work or reach age sixty-five and have twenty units. The pension system was not universalized until the 1970s, and so many members began marking quotas late into their working lives. Of course, the average retirement age has started to fall as the system matures.

41. Mesa-Lago, *Changing Social Security*, 98–99.

42. This fund covers primary through post-secondary teachers. The other two special funds that were not unified under the 1992 law belong to the deputies of the Legislative Assembly and to the judicial system. The former was eliminated in 1995 and the latter fund has not been an object of reform because of the small number of beneficiaries involved (4,000) and because it is solvent.

43. The teacher's own contribution was increased from 5 to 7 percent in 1991.

44. Beginning in 1992, new teachers had been offered a less-lucrative pension package into which they would contribute 6 percent of their salaries and the state 5.75 percent.

45. Economic Intelligence Unit, *Country Report: Costa Rica, 3rd Quarter 1995*, 22.

46. Information on these plans was obtained in interviews with Adolfo Rodríguez, Advisor to the Second Vice President and director of the pension reform project, San José, 18 July 1996 and 18 July 1997. The Figueres administrations' initiatives on pension reform were clearly the result of work by a domestic team, as opposed to being designed by the IFIs. In fact, in 1996 the World Bank refused to supply Costa Rica with a sectoral loan for the modernization of the pension system because the

administration's plans were not sufficiently market-oriented. Nevertheless, the pension reform team received about five million dollars in technical assistance loans from the Bank to help develop the enabling legislation for the changes discussed below.

47. Until recently, pensions were based on the average salary obtained by an employee during the last five years of work. This tended to favor public-sector workers and the best-paid private-sector workers whose wages went up over time. But the lowest paid private-sector workers (i.e. those in construction and agriculture) do not in general benefit from rising wages and are able to work less as they age. Thus, the system was skewed toward the more fortunate. The new formula uses an average of the salaries obtained by a employee over the last twenty years of work as a base for the pension.

48. The latter figure does not include administrative personnel located in the central bureaucracy. All statistics from John Ickis, Carlos Sevilla, and Miguel Iñiguez, "Estudio del sector salud de Costa Rica."

49. Trejos, "Enhancing Social Services," 56.

50. Ickis, "Estudio del sector salud," 108.

51. Trejos, "Enhancing Social Services," 59.

52. Ickis, "Estudio del sector salud," 93.

53. Interview with Dr. Manuel Piza, director of medical administration, College of Physicians and Surgeons of Costa Rica, San José, 31 July 1997.

54. Trejos, "Enhancing Social Services," 60–61.

55. Ickis, "Estudio del sector salud," 87.

56. Giannina Segnini, "Nicaragüenses no superan los 400 mil," *La Nación*, 5 December 1999. <http://www.nacion.co.cr/ln_ee/1999/diciembre/05/>

57. Giannina Segnini, "Nicaragüenses impactan salud," *La Nación*, 7 December 1999. <http://www.nacion.co.cr/ln_ee/1999/diciembre/07/>. In 1998, the CCSS reported that approximately one-third of children treated at its hospitals were those of illegal immigrants as were one-fourth of mothers giving birth in its facilities. Figures from "Illegal Nicaraguan immigrants good for business," *Central America Report* 26:31 (13 August 1999), 7.

58. Interview with Roger Ballestero, Coordinator of the CCSS-IDB reform project, San José, 22 July 1997.

59. France was the first country to use performance contracts to improve the efficiency of public enterprises instead of privatizing them.

The Harvard Institute for International Development and Andersen Consulting have helped spread this practice in Latin America. See Ickis, "Estudio del sector salud," 127.

60. Interview with Dr. Luís Bernardo Sáenz, Director of the CCSS's Proyecto de Modernización (the World Bank-funded Modernization Project), San José, 30 July 1997, and Montserrat Solano, "Más hospitales asumen retos," *La Nación*, 3 January 1998. <http://www.nacion.co.cr/ln_ee/1998/03/>

61. Interview with World Bank official, Washington D.C., 16 October 1996.

62. Ickis, "Estudio del sector salud," 131.

63. Interview with Roger Ballestero.

64. School enrollment data for 1993 from: World Bank, *World Development Report 1997*, 227. Ministry of Education officials believe that Costa Rican high school enrollment rates lag behind the Southern Cone countries because of the higher number of students who fail the post-primary school exams needed to advance in grade level and because more of them come from rural families, among whom dropping out to enter the agricultural labor force is more common.

65. Montiel, "La educación en Costa Rica," 59.

66. Ibid., 9.

67. World Bank, "Costa Rica: Public Sector Social Spending," 42.

68. See Ministerio de Educación Pública, "Estadísticas del sistema educativo costarricense, 1980–1996."

69. Trejos, "Enhancing Social Services," 68.

70. Ibid., 68.

71. Montiel, "La educación en Costa Rica," 20, 26, 53.

72. Ibid., 43.

73. Guillermo Acuña González and Edith Olivares Ferreto, "Diagnóstico global: La población migrante nicaragüense en Costa Rica: realidad y respuestas," 14.

74. Ministerio de Educación Pública, "Estadísticas," 47.

75. Juan D. Trejos, et. al., "Costa Rica: La respuesta estatal frente a la pobreza: instituciones, programas y recursos," 34.

76. Reforming higher education seems all but politically impossible. For example, when President Calderón's finance minister Thelmo Vargas

attempted to cut funding to the university system in 1991, its employees struck. The president restored the funding and Vargas resigned.

77. PROMECE, "Sistematización del proyecto."

78. Interview with Carlos Barrantes, Director, PROMECE, San José, 23 July 1997.

79. Montiel, "La educación en Costa Rica," 53.

80. In "After the Golden Age?" Gosta Esping-Andersen uses the term creeping privatization in the same way.

81. Wilson, *Costa Rica*, 143.

Chapter 5. Costa Rican Outcomes

1. Interview with Daniel Chaij, former Director of USAID/Costa Rica, Washington D.C., 18 October 1990.

2. Calculated using GDP data from Figure 5.3.

3. Instituto Costarricense de Turismo (ICT), unpublished data, 1997.

4. PROCOMER data, 1997.

5. Tourism and export data from figure 5.1. GDP data from the Central Bank of Costa Rica and United Nations Development Office, *Estado de la nación* (1999).

6. Pamela Méndez Rodríguez, "Intel: A la cabeza del desarrollo tecnológico," 34.

7. Ibid., 36.

8. "Government Touts Intel Success," *Central America Report*, 26:48 (10 December 1999), 5.

9. Peter Bate, "Costa Rica Brews a New Blend of Java," 2–3.

10. This statement is based on data supplied by the U.S. Department of Commerce and Marvin Barquero, "Textiles lideran exportaciones," *La Nación*, 23 February 1998. <http://www.nacion.co.cr/ln_ee/1998/febrero/23/>

11. These explanations were given in interviews with industry businesspeople, San José, August, 1994.

12. Dixie Mendoza, "Buscan nuevas opciones en ICC," *La Nación*, 24 March 1998. <http://www.nacion.co.cr/ln_ee/1998/marzo/24/>

13. Eduardo Lora and Felipe Berrera, "A Decade of Structural Reforms in Latin America: Growth, Productivity and Investment Are Not

What They Used to Be." The study was used as the basis for text and graphics in: Inter-American Development Bank, *Economic and Social Progress* (1997), 59–61.

14. Nora Lustig, "Introduction," 3.

15. In 1996, 51 percent of Costa Rica's population was still found in rural areas. See Inter-American Development Bank, *Economic and Social Progress* (1997), 220.

16. Former Central Bank President Eduardo Lizano painted this scenario during an interview in San José, 30 July 1990.

17. ECLAC, *Statistical Yearbook for Latin America and the Caribbean* (1997), 66. The discrepancies in results between this and other studies arise from methodological differences. They all use raw data from household surveys conducted by Costa Rica's Department of Census and Statistics, but the ECLAC statisticians adjust aspects of the data (such as the composition and costs of minimum caloric requirements and income reports) in such a way that a greater number of households end up defined as poor.

18. Samuel A. Morley, *Poverty and Inequality in Latin America*, 139–141.

19. Mitchell Seligson, Juliana Martínez, and Juan Diego Trejos, "Reducción de la pobreza en Costa Rica: el impacto de las políticas públicas," figures 2 and 3.

20. Victor Hugo Céspedes and Ronulfo Jiménez, *La pobreza en Costa Rica*, 85. Social scientists remain concerned about the validity of Costa Rican poverty estimates, because household surveys are still conducted on the basis of 1984 census data. A new census was to be taken in 1997 but has been postponed indefinitely.

21. In yet another series, official government statistics for the 1990s show that the recession of 1996 was accompanied by a slight increase in poverty, from 20 percent in the two previous years to 22 percent in 1996, and then a drop back down to 21 percent during the recovery in 1997. These statistics were reported in Patricia Leitón, "Menos hogares son pobres," *La Nación*, 22 January 1998. <http://www.nacion.co.cr/ln_ee/1998/enero/22/>

22. Ariel Fiszbein and George Psacharopoulos, "Income Inequality Trends in Latin America in the 1980s," 73 (table 3–1). According to their data, Costa Rica's Gini coefficient decreased from 0.451 to 0.410 between 1981–89. The standardized Theil index dropped from 3.76 to 3.49 over the same period.

23. George Psacharopoulos, "Poverty and Income Distribution in Latin America: The Story of the 1980s," Annex 3. This study shows a decline in the Gini index from 0.475 to 0.460 between 1981–89.

24. Andreas Stamm, "Una nueva dinámica para las zonas rurales?" 36.

25. Jürgen Weller, "Efectos del ajuste estructural en el empleo y los ingresos agropecuarios, con énfasis en las exportaciones no tradicionales," 220.

26. Stamm, "Una nueva dinámica," 36.

27. Data in Samuel A. Morley, *Poverty and Inequality in Latin America: Past Evidence, Future Prospects*, 68 and Morley, *Poverty and Inequality in Latin America*, 143–46 show this shrinkage during 1980–93. Data from the Department of Census and Statistics show a further reduction in the number of people employed in agriculture between 1987–1996.

28. Morley, *Poverty and Inequality in Latin America: Past Evidence, Future Prospects*, 68.

29. Jorge Nowalski, Pedro Morales, and Gregorio Berliavsky, *Impacto de la maquila en la economía costarricense*.

30. There are no statistics that separate tourist-sector employment from other types but unpublished data from the Department of Census and Statistics show a near doubling in the number of people working in hotels and restaurants between 1987–1996.

31. There are legally registered prostitutes in Costa Rica.

32. United Nations Development Program, *Estado de la Nación*, (1995), 169–171.

33. Possible explanations for the crime wave unrelated to economic reform include the infiltration of criminals and arms from Costa Rica's war torn Central American neighbors and spillover effects from the growing traffic of narcotics throughout the isthmus.

34. At the time, the number of items in the basket was fourteen (including rice, sugar, beans, milk, water, electricity, soap, bus fares, school supplies, and shoes) but it rose to sixty-one by 1986. See Victorino Cardozo Rodas, *Política salarial del estado costarricense*, 54.

35. Céspedes and Jiménez, *La pobreza en Costa Rica*, 62.

36. Morley, *Poverty and Inequality in Latin America*, 147, and Victor Hugo Céspedes and Ronulfo Jiménez, *Apertura comercial y mercado laboral en Costa Rica*, 86.

37. Data from Trejos, "Enhancing Social Services in Costa Rica"; Trejos, "Costa Rica: The State's Response to Poverty"; and World Bank, "Costa Rica: Public Sector Social Spending."

38. Data on FODESAF funding from Seligson, "Reducción de la pobreza en Costa Rica," 71–73.

39. The closest thing to a private social investment fund in Costa Rica is ACORDE (Asociación Costarricense para Organizaciones de Desarrollo), an organization which began as a unit of CINDE and was spun off in 1987. ACORDE supports private voluntary associations which represent small producers (e.g. cooperative banks and groups of microentrepreneurs and artisans). ACORDE has been almost entirely funded by USAID, receiving a total of $14.5 million between 1983–1991, according to the minutes of the CINDE Board of Directors and Sojo, *La mano visible*, 77. Still, ACORDE's budget is dwarfed by FODESAF, which operated with $133.4 million in 1993. See Seligson, "Reducción de la pobreza en Costa Rica," 74.

40. For a broader discussion on this issue see Forrest Colburn, "Exceptions to Urban Bias in Latin America: Cuba and Costa Rica."

41. Nelson, "Politics of Adjustment in Small Democracies," 208; Sojo, *La mano visible*, 77; and Carol Graham, *Safety Nets, Politics, and the Poor*, 272. Sources disagree over number of households benefited by the program.

42. Interview with Oscar Arias S., Madison, WI, 25 October 1992.

43. The bank is a public-private venture with a board of directors composed of four private-sector representatives and three public-sector directors.

44. USAID, "Action Plan FY 1990–FY 1991, Part IIA: Plans by Goal and Objective."

45. Trejos, "Costa Rica: The State's Response to Poverty," 176.

46. Ibid., 196.

47. CENPRO data, 1996.

48. See Alexander Hoffmaister, "The Cost of Export Subsidies: Evidence from Costa Rica," 1.

49. The author was shown official statistics for 1993 demonstrating that PINDECO continued to receive the largest single CAT, and that concentration among the CAT awards had decreased only slightly.

50. Several interviewees mentioned the corruption problem but asked not to be quoted.

51. At this date, five separate CAT schedules are in effect (one each for the original contracts at 15 or 20 percent plus the three reduced tables).

52. In 1991, those holding the oldest and most lucrative CAT contracts were given a choice: they could take a 30 percent reduction in the subsidy and extend the contract to 1999, or start paying a 25 percent per year tax on their CAT until it expired in 1996.

53. Yanancy Noguera, "62,930 millones en CAT," *La Nación*, 24 November 1997. <http://www.nacion.co.cr/ln_ee/1997/noviembre/24/>

54. A more complete discussion of the effects of the CAT's elimination can be found in Mary A. Clark, "Nontraditional Export Promotion in Costa Rica: Sustaining Export-led Growth."

55. The drop was thought to be caused by negative publicity due to several kidnappings of European tourists in the northern part of the country and to competition from cheaper destinations.

56. Edgar Delgado and Marvin Barquero, "Exigen menos distorsiones," *La Nación*, 12 June 1998. <http://www.nacion.co.cr/ln_ee/1998/junio/12/>

57. Alan Angell and Carol Graham, "Can Social Sector Reform Make Adjustment Sustainable and Equitable?" 218.

58. Yasher, "Civil War and Social Welfare," 82.

59. Mitchell Seligson and John Booth, "Political Culture and Regime Type: Evidence from Nicaragua and Costa Rica," 784.

60. Another survey study found that Costa Ricans are even more anticommunist than U.S. respondents. See Jon Hurwitz, Mark Peffley, and Mitchell Seligson, "Foreign Policy Belief Systems in Comparative Perspective: The United States and Costa Rica."

61. The survey was carried out be FLACSO and the results are reported in Sojo, *La gobernabilidad en centroamérica*, 126. Fifty-four percent of those surveyed said that laziness was the cause of poverty; this was the most common response. The survey included street vendors, microentrepreneurs, peasants producing nontraditional exports, peasants producing food crops for internal consumption, and the lowest paid workers from the ministries of health and education.

62. Leslie Anderson, "Mixed Blessings: Disruption and Organization among Peasant Unions in Costa Rica." Anderson notes that intentionally or not, the Costa Rican state was successful at co-opting elements of the peasant movement at different points during the 1980s.

63. José David Guevara, "3.000 millones al agro," *La Nación*, 20 December 1997. <http://www.nacion.co.cr/ln_ee/1997/diciembre/20/>

64. Shahid Javed Burki and Sebastian Edwards, *Dismantling the Populist State: The Unfinished Revolution in Latin America and the Caribbean*, 9.

65. See Maria Victoria Murillo, "Latin American Unions and the Reform of Social Service Delivery Systems: Institutional Constraints and Policy Choice."

66. ECLAC, *Statistical Yearbook for Latin America and the Caribbean* (1996), 95.

67. The key difference between the old CACM and the new one is the shift from import-substituting industrialization to "open regionalism." See Victor Bulmer-Thomas, "The Central American Common Market: From Closed to Open Regionalism."

68. International Labour Office, *Yearbook of Labour Statistics* (1997). During the same time period, 124 strikes took place in the public sector.

69. Based on data from United Nations Program for Development, *Estado de la Nación* (1997), 238.

70. Wilson, *Costa Rica*, 69, notes that Costa Rican strikes are only legal when 60 percent of a union's members sign a petition and a judge then decides that the complaint is legitimate. Nonetheless, it is not unheard of for strikes to occur without having passed this test.

71. "Costa Rica: Labour Sector," *Latin American Monitor*, September 30, 1984, 97.

Chapter 6. Conclusion

1. Pension data from: Mesa-Lago, *Changing Social Security in Latin America*, 22. The data are from the late 1980s, when structural adjustment began in most of these countries. The level of coverage reported for Costa Rica is 69 percent, lower than stated previously in this book because coverage of indigents and others not qualified through payroll contributions is not included here. The corresponding levels for Uruguay, Brazil, Argentina, Chile, and Cuba are 73 percent, 87 percent, 79 percent, 79 percent, and 93 percent, respectively.

2. Ranking from the Inter-American Development Bank, *Economic and Social Progress* (1997), 50. Using a 1995 structural policy index judging the scope and pace of change, Argentina is ranked as an above-average reformer and the other three are rated as below average.

3. Mainwaring and Shugart, "Conclusion," 432. I constructed an index from the data in table 11.6 by awarding each country a combined number representing its score on the president's constitutional powers (1–4) and the president's partisan powers (1–4). Total scores ranged from three (strongest executive authority) to six (weakest executive authority).

4. Venezuela is close to belonging to the set of welfare states examined here. But it is rated a gradual reformer primarily because of the rollback of radical reforms, and thus, it offers a somewhat different set of problems and lessons than those discussed in this comparison.

5. Carey, "Strong Candidates for a Limited Office," 218, and Aldo C. Vacs, "Between Restructuring and Impasse: Liberal Democracy, Exclusionary Policy Making, and Neoliberal Programs in Argentina and Uruguay," 160.

6. Vacs, Between Restructuring and Impasse," 165.

7. For information on the Lacalle administration's economic policy platform upon taking office, see: Economic Intelligence Unit, *Country Report: Uruguay, Fourth Quarter, 1989*, 9–10.

8. Clifford Krauss, "The Welfare State is Alive, if Besieged, in Uruguay," *The New York Times*, May 3, 3.

9. Scott Mainwaring, "Multipartism, Robust Federalism, and Presidentialism in Brazil," 55–56.

10. Ibid., 94.

11. David Fleischer, "The Cardoso Government's Reform Agenda: A View from the National Congress, 1995–1998," 122.

12. Ravi Ramamurti, "Why Haven't Developing Countries Privatized Deeper and Faster?" 141.

13. "Franco Brings Opposition Together," *Latin American Regional Reports: Brazil Report*, 27 April 1999, 3.

14. See, for example: James F. Hoge, "Fulfilling Brazil's Promise: A Conversation with President Cardoso."

15. Wallis, "Understanding the Role of Leadership," 39.

16. Ibid., 42. Wallis also argues that the politicians who demonstrated these traits while implementing radical reform in New Zealand were actually part of a collective leadership or policy conspiracy advocating neoliberalism.

17. Vacs, "Between Restructuring and Impasse," 151–2, and James W. McGuire, *Peronism without Perón: Unions, Parties, and Democracy in Argentina*, 218. McGuire says that in addition to the 217,000 civil servants dismissed, 85,000 additional state workers lost their jobs after the privatization of public enterprises.

18. Mark P. Jones, "Evaluating Argentina's Presidential Democracy," 285–86.

19. Ibid., 282–284. Jones notes that the 1994 constitutional reform reduced the executive's decree power and ability to influence the judicial branch as well as strengthening Argentine federalism.

20. Vacs, "Between Restructuring and Impasse," 153.

21. Javier Corrales, "Do Economic Crises Contribute to Economic Reform? Argentina and Venezuela in the 1990s."

22. For details, see: McGuire, *Peronism without Perón,* and Victoria M. Murillo, "Union Politics, Market-Oriented Reforms and the Reshaping of Argentine Corporatism."

Bibliography

Official Publications

Costa Rica

Dirección General de Estadística y Censos. *Encuesta de Hogares*. San José, July 1996.

Ministerio de Educación Pública. "Estadísticas del sistema educativo costarricense, 1980–1996." San José, October 1996.

Programa de Mejoramiento de la Calidad de la Educación General Básica (PROMECE). "Sistematización del proyecto." San José, July 1997.

Promotora del Comercio Exterior de Costa Rica (PROCOMER). "Costa Rica: Comparación de las exportaciones, 1995–1996," San José, January 1997.

——. "Perfil de productos no tradicionales: piña." San José, June 1997.

——. "Análisis de las estadísticas de exportación 1998." San José, 1999.

Other Sources

Economic Commission on Latin America and the Caribbean (ECLAC). *Statistical Yearbook for Latin America and the Caribbean*. Santiago: various years.

Inter-American Development Bank. *Annual Report*. Washington, D.C., various years.

——. *Economic and Social Progress in Latin America*. Washington, D.C. various years.

International Monetary Fund. *International Financial Statistics Yearbook*. Washington D.C., 1997.

International Labour Office. *Yearbook of Labour Statistics*. Geneva, various years.

United Nations Program for Development. *Estado de la nación*. San José, various years.

United States Agency for International Development (USAID). "Costa Rica: Project Paper, Economic Stabilization and Recovery Program III." Washington D.C. 1984.

———. "Costa Rica: Economic Stabilization and Recovery III." Washington D.C., 2 March 1984.

———. "Costa Rica: Economic Stabilization and Recovery IV." Washington, D.C., February 1985.

———. "Economic Stabilization and Recovery V." Washington D.C., 2 June 1986.

———. "Costa Rica: Economic Stabilization and Recovery VIII." Washington, D.C. March 1989.

———. "Economic Stabilization and Recovery IX." Washington, D.C., 1 May 1990.

———. *Latin America and the Caribbean: Selected Economic and Social Data*. Washington, D.C., 1995.

———. "U.S. Historic Assistance Levels." San José, 30 September 1989.

———. "Action Plan FY 1990–FY 1991, Part IIA: Plans by Goal and Objective." San José, n.d.

USAID, Regional Inspector General for Audit. "Audit of Selected USAID/Costa Rica Local Currency Activities." Tegucigalpa, January 1988.

World Bank. "Costa Rica: Public Sector Social Spending." Washington, D.C., 23 October 1990.

———. *Averting the Old Age Crisis*. New York: Oxford University Press, 1994.

———. *World Development Report*. New York: Oxford University Press, various years.

Newspapers and Journals

Aportes
Central America Report
La Nación

Bibliography

Latin American Monitor
Latin American Regional Reports
The New York Times
Tico Times
Wall Street Journal

Books, Articles, and Unpublished Manuscripts

Acuña González, Guillermo and Edith Olivares Ferreto. "Diagnóstico global: La población migrante nicaragüense en Costa Rica: realidad y respuestas." San José: Fundación Arias para la Paz y el Progreso Humano, October, 1999.

Aguero, Felipe. "Crisis and Decay of Democracy in Venezuela: The Civil-Military Dimension." In *Venezuelan Democracy under Stress*. Edited by Jennifer McCoy, Andrés Serbin, William C. Smith, and Andrés Stambouli. Coral Gables: University of Miami North-South Center, 1995.

Aguilar, Marielos, and Victoria Ramírez. "Crisis económica y acción sindical en Costa Rica 1980–87)." *Revista de Ciencias Sociales*. 44 (June 1989): 49–68.

Altenburg, Tilman, Wolfgang Hein, and Jürgen Weller. *El desafío económico de Costa Rica: desarrollo agroindustrial autocentrado como alternativa*. San José: DEI, 1990.

Ameringer, Charles. *Democracy in Costa Rica*. New York: Praeger, 1982.

Anderson, Leslie. "Mixed Blessings: Disruption and Organization among Peasant Unions in Costa Rica." *Latin American Research Review* 26, No. 1 (1991): 111–143.

Angell, Alan, and Carol Graham, "Can Social Sector Reform Make Adjustment Sustainable and Equitable? Lessons from Chile and Venezuela." *Journal of Latin American Studies*. 27 (1995): 189–219.

Arias, Cinthya, and José Mora. "Energía y telecomunicaciones: Tecnología demanda reformas." *Actualidad Económica*. San José 10, no. 22 (1996): 64–77.

Arthur D. Little International, Inc. "CENPRO: En el contexto de una estrategia para el desarrollo de las exportaciones de Costa Rica." San José, October 1982.

———. "Evaluation of the Private Sector Productivity Project as Implemented Through the Corporation Banex." San José, June 1983.

Aslund, Anders. "The Case for Radical Reform." *Journal of Democracy* 5, No. 4 (October 1994): 63–74.

Banks, Howard. "Bankruptcy without Pain." *Forbes*, 29 April 1985.

Bate, Peter. "Costa Rica Brews a New Blend of Java." *IDB America* 26, Nos. 9–10 (September-October 1999): 2–3.

Behn, Robert D. *Leadership Counts: Lessons for Public Managers.* Cambridge, MA: Harvard University Press, 1991.

Bell, John Patrick. *Crisis in Costa Rica: The 1948 Revolution.* Austin, TX: University of Texas Press, 1971.

Bolaños Rojas, Manuel. *Lucha social y guerra civil en Costa Rica: 1940–48.* San José: Editorial Alma Mater, 1986.

Booth, John A. "Socioeconomic and Political Roots of National Revolts in Central America." *Latin American Research Review* 26, No. 1 (1991): 33–62.

Brenes, Lidiette. *La nacionalización bancaria en Costa Rica.* San José: FLACSO, 1990.

Bresser Pereira, Luiz Carlos, José María Maravall, and Adam Przeworski. *Economic Reforms in New Democracies.* New York: Cambridge University Press, 1993.

Bresser Pereira, Luiz Carlos, and Jairo Abud. "Net and Total Transition Costs: The Timing of Economic Reform." *World Development* 25, No. 6 (1997): 905–914.

Brockett, Charles D. "The Structure of Political Opportunities and Peasant Mobilization in Central America." *Comparative Politics* 23, No.3 (April 1991): 253–75.

Bulmer-Thomas, Victor. *The Political Economy of Central America since 1920.* New York: Cambridge University Press, 1987.

———. "The Central American Common Market: From Closed to Open Regionalism." *World Development* 26, No. 2 (1998): 313–322.

Burki, Shahid Javed, and Sebastian Edwards. *Dismantling the Populist State: The Unfinished Revolution in Latin America and the Caribbean.* Washington, DC: The World Bank 1996.

Busey, James L. *Notes on Costa Rican Democracy.* Boulder, CO: University of Colorado Press, 1962.

Cardozo Rodas, Victorino. *Política salarial del estado costarricense.* San José: EUNA, 1990.

Carey, John M. "Strong Candidates for a Limited Office: Presidentialism and Political Parties in Costa Rica." In *Presidentialism and*

Democracy in Latin America. Edited by Scott Mainwaring, and Matthew Soberg Shugart. New York: Cambridge University Press, 1997: 199–224.

Carvajal, Mario. "Transformación del Estado: Diagnostico y Metas." San José: Office of the Presidency, 1995.

Céspedes, Víctor Hugo, and Ronulfo Jiménez. *Apertura comercial y mercado laboral en Costa Rica.* San José: Academia de Centroamérica, 1994.

———. *La pobreza en Costa Rica.* San José: Academia de Centroamérica, 1995.

Chalker, Cynthia. "Elections and Democracy in Costa Rica." In *Elections and Democracy in Central America, Revisited.* Edited by Mitchell A. Seligson, and John A. Booth. Chapel Hill, NC: University of North Carolina Press, 1995: 101–122.

Clark, Mary A. "Nontraditional Export Promotion in Costa Rica: Sustaining Export-led Growth." *Journal of Interamerican Studies and World Affairs* 37, No. 2 (Summer 1995): 181–224.

———. "Transnational Alliances and Development Policy in Latin America: Nontraditional Export Promotion in Costa Rica." *Latin American Research Review* 32, No. 2 (1997): 71–97.

Colburn, Forrest. "Exceptions to Urban Bias in Latin America: Cuba and Costa Rica." *Journal of Development Studies* 29, No.4 (July 1993): 60–78.

Coopers and Lybrand L.L.P. "Evaluación del proceso de privatización de subsidiarias y liquidación de activos de CODESA y del programa de reformar de estado." San José, November 1995.

Cornick Montero, Jorge and Gladys González Rodríguez. "La política bananera costarricense, 1974–85." Licenciatura thesis, National University, Heredia, Costa Rica, 1987.

Corrales, Javier. "Do Economic Crises Contribute to Economic Reform? Argentina and Venezuela in the 1990s." *Political Science Quarterly* 112, No. 4 (Winter 1997): 617–644.

Desai, Padma. "Beyond Shock Therapy." *Journal of Democracy* 6, No. 2 (April 1995): 102–112.

Development Group for Alternative Policies. *Structural Adjustment in Central America.* Washington, DC: Development GAP, 1993.

Dewatripont, Mathias, and Gerard Roland. "The Virtues of Gradualism and Legitimacy in the Transition to a Market Economy," *The Economic Journal* 102 (March 1992): 291–300.

———. "Economic Reform and Dynamic Political Constraints." *The Review of Economic Studies* 59 (October 1992): 703–30.

———. "The Design of Reform Packages under Uncertainty." *The American Economic Review* 85 (December 1995): 1207–23.

Doryan Garrón, Eduardo. *De la abolición del ejército al premio nobel de la paz.* San José: EDUCA, 1990.

Economist Intelligence Unit, *Country Report: Costa Rica, Second Quarter 1995*. London: Economist Intelligence Unit, Ltd.: 1995.

———. *Country Report: Costa Rica, 3rd Quarter 1995*. London: Economist Intelligence Unit Ltd.: 1995.

———. *Country Report: Uruguay, Paraguay, Fourth Quarter 1989*. London: Economist Intelligence Unit Ltd.: 1990.

———. *Country Profile: Uruguay, Paraguay (1997–98)*. London: Economist Intelligence Unit Ltd.: 1997.

Edelman, Marc. "Land and Labor in an Expanding Economy: Agrarian Capitalism and the Hacienda System in Guanacaste Province, Costa Rica, 1880–1982." Ph.D. diss., Columbia University, 1985.

Edelman, Marc, and Joanne Kenen, eds. *The Costa Rican Reader*. New York: Grove Weidenfeld, 1989.

Edwards, Sebastian. *Crisis and Reform in Latin America*. New York: Oxford University Press, 1995.

English, Burt H. *Liberación Nacional in Costa Rica: The Development of a Political Party in a Transitional Society*. Gainesville, FL: University of Florida Press, 1971.

Esping-Andersen, Gosta. "After the Golden Age?" In *Welfare States in Transition: National Adaptions in Global Economies*. Edited by Gosta Esping-Andersen. Thousand Oaks, CA: SAGE Publications, 1996: 1–31.

———. "Positive-Sum Solutions in a World of Trade-Offs?" In *Welfare States in Transition: National Adaptions in Global Economies*. Edited by Gosta Esping-Anderson. Thousand Oaks, CA: SAGE Publications, 1996: 256–268.

Facio, Rodrigo. *Obras de Rodrigo Facio*. San José: Editorial Costa Rica, 1975.

Fallas Venegas, Helio. *Crisis económica en Costa Rica: un análisis económico de los últimos 20 años*. San José: Nueva Decada, 1981.

Fiszbein, Ariel, and George Psacharopoulos. "Income Inequality Trends in Latin America in the 1980s." In *Coping with Austerity: Poverty and Inequality in Latin America.* Edited by Nora Lustig. Washington, D.C.: The Brookings Institution, 1995: 71–100.

Fleischer, David. "The Cardoso Government's Reform Agenda: A View from the National Congress, 1995–1998." *Journal of Interamerican Studies and World Affairs* 40, No. 4 (Winter 1998): 199–137.

Furst, Edgar. "Estabilización vs. industrialización: crisis económica, medidas de estabilización y políticas industriales durante la administración Carazo: 1978–1982." Heredia, Costa Rica: Department of Economics, Universidad Nacional, 1986.

———. "Liberalización comercial y promoción de exportaciones en Costa Rica (1985–1990)." Heredia, Costa Rica: Universidad Nacional, 1992.

González-Vega, Claudio. *Temor al ajuste: los costos sociales de las políticas económicas en Costa Rica durante la década de los 70.* San José: Academia de Centroamérica, 1984.

González-Vega, Claudio, and Víctor Hugo Céspedes. "Part I: Costa Rica." In *Costa Rica and Uruguay.* Edited by Simon Rottenberg. Washington, DC: The World Bank, 1993: 3–186.

Graham, Carol. *Safety Nets, Politics, and the Poor.* Washington DC: Brookings Institution, 1994.

Grindle, Merilee S., and John W. Thomas. *Public Choices and Policy Change: The Political Economy of Reform in Developing Countries.* Baltimore, MD: The Johns Hopkins University Press, 1991.

Gudmundson, Lowell. *Costa Rica before Coffee: Society and Economy on the Eve of the Export Boom.* Baton Rouge, LA: Louisiana State University Press, 1986.

Haggard, Stephan. "The Newly Industrializing Countries in the International System." *World Politics* 38, No. 2 (1986): 343–70.

———. *Pathways from the Periphery: The Politics of Growth in the Newly Industrialized Countries.* Ithaca: Cornell University Press, 1990.

Haggard, Stephan, and Robert R. Kaufman. "Introduction: Institutions and Economic Adjustment." In *The Politics of Economic Adjustment.* Edited by Stephan Haggard, and Robert R. Kaufman. Princeton: Princeton University Press, 1992: 3–40.

———, eds. *The Politics of Economic Adjustment: International Constraints, Distributive Conflicts, and the State.* Princeton: Princeton University Press, 1992.

———. "The Political Economy of Inflation and Stabilization in Middle-Income Countries." In *Politics of Economic Adjustment.* Edited by Stephen Haggard, and Robert R. Kaufman. 270–318.

———. *The Political Economy of Democratic Transitions*. Princeton: Princeton University Press, 1995.

Haggard, Stephan, and Steven B. Webb. eds. *Voting for Reform: Democracy, Political Liberalization, and Economic Adjustment*. New York: published for the World Bank by Oxford University Press, 1994.

Hoffmaister, Alexander. "The Cost of Export Subsidies: Evidence from Costa Rica." Washington DC: IMF Working Paper WP/91/94, 1991.

Hoge, James F. "Fulfilling Brazil's Promise: A Conversation with President Cardoso." *Foreign Affairs* 74 (July/August 1995): 62–75.

Honey, Martha. *Hostile Acts: U.S. Policy in Costa Rica in the 1980s*. Gainesville, FL: University Press of Florida, 1994.

Hurwitz, Jon, Mark Peffley, and Mitchell Seligson. "Foreign Policy Belief Systems in Comparative Perspective: The United States and Costa Rica." *International Studies Quarterly* 37 (1993): 245–270.

Ickis, John, Carlos Sevilla, and Miguel Iñiguez. "Estudio del sector salud de Costa Rica." Alajuela, Costa Rica: Instituto Centroamericano de Administración de Negocios (INCAE), June 1997.

Johnson, John H., and Sulaiman S. Wasty. "Borrower Ownership Adjustment Programs and the Political Economy of Reform." Discussion Paper 199, Washington DC: World Bank, 1993.

Jones, Mark P. "Evaluating Argentina's Presidential Democracy." In *Presidentialism and Democracy in Latin America*. Edited by Scott Mainwaring, and Matthew Soberg Shugart. New York: Cambridge University Press, 1997: 259–299.

Kahler, Miles. "External Influence, Conditionality, and the Politics of Adjustment." In *Politics of Economic Adjustment*. Edited by Stephen Haggard, and Robert R. Kaufman. Princeton: Princeton University Press, 89–136.

Katzenstein, Peter. *Small States in World Markets: Industrial Policy in Europe*. Ithaca: Cornell University Press, 1985.

Lagos, Marta. "Latin America's Smiling Mask." *Journal of Democracy* 8, No. 3 (1997): 125–138.

Lehoucq, Fabrice Edouard. "Class Conflict, Political Crisis and the Breakdown of Democratic Practices in Costa Rica: Reassessing the Origins of the 1948 Civil War." *Journal of Latin American Studies* 23, No. 1 (1991): 37–60.

———. "The Institutional Foundations of Democratic Cooperation in Costa Rica." *Journal of Latin American Studies* 28, No. 1 (May 1996): 329–355.

Bibliography

Linz, Juan J, and Arturo Valenzuela. *The Failure of Presidential Democracy.* Baltimore, MD: Johns Hopkins University Press, 1994.

Lizano, Eduardo. *Desde el Banco Central.* San José: Academia de Centroamérica, 1988.

Lora, Eduardo, and Felipe Berrera. "A Decade of Structural Reforms in Latin America: Growth, Productivity and Investment Are Not What They Used to Be." Washington DC: Inter-American Development Bank, Working Paper No. 350, 1997.

Lustig, Nora. "Introduction." In *Coping with Austerity: Poverty and Inequality in Latin America.* Edited by Nora Lustig. Washington DC: The Brookings Institution, 1995: 1–41.

Mainwaring, Scott. "Multipartism, Robust Federalism, and Presidentialism in Brazil." In *Presidentialism and Democracy in Latin America.* Edited by Scott Mainwaring, and Matthew Soberg Shugart. New York: Cambridge University Press, 1997: 55–109.

———, and Matthew Soberg Shugart. "Introduction." In *Presidentialism and Democracy in Latin America.* Edited by Scott Mainwaring, and Matthew Soberg Shugart. New York: Cambridge University Press, 1997: 1–11.

———. "Presidentialism and Democracy in Latin America: Rethinking the Terms of the Debate." In *Presidentialism and Democracy in Latin America.* Edited by Scott Mainwaring, and Matthew Soberg Shugart. New York: Cambridge University Press, 1997.

———. "Conclusion: Presidentialism and the Party System." In *Presidentialism and Democracy in Latin America.* Edited by Scott Mainwaring, and Matthew Soberg Shugart. New York: Cambridge University Press, 1997: 394–439.

McDonald, Ronald H., and J. Mark Ruhl. *Party Politics and Elections in Latin America.* Boulder, CO: Westview Press, 1989.

McGregor Jr., Eugene B. "Toward a Theory of Public Management Success." In *Public Management: The State of the Art.* Edited by Barry Bozeman. San Francisco: Jossey-Bass Publishers, 1993.

McGuire, James W. *Peronism without Perón: Unions, Parties, and Democracy in Argentina.* Stanford, CA: Stanford University Press. 1997.

Meléndez, Dennis, and Mauricio Meza. "CODESA: Origen y Consequencias." San José: FINTRA, 1993.

Méndez Rodríguez, Pamela. "Intel: A la cabeza del desarrollo tecnológico." *Actualidad Económica* 13, No. 205 (20 July 1999): 30–38.

Mesa-Lago, Carmelo. *Changing Social Security in Latin America.* Boulder, CO: Lynne Rienner, 1994.

Monge Alfaro, Carlos. *Historia de Costa Rica,* 16th ed. San José: Librería Trejos, 1980.

Montiel, Nancy, Anabelle Ulate, Luis C. Peralta, and Juan Diego Trejos. "La educación en Costa Rica: un solo sistema?" San José, Instituto de Investigaciones en Ciencias Económicas, University of Costa Rica, February 1997.

Morley, Samuel A. *Poverty and Inequality in Latin America: Past Evidence, Future Prospects.* Washington DC: Overseas Development Council, 1994.

———. *Poverty and Inequality in Latin America: The Impact of Adjustment and Recovery in the 1980s.* Baltimore, MD: Johns Hopkins University Press, 1995.

Mosley, Paul, Jane Harrigan, and John Toye. *Aid and Power: The World Bank and Policy-Based Lending.* Vol. 1. New York: Rouledge and Kegan Paul Press, 1992.

Murillo, Maria Victoria. "Latin American Unions and the Reform of Social Service Delivery Systems: Institutional Constraints and Policy Choice." Washington DC: IDB, Working Paper Series No. 332, 1996.

———. "Union Politics, Market-Oriented Reforms and the Reshaping of Argentine Corporatism." In *The New Politics of Inequality in Latin America.* Edited by Douglass Chalmers. New York: Oxford University Press, 1997: 72–94.

Naím, Moisés. "Latin America: The Second Stage of Reform." *Journal of Democracy* 5, No. 4 (October 1994): 32–48.

———. "Washington Consensus or Washington Confusion?" *Foreign Policy,* No. 118 (Spring 2000): 87–103.

Nelson, Joan M. "The Politics of Adjustment in Small Democracies: Costa Rica, the Dominican Republic, and Jamaica." In *Economic Crisis and Policy Choice: The Politics of Adjustment in the Third World.* Edited by Joan M. Nelson. Princeton: Princeton University Press, 1990: 169–214.

———. *Intricate Links: Democratization and Market Reforms in Latin America and Eastern Europe.* New Brunswick: Transaction Publishers, 1994.

Newton, John. "The Effectiveness and Economic Development Impact of Policy-Based Cash-Transfer Programs: The Case of Costa Rica." Washington, DC: USAID, 1988.

Nickson, Andrew R. *Local Government in Latin America*. Boulder, CO: Lynne Rienner, 1995.

North, Douglass C. *Institutions, Institutional Change and Economic Performance*. New York: Cambridge University Press, 1990.

Nowalski, Jorge, Pedro Morales, and Gregorio Berliavsky. *Impacto de la maquila en la economía costarricense*. San José: Fundación Friedrich Ebert, 1994.

Pierson, Paul. *Dismantling the Welfare State?* New York: Cambridge University Press, 1994.

Przeworski, Adam. *Democracy and the Market: Political and Economic Reforms in Eastern Europe and Latin America*. New York: Cambridge University Press, 1991.

———. *Sustainable Democracy*. New York: Cambridge University Press, 1995.

Przeworski, Adam, and Fernando Limongi. "Political Regimes and Economic Growth." *Journal of Economic Perspectives* 7, No. 3 (Summer 1993): 51–69.

Psacharopoulos, George. "Poverty and Income Distribution in Latin America: The Story of the 1980s." Washington, DC: Latin America and the Caribbean Technical Department Regional Studies Program Report 27, World Bank, 1993.

Ramírez, Francisco, Jaime Lobo, and Marvin Acuña. "El estado de los regimenes: el caso del regimen de invalidez, vejez y muerte de la CCSS." Heredia, Costa Rica: Maestría en Política Económica, Universidad Nacional, October 1991.

Ramamurti, Ravi. "Why Haven't Developing Countries Privatized Deeper and Faster?" *World Development* 27, No. 1 (1999): 137–155.

Raventos, Ciska. "The Construction of an Order: Structural Adjustment in Costa Rica (1985–1995)." Ph.D. diss., New School for Social Research, 1995.

Remmer, Karen L. "Democracy and Economic Crisis: The Latin American Experience." *World Politics* 42, No. 3 (April 1990): 315–335.

Reuben Soto, Reuben. "El potencial de la economía campesina en la reactivación económica y el desarrollo de Costa Rica." In *Los campesinos frente a la nueva década*. Edited by William Reuben Soto. San José: Editorial Porvenir, 1989: 213–242.

Rivera Urrutia, Eugenio. "El Fondo Monetario Internacional y las políticas de estabilización en Costa Rica: 1978–82." In *Costa Rica hoy: la crisis y sus perspectivas*. Edited by Jorge Rovira Mas. San José: Universidad Estatal a Distancia, 1984: 175–200.

Rivera Urrutia, Eugenio, Ana Sojo, and José Roberto López. *Centroamérica: política económica y crisis*. San José: DEI, 1986.

Rodrik, Dani. "Promises, Promises: Credible Policy Reform via Signalling." *The Economic Journal*. 99 (September, 1989): 756–72.

Rosenberg, Mark. *Las luchas por el seguro social en Costa Rica*. San José: Editorial Costa Rica, 1983.

Rovira Mas, Jorge. *Estado y política económica en Costa Rica, 1948–1970*. San José: Editorial Costa Rica, 1988.

———. *Costa Rica en los años ochenta*. San José: Porvenir, 1989.

Saborio, Sylvia. "Central America." In *Latin American Adjustment: How Much Has Happened?* Edited by John Williamson. Washington DC: Institute for International Economics, 1990.

———. "U.S.-Central America Free Trade." In *The Premise and the Promise: Free Trade in the Americas*. Edited by Sylvia Saborio. New Brunswick: Transaction Publishers, 1992.

Salazar, José, Pedro Morales, Eugenio Morales, and F. Salas. "Precios, incentivos, y reformas de política." San José: Ministerio de Planificación, 1988.

Schifter Sikora, Jacobo. "La democracia en Costa Rica como producto de la neutralización de clases." In *Democracia en Costa Rica: cinco opiniones polémicas*. Edited by Chester Zelaya. San José: Editorial Universidad Estatal a Distancia, 1983: 172–246.

Seligson, Mitchell A. *Peasants of Costa Rica and the Development of Agrarian Capitalism*. Madison, WI: University of Wisconsin Press, 1980.

Seligson, Mitchell A., and John Booth. "Political Culture and Regime Type: Evidence from Nicaragua and Costa Rica." *Journal of Politics* 55, No. 3 (August 1993): 777–792.

Seligson, Mitchell A., Juliana Martínez, and Juan Diego Trejos. "Reducción de la pobreza en Costa Rica: el impacto de las políticas públicas." San José, Instituto de Investigaciones en Ciencias Económicas, University of Costa Rica, 1996.

Shugart, Matthew S., and John M. Carey. *Presidents and Assemblies: Constitutional Design and Electoral Dynamics*. New York: Cambridge University Press, 1992.

Sojo, Ana. *Estado empresario y lucha política en Costa Rica*. San José: EDUCA, 1984.

Sojo, Carlos. *La utopía del estado mínimo: influencia de AID en Costa Rica en los años ochenta*. Managua: CRIES, 1991.

―――. *La mano visible del mercado: la asistencia del Estados Unidos al sector privado costarricense en la década de los ochenta*. Managua: CRIES, 1992.

―――. *La gobernabilidad en Centroamérica: La sociedad después del ajuste*. San José: FLACSO, 1995.

Stallings, Barbara, ed. *Global Change, Regional Response: The New International Context of Development*. New York: Cambridge University Press, 1995.

―――. "International Influence on Economic Policy: Debt, Stabilization, and Structural Reform." In *Politics of Economic Adjustment*: Edited by Stephen Haggard, and Robert R. Kaufman. Princeton: Princeton University Press, 41–88.

Stallings, Barbara, and Robert Kaufman, eds. *Debt and Democracy in Latin America*. Boulder, CO: Westview Press, 1992.

Stamm, Andreas. "Una nueva dinámica para las zonas rurales?" In *Apertura comercial en centroamérica: Nuevos retos para la agricultura*. Edited by Helmut Nuhn, and Andreas Stamm. San José: Editorial DEI, 1996: 23–48.

Stoakes, Susan C. "Public Opinion and Market Reforms: The Limits of Economic Voting." *Comparative Political Studies* 29, No. 5 (October 1996): 499–519.

Trejos, Juan Diego. "Costa Rica: The State's Response to Poverty." In *Strategies to Combat Poverty in Latin America*. Edited by Dagmar Raczynski. Washington DC: Inter-American Development Bank, 1995.

Trejos, Juan Diego, Leonardo Garnier, Guillermo Monge, and Roberto Hidalgo." Enhancing Social Services in Costa Rica." In *Social Service Delivery Systems: An Agenda for Reform*. Edited by Cristián Aedo, and Osvaldo Larrañaga. Washington, DC: Inter-American Development Bank, 1994.

Trejos, Juan Diego, Xinia Picado, Adriá Rodriguez, and Maria Saénz. "Costa Rica: La respuesta estatal frente a la pobreza: instituciones, programas y recursos." San José: Instituto de Investigaciones en Ciencias Económicas, University of Costa Rica, August 1994.

Tsebelis, George. "Decision Making in Political Systems." *British Journal of Political Science* 25, No. 3 (July 1995): 289–325.

Vacs, Aldo C. "Between Restructuring and Impasse: Liberal Democracy, Exclusionary Policy Making, and Neoliberal Programs in Argentina and Uruguay." In *Deepening Democracy in Latin America*. Edited by Kurt von Mettenheim, and James Malloy. Pittsburgh: University of Pittsburgh Press, 1998: 137–172.

Vargas-Cullell, Jorge. "Privatization in Costa Rica: Democratic Constraints to Institutional Reform." Paper presented at the International Congress of the Latin American Studies Association. Guadalajara, Mexico, March 1997.

———. "Democratic Constraints to Reform." *Hemisphere* 8, No. 2 (Winter/Spring 1998): 12–16.

Vega Carballo, José Luis. *Poder político y democracia en Costa Rica*. San José: Editorial Porvenir, 1982.

Wade, Robert. *Governing the Market: Economic Theory and the Role of Government in East Asian Industrialization*. Princeton: Princeton University Press, 1990.

Wallis, Joe. "Understanding the Role of Leadership in Economic Policy Reform." *World Development* 27, No. 1 (1999): 39–53.

Walton, John. *Free Markets and Food Riots: The Politics of Global Adjustment*. Cambridge, MA: Blackwell, 1994.

Weller, Jürgen. "Efectos del ajuste estructural en el empleo y los ingresos agropecuarios, con énfasis en las exportaciones no tradicionales." In *Apertura comercial en centroamérica*. Edited by Helmut Nuhn, and Andreas Stamm. San José: Editorial DEI, 1996: 195–224.

Williams, Robert G. *Export Agriculture and the Crisis in Central America*. Chapel Hill, NC: University of North Carolina Press, 1986.

———. *States and Social Evolution: Coffee and the Rise of National Governments in Central America*. Chapel Hill, NC: University of North Carolina, 1994.

Williamson, John. "What Washington Means by Policy Reform." In *Latin American Adjustment: How Much Has Happened?* Edited by John Williamson. Washington, DC: Institute for International Economics, 1990.

Wilson, Bruce. "When Social Democrats Choose Neoliberal Economic Policies: The Case of Costa Rica." *Comparative Politics* 26 (January 1994): 149–68.

———. *Costa Rica: Politics, Economics, and Democracy*. Boulder, CO: Lynne Rienner, 1998.

Winson, Anthony. "Confronting the Coffee Oligarchy: The Roots of Costa Rica's Middle Road." *Canadian Journal of Latin American and Caribbean Studies* 9, No. 17 (1984): 33–50.

———. *Coffee and Democracy in Modern Costa Rica*. London: Macmillan, 1989.

Yashar, Deborah J. "Civil War and Social Welfare: The Origins of Costa Rica's Competitive Party System." In *Building Democratic Institutions: Party Systems in Latin America*. Edited by Scott Mainwaring, and Timothy R. Scully. Stanford: Stanford University Press, 1995: 72–99.

Zimbalist, Andrew. "Costa Rica." In *Struggle Against Dependence: Nontraditional Export Growth in Central America and the Caribbean*. Edited by Eva Paus. Boulder, CO: Westview Press, 1988: 21–40.

Index

Acción Demócrata (AD), 20
Agriculture, 130–131; basic grains, 35, 63–65; and CACM, 38; employment in, 118; nontraditional exports, 59, 106–110
Angell, Alan, 129
Argentina, 6, 144–145
Arias, Oscar, 26, 123, and economic reforms, 136; and education, 98; and export contracts, 127; and housing, 121; and United States, 46, 50
Asociación Nacional de Fomento Económico (ANFE), 27, 46, 61, 70
Asociación Nacional de Hoteles y Afines (ACHA), 123, 128
Autoridad Reguladora de Servicios Públicos (ARESEP), 80

Banana industry, 36–37, 133, 155$n60$
Banking system, private, 60–63, 110, 161$n63$; public, 34, 60–63, 161$n57$
Booth, John, 130
Brady Plan, 70
Brazil, 143–144
Bulmer-Thomas, Victor, 39

Calderón Fournier, Rafael Angel, 27–28, 79, 103, 122

Calderón Guardia, Rafael Angel, 19, 26, 32, 122, 137
Cámara de Exportadores (CADEXCO), 123
Cámara de Industrias, 37, 61, 67, 123, 129, 132
Cámara Nacional de Turismo (CANATUR), 123, 128
Carazo Odio, Rodrigo, 28, 40, 44–45
Cardoso, Fernando Henrique, 143–144, 146
Carey, John M., 24
Caribbean Basin Initiative (CBI), 47, 110, 157$n10$
Castillo, Carlos Manuel, 72
Central American Common Market (CACM), 37–39, 45, 65–67, 132
Centro de Promoción de Exportaciones e Inversión (CENPRO), 56–58, 78
Certificado de Abono Tributario (CAT), 58, 127–128, 160$n44$
Céspedes, Victor, 113
Chaij, Daniel, 51–52, 57
Chalker, Cynthia, 18
Chamber of Exporters, 123
Chamber of Industries, 37, 61, 67, 123, 129, 132
Chamber of Tourism, 123, 128
Civil war (1948), 19–21, 152$n11$

Class, middle, 22, 25, 112; upper-middle, 20; urban lower, 20, 27
Coalición Costarricense de Iniciativas para el Desarrollo (CINDE), 57–60, 119, 23
Coffee industry, 35–36
Collor, Fernando, 143
Comptroller (Contraloría General de la República), 7, 29, 54–55, 72
Confederación de Trabajadores de Costa Rica (CTCR), 22
Consejo Nacional de Investigaciones Científicas y Tecnológicas (CONICIT), 78
Consejo Nacional de Producción (CNP), origins of, 35; reform of, 63–65, 76
Constituent Assembly, 22–23
Constitution (1949), 23
Cooperatives, coffee, 36; and the CNP, 76; and CODESA, 54, 56; health care, 94–95
Corporación Costarricense de Desarrollo (CODESA), 39–40, 44, 137; privatization of, 52–56
Corruption, 44, 60, 76–77, 109
Costa Rican Social Security Fund (CCSS), 32–33, 84–95
Crime, 108, 119, 171$n33$
Customs Administration, 76

Debt crises, external, 45, 70; internal, 71
Democracy in Costa Rica, origins of, 17–19
Dirección Nacional de Desarrollo Comunal (DINADECO), 79
Doctors, 32, 88–89, 91, 94, 132
Doryan, Eduardo, 72, 100

Echandi, Mario, 26, 37–38
Economic aid, multilateral, 48–50, 70; United States, 47–51, 69

Economic crisis, 44–46; and foreign debt, 45, 51, 70, 135
Economic development, 34–40
Economic growth. See Economic performance
Economic liberalization. See Economic reforms
Economic performance, pre-1979, 40; post-1979, 105–112, 115–119, 132
Economic reforms, 52–53, 59, 61, 136–137, 147$n2$; in Argentina, 144–145; in Brazil, 143–144; and Comptroller, 29–30; and consensus-building, 129–130; and democratic regimes, 3–4, 137; and economic distortions, 111–112; first-stage, 8–9, 136; and inequality, 112–122; leadership of, 9–10, 102, 144–145; origins of, 33–34, 151$n42$; and poverty, 112–122; and presidentialism, 5–8; and private sector, 70; resources needed, 10; second-stage, 8–9, 78, 83, 131, 134, 136, 137, 139; and Supreme Court, 29; in Uruguay, 142
Education sector, origins of, 33–34; problems in, 97–98; reform of, 99–101
Elections, 23–27; constitutional provisions on, 23; 1899, 18; 1948, 21; 1953, 24; 1978, 44
Employment, and the new economy, 117–119, 171$n30$
Equipos Básicos de Atención Integral de Salud (EBAIS), 91
Exchange rate, 51, 58, 123–125
Executive branch, constitutional provisions on, 23; strength of, 6–7, 110
Export contracts, 58–59, 126–128
Exports, bananas, 36–37; to CACM, 37–39, 45; under CBI, 47; coffee, 35–36; nontraditional, 56–60, 106–110

Fábrica Nacional de Licores
  (FANAL), 78–79
Federation of Cooperatives of Coffee
  Growers (FEDECOOP), 36
Fiduciaria de Inversiones
  Transitorias (FINTRA), 54–56
Figueres Ferrer, José (Pepe), and
  bananas, 36; and banks, 60; and
  CODESA, 40, 44; and education,
  34; in 1948 civil war, 20–22; and
  PLN, 24
Figueres Olsen, José María, and
  economic reforms, 74, 79, 86–87,
  100, 102, 122–123, 131, 142,
  146; as "New Democrat," 26, 72,
  103; pact with PUSC, 70
Fondo de Desarrollo Social y
  Asignaciones Familiaries
  (FODESAF), 120–122
Franco, Itamar, 143–144
Free Zone Corporation, 78
Free zones, 59, 124–127
Fundación de Cooperación Estatal
  (FUCE), 69, 73–78
Fundación Costa Rica-USA
  (CRUSA), 69

Garnier, Leonardo, 72
González-Vega, Claudio, 39
Gradualism, 110, 136–138; practical implications, 145–146;
  results of, 122–123, 134; theoretical perspectives, 11–12
Graham, Carol, 129
Gutiérrez, Francisco de Paula, 72

Health sector, doctors; 89, 91, 93;
  origins of, 32–33; and physicians' unions, 32; private
  providers, 88, 94–95; problems
  in, 89–90; reform of, 88–95
Honeymoon period, 4, 44
Housing, 121–122

Import-substitution industrialization (ISI), 39, 57, 65, 135

Income inequality, 26, 113–115,
  170n22
Industry, 132; employment in, 118;
  and nontraditional exports, 59,
  106–110; state-owned enterprises, 39–40
Infrastructure, 81, 91, 108, 111
Instituto Costarricense de
  Electricidad (ICE), 78–80, 111
Instituto Costarricense de
  Ferrocarriles (INCOFER), 78
Instituto Costarricense de Puertos
  del Pacífico (INCOP), 81
Instituto Costarricense de Turismo
  (ICT), 128
Instituto Nacional de Seguros
  (INS), 33, 78–79, 111
Intel Corporation, 60, 108, 119
Inter-American Development Bank
  (IDB), 111, 139, education
  reform, 99–100; health reform,
  91, 93; loans, 70, 74, 124, 136
Interest groups, 30–31
International Monetary Fund
  (IMF), conditionality, 49, 84, 93,
  124; loans, 45, 48, 51, 70, 136
Investment, diversion, 109; foreign,
  38, 108; public, 82, 84–85, 90,
  97, 119

Jiménez, Ronulfo, 113
Junta (1948–49), 21–22
Junta de Administración Portuaria
  y de Desarrollo Económico de la
  Vertiente Atlántica (JAPDEVA),
  81

Labor unions, 31; in Argentina,
  144–145; in Brazil, 144; in civil
  war, 20, 22; private-sector, 132;
  public-sector, 73–74, 80–82, 86,
  123, 131; in Uruguay, 142
Lacalle, Luis, 142, 146
La Nación, 61, 70, 80, 97
Legislative Assembly, and civil service law, 75; constitutional pro-

Legislative Assembly *(continued)* visions on, 23; and economic reform bills, 7, 71, 77; and education reform, 100; and 1995 tax package, 70; party representation in, 25; and pension funds, 85–87; and privatizations, 79; and public-sector layoffs, 74
Lehoucq, Fabrice, 18
Ley de concesión de obra pública, 79, 81, 111
Ley de contratación administrativa, 79
Liberalization. *See* Economic reforms
Lizano, Eduardo, 58, 62–64, 72

McDonald, Ronald H., 18
Mainwaring, Scott, 6, 140
Market reforms. *See* Economic reforms
Menem, Carlos, 144–145
Meoño, Johnny, 73
Mesa-Lago, Carmelo, 85
Ministry of Education (MEP), 34, 95–100
Ministry of Finance, 76, 93, 98, 128; reform of, 77
Ministry of Foreign Trade, 127
Ministry of Health, 33, 88, 92–93
Monge, Luis Alberto, and economic reforms, 61–62, 133; and external creditors, 45, 51; and social policy, 119, 121
Morley, Samuel, 113
Movilidad laboral, 73–77
Movimiento Costa Rica Libre, 29
Municipal government, 24

Naranjo, Fernando, 72
National Banana Association (ASBANA), 36
National Investment Council, 78
Neoliberalism, 147n2. *See also* Economic reforms
Nicaraguan immigrants, 90, 97

North American Free Trade Association (NAFTA), 109–110

Oduber, Daniel, 26, 28, 37, 40, 44
Overseas Private Investment Council (OPIC), 47

Partido Comunista (PC), 20, 22
Partido Liberación Nacional (PLN), 24–26, 61, 75, 146; and CODESA, 54; and neoliberalism, 46, 51, 61, 71–72, 80, 103–104
Partido Republicano Nacional (PRN), 19, 26, 27
Partido Social Demócrata (PSD), 20–22
Partido Unidad Social Cristiana (PUSC), 26, 28, 46, 61, 70, 146; and neoliberalism, 103–104
Partido Unión Nacional (PUN), 20–21, 26–27
Path dependence, 9
Peasants, 64–65; protests, 130–131
Pension plans, origins of, 32–33; problems of, 84–85; reform of, 84–94; teachers', 86
Political culture, 7, 130
Political institutions, in Argentina, 144–145; in Brazil, 143–144; in Costa Rica, 23–31, 137; in Uruguay, 140, 142
Political parties (party system), 24, 29; bipartisanship, 31; leftist, 28–29, 130
Postal system (CORTEL), 77, 111
Poverty, data, 113–115; and government programs, 26, 120–122; and resistance to reforms, 112
Privatization, 12, 31, 49, 74, 101, 163n85; in Argentina, 144; in Brazil, 143; and CODESA, 51, 53–56, 71, 135–137; complex, 78–82; easy, 8; in health care, 95; in Uruguay, 142
Programa de Mejoramiento de la Calidad de la Educación

General Básica (PROMECE), 99–101
Promotora del Comercio Exterior de Costa Rica (PROCOMER), 78
Prostitution, 119
Public employees, 26, 34, 73–75, 77, 137; and civil service regulations, 75; and *salario escolar*, 122
Public opinion, 80, 137
Pueblo Unido (PU), 28

Refinadora Costarricense de Petróleo (RECOPE), 39, 78
Reforms. See Economic reforms
Rodríguez, Miguel Angel, 28, 78, 110, 123, 128–129, 137
Ruhl, Mark J., 18

Salazar, José Manuel, 72
Sandinistas, 3, 45–46, 136
Sanguinetti, Julio, 143, 146
Sarney, José, 143
Seligson, Mitchell, 130
Semi-automomous institutions, 7–8, 30, 32, 41, 60, 153n35
Shock therapy, 111, 122, 138, 146, 150n30; theoretical perspectives, 11
Shugart, Matthew, 6, 140
Socialism, 26
Social safety-net, 8, 129–130, 146
Social welfare, 20, 40, 112–122
Society, middle-class, 25; nineteenth century, 17–18; and preventative health, 91; and resistance to reforms, 53, 64–65, 81, 86, 130–131, 145
Solidarismo, 22, 133
State intervention (in economy), 26–27; in agriculture, 35–37; in banking, 34; in industry, 37–40, 44
State reform, 8, 12, 83, 103, 134, 137; and Figueres administration, 75–76, 78

Structural adjustment, 71, 122, 130, 147n2; loans, 49, 64, 66, 74, 136. *See also* Economic reforms
Subsidies, to agriculture, 35, 63–65, 136; to coffee, 36; to exporters, 58, 124, 127–128
Supreme Court, 7, 29, 79

Tariffs, under CACM, 38–39, 65, 67; and CBI, 47; import, 66–67, 131, 162n76; reform of, 65–67, 136
Tax(es), from bananas, 36–37; from coffee, 35; exemptions on, 37–38, 58, 106, 126; and FODESAF, 120; package of 1995, 31, 70; and tourism industry, 128; on wealth, 22
Tourism, 106–108, 128
Trade, and CBI, 47; with Central America, 37–40, 67; international agreements, 132; and United States, 109–110; and WTO, 110
Transnational alliances, 10, 46, 51–52, 137; and banking, 62; and CODESA, 53–54; and export promotion, 57–59; and Ministry of Finance, 76. *See also* United States Agency for International Development
Tribunal Supremo Electoral (TSE), 23–24

Ulate, Otilio, 21, 27
Unemployment, 81, 117–119, 133
Unidad (coalition), 28, 44
Unión Costarricense de Cámaras y Asociaciones de la Empresa Privada (UCCAEP), 31, 70
Unions. *See* Labor unions
United Nations Economic Commission for Latin America and the Caribbean (ECLAC), 37–38, 173
United States, 3, 135–136; and CBI, 47; and Nicaraguan contras, 47, 50

United States Agency for
International Development
(USAID), 2, 69, 73, 98, 121, 136;
and aid conditionality, 49–51,
158nn12, 18; and bank reform,
60–63; and CNP, 64; and CODE-
SA, 53–56; and nontraditional
exports, 57–60; and tariff
reform, 66; and transnational
alliances, 46, 51–52
Universities, 34, 96–98, 100–101
Uruguay, 140–143;

Venezuela, 174n4
Veto points (players), 7, 29, 142,
149n9, 153n35; in economic
reforms, 72, 136–137

Wage Policy, 119–120
Wallis, Joe, 144, 150n28
Washington Consensus, xi,
147n1
Welfare state, assistance to poor,
120–122; in comparison,
139–141; employment in, 34;
origins of, 32–34; and PLN, 26;
problems of; 82; size of, 7–8,
139–140; in Uruguay,
142–143
World Bank, and education reform,
99; and health reform, 91, 93;
and liberalization, 64, 66; loans,
48–49, 74, 136

Yashar, Deborah, 22